D1807756

The Mental Performance Index

Ranking the Best Teams in Super Bowl History

John F. Murray, Ph.D.

Published by World Audience, Inc.
(www.worldaudience.org)
303 Park Avenue South, Suite 1440
New York, NY 10010-3657
Phone (646) 620-7406; Fax (646) 620-7406
info@worldaudience.org

ISBN 978-1-935444-89-3

© 2011, John F. Murray

Edited by M. Stefan Strozier

Copyright notice: All work contained within is the sole copyright of its author, 2011, and may not be reproduced without consent.

World Audience (www.worldaudience.org) is a global consortium of artists and writers, producing quality books and the journal *audience*, and *The audience Review*. Our periodicals and books are edited by M. Stefan Strozier and assistant editors.

The Mental Performance Index:
Ranking the Best Teams in Super Bowl History

John F. Murray, Ph.D.

A World Audience Book
www.worldaudience.org

March, 2011

New York, Newcastle (Australia)

TABLE OF CONTENTS

Praise and Comments for *The Mental Performance Index*

"You've got to continually eliminate errors and take pride in not making mental and physical mistakes. It takes extra work, extra thoughts, and extra practice to get it all done. It just doesn't happen on Sunday. You have to make up your minds to get it done and make up your minds to win."
—Don Shula, Head Coach, Baltimore Colts (1963-1969) and Miami Dolphins (1970-1995). Most Career Wins (347), Most Super Bowl Appearances (6), Only Perfect Season (1972 Miami Dolphins), and 2 Super Bowl Titles with the Miami Dolphins (VII & VIII)

"This is a fascinating work of remarkable scope and scholarship. Dr. Murray has devised a valid new way to measure and predict greatness in the game of football."
—Steve Sabol, President of NFL FILMS

"Everyone is gifted, but not everyone opens the package. Open this package and you will understand the secret advantage that helped keep me in the NFL for 12 years!"
—Jim "Crash" Jensen, Miami Dolphins All Purpose Player (1981-1992), NFL Special Teams Player of Year (1988), "Miami Dolphins Unsung Hero" (2006)

"As a professional kicking coach, who has spent my entire career working with professional athletes, I feel that John has done a brilliant job of demonstrating the importance of mental toughness, and intelligent play in professional football! 'The Mental Performance Index: Ranking the Best Teams in Super Bowl History' should be required reading for all football coaches at every level of the game. His book is masterfully done, and clearly outlines that mental preparedness, and intelligence on the playing field, is equally as important as physical ability and athletic talent!"

"John, I truly believe that you have created a masterpiece! As a kicking coach, I am very excited about what you have done."
—Doug Blevins, President, DOUG BLEVINS KICKING AND PUNTING, Ex-Miami Dolphins Kicking Coach, Football Consultant

"Dr. John F. Murray is trailblazing a new frontier in understanding and appreciating football and helping teams win! This is a must read for coaches, reporters and anyone who loves the sport."
—Jim Martz, Miami Herald sports writer (1970-1990), Editor of Cane Sport (University of Miami fan magazine), Author of 4 Miami Hurricanes books

"Today's athletes are blessed with unprecedented physical talent, speed, strength, grace, facilities, technologies, and coaching. Unfortunately, they are often plagued by an ADD culture that inhibits their most important asset in performance - bringing their passion and focus to the moment. Whether the placekicker with a last minute game-winning field goal, an offensive lineman who goes off-sides on a key 4th down in the 4th quarter, or the safety who blows a coverage that costs a game, it is the individuals, but more importantly the TEAMS that play with collective intelligence that consistently win championships. Dr. John F Murray's Mental Performance Index helps us finally understand *how and why* teams like Bill Belichick's New England Patriots play smarter. I learned in almost 20 years in the NFL that it was improving my capacity to focus on the right things in the moments of truth that took me from a good college placekicker to the most accurate kicker in NFL History. Read this book and carve out new space in your life for lasting success!"
—Nick Lowery, New England Patriots, Kansas City Chiefs & New York Jets Placekicker (1978-1996)

"Catching or dropping the big pass in a game actually happens long before the game in great or poor mental preparation. By measuring terrific execution, or it's opposite in carelessness and mental errors, Dr. Murray is also capturing how well players prepare mentally before the big game!"
—Dan Johnson, Miami Dolphins tight end (1983-1987), Caught a touchdown pass from Dan Marino in the first quarter of Super Bowl XIX

Foreword

Sports have gone through many evolutions. Players have improved in strength, size, abilities and most of all intellectual maturity. By intellectual maturity, I mean the modern day athlete no longer just shows up for an event and competes. That individual prepares long before his or her performance by training physically and mentally.

Dr. Murray has developed an approach toward preparation that has probably been around for years in some form but never defined. He has perfected a system of self evaluation and taken it to a new and modern level. His approach is an introspective system of grading performance levels that separate winning teams from the others.

I have been in professional football for fifty years at every level: player, coach, head coach, president/general manager and now radio analyst. I have seen and experienced almost every aspect of the game and been very fortunate in doing so. In my career, I have been a member of four winning Super Bowl teams. In 1969, I was a member of the Kansas City Chiefs in Super Bowl IV. In 1976, I was an assistant coach with the Oakland Raiders in Super Bowl XI. In 1980 and 1983, I was the Head Coach of the Oakland/Los Angeles Raiders in Super Bowls XV and XVIII.

The reason I mention my accomplishments is not to pound my chest but to emphasize one thing. Every one of those teams had one thing in common, other than excellent players. They were very smart players, prepared intellectually and performed at a high level of intelligence. They did not make mistakes.

I've always believed that successful athletes and coaches visualize and conceptualize what they are about to experience. This process prepares one to face any situation and to respond favorably in spite of what actually occurs.

Some of the great players that I coached had one thing in common. They had the ability to visualize what was about to happen before it happened without realizing why. Hall of Fame players like Marcus Allen, Ted Hendricks and Mike Haynes made great plays, over and over. When asked why they did what they did, they would usually respond: 'I'm not sure.' They were so mentally prepared that they automatically responded physically to any stimulus.

Dr. Murray has developed a system that is part of the evolution of football: The ability to identify, quantify and utilize a grading system that will aid coaches and players. It is a method of identifying the strengths and weaknesses of every aspect of a team and or individual. It is a system that can point out the direction needed for improvement.

Sports have come a long way in the past century. The future, compared to the past, is vast. Innovation was frowned upon for years but not any longer. Teams, coaches and players are always looking for an edge and a way to stay ahead of the field. Dr. Murray's Mental Performance Index can be and will be the next part of sports evolution in the 21st Century.

—Tom Flores

Acknowledgments

I would like to start by honoring my father, a great man and my constant companion. He sparked this book by taking me to my first NFL game 41 years ago. Our many illuminating discussions, his sense of humor, his remarkable creativity, and his tireless efforts helping shape this manuscript will be forever appreciated.

I thank my gorgeous wife, Charlotte, and our amazing and beautiful 7-year-old daughter, Caroline, for understanding my days and evenings away to finish this project. I can still hear Caroline asking, "Daddy, are you still writing that book?"

I thank both my parents for their love, support, encouragement, and optimism. My three sisters and I are lucky to have such positive role models.

I am grateful for all my rivals and teammates who've kept me on my toes over the years from heated neighborhood games to organized sports in the '60s and '70s, fraternity rivalries and worldwide tennis in the '80s, college athletics in Gainesville, Florida and Pullman, Washington in the '90s, and a rich variety of pro, Olympic and amateur athlete clients for whom I've been honored to serve as sports psychologist.

Huge thank to Steve Sabol, President of NFL Films, for sending his crew my way to talk football psychology on The NFL Network and ESPN2 in November, 2009. I also thank the hundreds of radio and television show hosts who've invited me to discuss the Super Bowl and the MPI over the past 8 years. Thanks also to the late Dr. Stephan Tchividjian who encouraged me to produce my own radio show and follow my passion in sports.

Hugs and thanks to Lesley Visser who immediately grasped the concept of the MPI and never wavered in her support. Unfortunately, her first question was, "It is brilliant and it makes total sense, but how did YOU come up with it?" as if I was incapable of such insight (just kidding!). Lesley is a true American pioneer as the first in an entire industry of fantastic female sportscasters that we have today. She knows about a good healthy struggle to improve the landscape of sports for all.

Student intern David Annetta was fabulous in preparing first draft Super Bowl game reviews on 29 games, and he continued on this project even long after his official duties were completed. I also appreciate Dr. Juan A. Sanchez-Martinez for his insights from the field of medicine, for helping to organize statistical data, and for summarizing a handful of games at crunch time.

I sincerely thank my Alpha Delta Gamma fraternity brothers and especially Lewis Waldheisen and Mike Horvath for their assistance toward the completion of this project. Both demonstrated the spirit of a "city walled" and I am proud to call them brothers.

Enormous thanks to my patient publisher Mike at World Audience, to Neil Salkind, my agent and great backup statistician, and to Professor Victor Pestien and his student Daniel Kirsner at the University of Miami Department of Mathematics for their early ideas, support, and direction.

Big thanks to Don Shula who inspired this book in many ways and then later graciously agreed to allow me to share with my readers an actual quote taken from his coaching days with the Miami Dolphins.

Everyone needs a great sounding board and advisor, and having one like Sven W. Hanson, who is a brilliant lawyer and friend, has been more valuable than words can convey. I've navigated a variety of challenging situations with him over the years and he always comes through.

Finally, I am thrilled to claim one of the most successful coaches in NFL and Super Bowl history, Tom Flores, as a partner in my mission. He freely wrote the foreword, wished me good luck and asked for nothing in return. There is no man more qualified for the Pro Football Hall of Fame than Tom Flores, a winner on and off the field of play!

—John F. Murray, Palm Beach, January 2011

Author's Note

Something was astonishingly missing in the measurement of team performance and I had to do something about it. While the product of the mind in competition (e.g., smarts, intelligent play) was vital to performing and winning, it was rarely, if ever, professionally quantified. Smarter and more disciplined athletes consistently outfoxed their more careless opponents. Yet as influential as smart play was to success, it was overlooked in team performance statistics resulting in less precision. The result was that coaches, media and fans received a limited understanding of team performance.

Imagine the errors that have occurred over the years in scouting opponents, understanding success, and grasping the impact of the mental game. This book corrects this historical omission by introducing the Mental Performance Index (MPI), a new rating system for performance in football that includes the mental game. Like our first a view of stars from the Hubble telescope, the MPI illuminates football and the Super Bowl as never before.

The organ of the mind is the brain, and it is such a smart computer that it invented the computer. It monitors and controls actions, makes rapid and accurate decisions, creates and interprets emotions, and causes both smart sports play and its opposite in carelessness and mental mistakes. Like any computer needing regular updates, the brain requires proper training and maintenance too in order to perform flawlessly. Smart football teams commit fewer mental mistakes and operate more efficiently than careless teams, but mental mistakes still occur.

Perfection is almost impossible for a team of 11 football players over approximately 150 plays in a game. That would require 1,650 perfectly executed assignments (11 players times 150 plays), and just never happens with fatigue, distractions, opponents, snap counts, and so much more. Consider how one player's mental mistake on one small part of one play may sabotage an entire team and lead to defeat. The winning team is often the one that made just one or two fewer mental errors over a three hour contest.

Given this fragility of victory, and benefits of solid mental performance, isn't it amazing that this factor has been disregarded in quantifying sports performance? It is almost as if for every baseball team that played nine innings, only the first seven innings counted in their team statistics, ignoring what happened in the final two innings. It is almost as if yards gained in the first quarter of a football game were not counted in total yards gained. What good is a last second touchdown if a player commits a careless personal foul that negates the score and his team loses? Think of how much better the analysis of any game would be if mental performance, or smart play, were computed too.

The Mental Performance Index (MPI), which captures both mental and physical team performance in a simple statistic developed over eight years, puts the mind and body back together. The products of mind and body always contribute to a team's performance, so mental performance cannot be excluded any longer among the statistics if you want a complete understanding of how a team played. Truth speaks more eloquently than words, so it is truly exciting, if not surprising, that MPI statistics correlate with winning better than any other football statistic yet created, even points scored or given up! This suggests that while teams obviously need scoreboard points to win, scoring high on the MPI, which is another way to say performing well mentally and physically in every possible moment, may win even more games.

The MPI gets its power by more fully, and accurately, representing what happens in a game by respecting the influences of both mind and body, and reversing years of ignorance. Sports will never be the same and the mental game gains new respect with this book. Call it a revolution in sports … or just evolution.

—John F Murray, Palm Beach, January, 2011

Preface

American Football is as thrilling and beautiful a sport as was ever played, coached, watched, or analyzed. While it showcases sheer brutality, amazing strength, raw speed, and years of refined position skill, it also requires the intelligence, decision making, and mental prowess of a chess master, day trader, or trial lawyer. A team sport through and through, it's also one of great emotional intensity.

I love football so much that I made it the topic of my doctoral dissertation on how players on a national championship football team coped with injuries. So my first aim in this book is to share my passion and excitement for football, the Super Bowl, and the new mega-Super Bowl this book creates each year, with each team ranked from top to bottom. This first task is easy as I've been inspired during more than 40 years as a fan, athlete, coach, and more recently as a paid consultant to NFL, college and high school players to enhance performance. If you love football, you will enjoy rare insights into our nation's most popular sport played on its biggest stage. I have meticulously studied every one of the almost 15,000 plays in Super Bowl history and will provide these insights while introducing the breakthrough approach to understanding and quantifying the game that has made this possible.

America's most beloved sportscaster, Lesley Visser, liked the idea of this book so much that she contributed its Epilogue on the genius of Bill Walsh and the San Francisco 49ers that I am sure you will find fascinating. Lesley's many accomplishments include first and only woman assigned to a Super Bowl sideline, first assigned to Monday Night Football and first to handle a Super Bowl trophy presentation. She is also the first and only woman enshrined into the Pro Football Hall of Fame. She doesn't disappoint in her chapter. Even if football is not a passion for you as it is for Lesley and me, you will hopefully acquire a different view on the game after reading this book.

A second and equally vital task in this book will be to introduce the Mental Performance Index (MPI), a new quantitative way of measuring on field performance that has undergone eight years of successful testing and validation. I will explain why many consider the MPI a revolutionary breakthrough in understanding football and sports performance. The performance philosophy behind the MPI helps people with needs far beyond the gridiron and the success of the MPI gives the mental game a big boost. It is very hard to think of "mental" as weak when we know how much influence it has on the biggest stage in history!

Knowledge is power. The knowledge I gained by applying the MPI to the Super Bowl games was more than I could have expected. The development of the MPI began by finding a reliable and valid means of collecting observable football performance data followed by state-of-the-art statistics to organize, analyze, and interpret the data. I've taught statistics at the college and graduate school levels, I know football, and I'm an expert in training the mind for peak performance. I know what is statistically fair and I kept my data collection simple enough to reduce mistakes yet sophisticated enough to capture the essence of football team execution. Integrating this knowledge of statistics, football, and mental skills turned out to be the winning combination in developing the MPI.

I also involved outside statisticians and football experts to review my project and ensure that I had developed a fair and football smart quantification of observable team performance. As a former coach and strategist wanting to help my teams win, showing them how they performed with just one statistic, was thrilling and profound beyond words. Since the MPI allows direct comparisons of teams by using a standard scale of .000 to 1.000 like a baseball batting average, where in this case .500 is roughly average, the football coach or executive can now more precisely track team or unit performance, or scout an upcoming opponent for strengths and weaknesses much better than before.

The standard scale of 0 to 1 allows the football historian to go back and compare teams across decades. It also allows us to answer age-old questions and learn more about the game. For example, the MPI can answer hot questions in this book such as which football team of all was best and why? What wins more championships, great offense or great defense? How do the best teams rank in traditional statistics and in 14 new areas? So while introducing a revolutionary new statistic that is destined to take its place alongside such statistical advances as baseball's WHIP (walks and hits per inning) and football's quarterback rating, you will also be entertained and taught many important lessons learned from the battles on Super Bowl gridirons. At the end of each game review is "Dr. John's Super Bowl Lesson" and they are again presented all together in an appendix.

As a sports psychologist paid by athletes and teams to train the subtle mental keys to success, I find that coaches and even athletes at times have an initial negative view about the word "psychology" as it may elicit thoughts of poor health, weakness, or insanity. This stereotype may come from a history of mental health care that is far from noble in the early years, but has nothing to do with today's positive brand of sports psychology. As a former international athlete and coach focused on building winning team strategies, I think we trip over labels. Psychology is just a science suited to study human behavior and mental processes, and a profession to help people improve. Since human behavior is complex, this expertise is needed to understand and help my clients. I want people to leap out of the dark ages after reading this book and to realize that any achievement is facilitated by excelling mentally as well as physically.

I consciously went right to the top to study the NFL Super Bowl. It was my belief that by understanding what happened on this monumental platform, when the eyes of the world were upon players and coaches with the greatest scrutiny, and the biggest prize loomed, we would learn lessons of success, teamwork, and passion in whatever we are doing in life, and especially in demanding pressure situations. I studied each play a little differently than in the past, looking not only for traditional performance as seen in yards gained, first downs, turnovers etc., but also for observable aspects of mental performance that could be incorporated into the team performance ratings in a fair and balanced way. Smart playing teams would score higher in my system. Careless teams making mental errors (e.g., running before a catch and dropping passes, managing the clock poorly, making careless penalties) would rate lower on this factor than teams with fewer mental errors and superior execution in pressure moments such as 3rd and 4th down, for example.

After reviewing every play of Super Bowl history from this new perspective of including observable mental performance too, I am excited to say that I have captured a more realistic picture of actual performance than was before possible. By including how smart each team performed,

I've obtained a more accurate picture of team performance. With this added measurement of mental as well as physical performance, knowledge wins big by flexing its mighty muscles and empowering us to see more of what really happened on the field.

That which reporters, coaches and fans call intangibles, mental factors, or smart play, is usually forgotten after the game. It now becomes a critical and measurable aspect of behavior. The football purist and fan alike will be pleased that we are not satisfied ignoring a part of the game so crucial to success - mental performance!

Imagine the following scenario. With 5 seconds remaining and down by 5 points in the 4th quarter of the Super Bowl, a New York Giants future Hall of Fame wide receiver makes a brilliant leaping touchdown reception with the Steelers in tight coverage, but just before making the catch, he commits a careless personal foul, or he loses focus and runs out of bounds. The zebras convene for longer than usual, reverse the touchdown and the Giants lose when they would have won without the player's mental lapse. This star receiver's brief loss of focus reverses all of his brilliance on this play and changes Super Bowl history forever. The Steelers go to Disney once again and the Giants lament over what could have been. In the past this receiver's mental error would be largely forgotten to history. We only remember winners. His gaffe would register statistically as a mere penalty or incompletion. The numbers would have missed his loss of focus and the fact that it occurred in a pressure situation on the last play. Now with the MPI, his mental error would contribute to a lower overall MPI team rating, lower offense rating, lower offense pressure rating, lower offense pressure difference rating, and lower overall pressure rating! We'll explain these different scores later in the book, and it's not as complicated as it sounds, but this receiver's obvious mental error now contributes as it should to team statistics. What about the other 149 plays executed by the Steelers and Giants in the game where carelessness or smart play would have been overlooked without the MPI? So much was missing before!

I rated every play in Super Bowl history and the precision of the MPI helped me more accurately determine which the best performing and most dominant teams were. A football team coming together to win a championship is a terrific story in itself. It creates a magnificence of spirit and comradeship that can only be equated to the finest crack combat force. Knowing how 88 different teams competed on Super Bowl Sunday, I believe, also holds clues to winning more in our sports, jobs, families and lives. You will learn how the mental game was critical in helping each Super Bowl team win. You will realize that mental performance is always present, either helping or hurting, and that monitoring it regularly is the first step toward knowing what to emphasize in practice and training. Regular mental training helps teams perform better in the same way that regular technical, strength, and endurance training also helps.

Each year after the Super Bowl, new MPI data from that game will be added to the previous database to determine where these two new teams stand in comparison to the others. This creates a slightly new overall ranking each year, and we'll all know if there is a new best performing or more dominant team of all time, or a new best in 28 other categories. Fans in New York, Pittsburgh, Chicago, Miami or Dallas will wonder if their new Super Bowl champion is the Super Bowl team for the ages, better than all previous teams that played. Exciting? You bet. Almost as exciting as the actual game!

In Chapter 1, I share my background and the many fascinating experiences and people that shaped my views on sports and football and ultimately inspired me to develop a way to measure degree of perfection in team sport performance. I discuss the awe of discovering an historic oversight in team performance measurement compelling me to correct it by developing the MPI. In Chapter 2, I demonstrate how I tested my theory that mental performance, ignored in team performance ratings, was actually crucial to success. Signaling a paradigm shift in sports, I provide empirical evidence that MPI scores relate to winning better than more traditional football statistics. I explain the MPI and how it allows us to see games more clearly than ever, revealing previously hidden elements that allowed each winning team to raise the vaunted Lombardi Trophy. In Chapter 3, I review every Super Bowl played, provide MPI graphs and statistics, and show how mental performance impacted outcome. Every Super Bowl game is placed into a single category according to how the game was played and won using MPI data and other team performance statistics. This meaning based grouping of games was viewed as superior to an arbitrary chronological listing. A keen examination of what happened in each game reveals new lessons about success for us all. In Chapter 4, I introduce the first ever MPI Bowl with tables showing which teams were the 32 best teams in history and on specialized categories. Let the controversy begin. Wherever you live or whatever team you love, you might be surprised where your team ranks. Chapter 5 explores how the mental game holds keys to solving many problems in today's game. Topics include athletic counseling, mental coaching, weekly team ratings, and the advantage of scouting opponents' MPI scores and reviewing the data frequently. Finally, Lesley Visser's superb Epilogue gives us a unique perspective on the Super Bowl and the genius of coaching legend Bill Walsh. She knew Coach Walsh well, and shares never-before-revealed secrets to his influence and success.

Whatever your reason for reading this book, I appreciate your openness to these ideas. The MPI and the thought of measuring mental performance might not agree with some football traditionalists, but why should that discourage anyone? The data speaks for itself and its success cannot be denied. New ideas are rarely accepted immediately because people are stubborn. Learning and growing is often a slow and painful process. But those who use the MPI and include smart play in their analyses and team preparation gain a distinct performance advantage over those who do not. Those who ignore reality usually face competitive extinction. I have not changed the great sport of football, just discovered a new way to describe, understand, and appreciate it that is more comprehensive and precise.

I predict you'll grow to respect the MPI for the insights it provides. You'll wonder where the MPI has been hiding. Ratings can be done on games currently in progress with partial scores provided, or on games played many years ago. I've always been fascinated by going back in time and looking at history in a slightly different way. My hope is that after reading this book you will be more inspired than ever about football, the Super Bowl, the proven power of the mental game, and the unlimited possibilities this paradigm shift creates.

Chapter One: Experiences Shaping a New Idea

"Because it's familiar, a thing remains unknown." - Hegel

Every so often in history an improved idea appears - a shift in thinking that challenges our actions and forces us to change in order to improve to a higher level, or stubbornly resist and stagnate. This is the story about just such an idea that begins in the world of sports, travels back in time to re-examine 44 Super Bowl games, and is now on its way to you.

Since we've always assumed that smart play wins more games in sports than its opposite in carelessness, mental mistakes or poor mental performance, isn't it then astonishing that the magnitude of this mental performance, and whether good or bad, has never been professionally quantified or represented in team performance statistics? I'm not sure it has been done in any sport. It never has, that is, until now, with American football.

Given the need to play smart, one would think that football coaches and analysts would have years ago demanded some kind of mental performance statistic, and that you would read and hear about this numerically, as you do with net yards gained or time of possession, rather than only in anecdotes about how dumb or smart a player or team was, or in post-game columns exploring the importance of smarter play but never defining or measuring it. You hear about smart play and the intangibles in almost any sports press conference or interview. In just one example, I found in a two-second Google search, Mike Pesca, on NPR Radio November 25, 2010 discussing the New England Patriots, and writing: "They're just really a smart football team … So they come in as a very good team."

While these comments about the intelligence or mental aspects of a team's play are made every day, and we all assume that playing smart is so crucial to success, isn't it amazing that so few have tested this assumption or measured mental performance? That's why I chose Hegel for the opening quote in this chapter. It was so familiar, so talked about and so apparently understood that it hid right in front of our noses and remained unknown at a deeper level! We chatted about "smart" so much that we assumed we already knew what it meant, when in fact we never really stopped to look at it carefully.

There came a time in my professional life an "ah-ha moment" when I chose to attempt to correct this historical oversight and create a valid measurement that included the mental aspects of football performance. The experiences and motivations leading me there are a big part of this first chapter. I decided to find a way to measure this supposedly intangible or elusive factor in developing the Mental Performance Index.

The findings I later share suggest that what we have ignored, or only given casual lip service to, has never once ignored sports. It was always right there exerting a remarkable impact on both performance and winning. This book will show this truth, and also reveal the treasure awaiting those who dig a little deeper and exploit the mental side of performance.

Mental Flexes its Muscle and Fights Back

There are other important influences to consider when discussing the mental game. Our sports culture has been telling psychology to sit in the back of the bus for years and "mental" has long been viewed as subservient to "physical" in sports. This is perhaps because physical qualities like grace, strength, power and coordination are easier to spot than the even more amazing and complex neural transmissions and linguistic associations occurring out of sight and beneath our skulls. Contact sports like football, hockey, and mixed martial arts worship smashing hits and everything physical, and this is fun to watch and even more fun to release on the opponent. Huge displays of organized aggression have mesmerized the people for thousands of years in stadiums with addresses from the Piazza del Colosseo in Rome, to 1265 Lombardi Avenue in Green Bay.

"No matter how much a 325 pound offensive lineman wants to admit it, a thought always precedes an action"

– Dr. Lem Burnham, Former NFL Director and Vice President of Player and Employee Development (in phone communication from Pullman, WA 1998)

Being exposed to physical excitement or danger evokes our most basic instincts for attack and survival including a quick rush of adrenaline interpreted as either thrill or terror. Managing these emotions is a key to success in the NFL, so "NFL Films Presents" hosted by Steve Sabol came to my office and filmed me for a segment called "Love, Hate, and Grief in the NFL" that aired six or seven times in November 2009 on the NFL Network and ESPN2. But while I discussed the exciting and potentially dangerous aspects of the adrenaline rush and the adrenaline dump to NFL teams, I was also able to discuss the more cerebral differences between strategy on offense and defense. What started as an expose on the thrill of the physical excitement and passion of football merged into a discussion of the intelligence of the inner game and the importance of proper mental skills.

Physical aspects of sport are indeed thrilling or frightening, but what is easy to overlook is that the puppet master of aggression and violence is not the big hit or body that delivers it, but really the noggin that plans and carries those actions out! Humans rose to the top of the evolutionary heap not with sharper teeth or larger biceps, but with larger and more wrinkled frontal lobe gyri and sulci, those folds in the brain that increased cortical surface area and allowed us to better plan, strategize, and reason than our more beastly or venomous rivals. This is where our true advantage in football lies too. T-Rex was big, but in the hierarchy of survival skills it was the mammals and ultimately humans who found that mental skills could trump even sheer size and speed. Bone crushing hits in football are exciting, but they also require proper desire and skilled focus that begins in the brain.

Consider the following military analogy. Navigational computer technology in a smart weapon is far more advanced and influential in destroying an enemy target than the cheap explosives packed into the cone. In much the same way, the brain monitors and controls every exciting pass, catch, sack, or kick that you have ever enjoyed in football. Other subtle mental qualities such as motivation, habit, attention to detail, patience, grit and consistency win in combat too. No computer could even match that. Despite these facts, we overestimate the influence of the end product of physical motion and contact when a player scores a touchdown. Rarely do we talk about the phenomenal mental consistency and focus required to protect a quarterback's blind side all game, or the developed confidence that makes an average player superb. We credit the final physical product and underestimate the true origin of all this excitement in sports!

Physical skills for a professional athlete are well developed and embodied in complex motor programs in the brain. Once initiated, they drive behavior almost automatically and often outside of conscious awareness. But doing it all under the pressure and scrutiny of serious competition with perfect execution, focus, lack of error, and proper intensity almost always requires excellence in mental integrity and mental performance too! Sports will always look physical, but the end products of ugly or extraordinary mental performance are not at all hard to spot. This was a great realization for me. Especially in the play by play methodical stop and start nature of football where 11 players are asked to execute as one, deviations in performance based on mental slip-ups are not only possible, but common. And what I discovered is that mentally brilliant acts usually have directly observable qualities too. What might look completely physical at first glance is soon understood at a deeper level when analyzed by the quality of its mental performance.

Adapt Now or Perish

Nothing short of a paradigm shift is now underway and this book shows the reasons for that shift. It also encourages those willing to risk being the very best to step forward and train their minds, whether in football, other sports, or even business. We've almost maxed out what we can do with a human body to improve physical performance, but the brain is still the last frontier of unexplored territory in evaluating human performance. Mental performance is and always was essential for peak performance, and after the empirical findings I share in chapter two of this book, coaches will have no more excuses for not ensuring that every player on the team receives the best mental training possible. The alternative is stagnation and extinction. As has always been the case in evolution, the more advanced adapt, survive and win. Those who ignore truth will remain in the past, lose an advantage, and fall to more well prepared rivals.

I had no interest in MRI results or the neural activity or blood flow patterns of 11 different brains, and I did not stop each player after the game and administer an IQ or personality test. I looked for something much more obvious but profound in what counts in a team sport - how smart or not the team performed on each and every meaningful play of the game. Coaches, players and reporters were not hallucinating when they described a smart performing team and neither was I. We all saw it and it was almost too real and easy to see that we never went deeper. I took eight years to measure it, carefully analyzing the results of more than 60,000 teams' plays in football. And it wasn't until I studied all the data and ran the analyses that I knew that I had stumbled upon a magnificent find, and something possibly more important for teams to do if they wanted to win than score points! That may sound absurd, but it may be true as you will later read from the data. The statistic created was quite reliable and valid in measuring what it was supposed to, and more related to winning than anything else I looked at. I had never felt the excitement of discovery like this before and knew this book was needed.

While my first book "Smart Tennis: How to Play and Win the Mental Game" is a commercial best-seller in three languages to help teach the mental skills to individual players, and still found in bookstores worldwide, twelve years after its publication as a "how to" manual, this new book is much more about my personal discovery and overwhelming realization, and then a new way of helping teams win championships. The story begins in my childhood and has not yet ended. Each year an update to this book will be made after the Super Bowl to bring it current. I'm the most fortunate guy on the planet at the start of 2011. All the hard work of the past now allows me to excitedly share this entirely new way of looking at sports performance and a refined way to measure it.

Looking at what actually happens on a football field, one play at a time, and only looking at what is directly observable and measurable, I have more precisely captured how well teams perform in an entire game relative to their opponents. A big part of this precision is that I adjust the rating based on observable mental performance that anyone savvy in football would agree upon. While I am a scientist and readily admit that no data or measurement system could possibly be perfect, especially with human behavior, what I found appears to be much better than what we had before. This is partly because I closely examined every single play in a game and this greater amount of data provided increased statistical power. More observations also minimized statistical error. But it is also, as mentioned, about being more inclusive in allowing mental performance to shine too.

This is not a heavy book on numbers and statistics as the title might suggest. At the same time, numbers add precision that has been sorely missing and statistics allow us to make sense of scientific findings. This is mainly an inspiring story with a serious side too, and you will hopefully learn from the success of the teams throughout Super Bowl history and learn from what we have found adding mental performance to the mix. Enjoy the serendipity of discovery and motivational forces guiding me from a childhood athlete and dedicated sports fan to international coach, sport psychologist and radio talk show host. Only when I had the responsibility of telling thousands of on air listeners how their team had performed mentally, did I stumble upon this major flaw in team performance statistics, and realized that I needed to attempt to do something about it. I called it the Mental Performance Index (MPI), and as stated, the MPI measures team performance overall that is adjusted with observable mental performance too. So finally we have a team performance statistic that is comprehensive in showing both physical and mental performance together.

My analysis of every play of the first 44 NFL Super Bowl games, and eight consecutive seasons of playoff games with the MPI, demonstrated that smart play was even more important to success than I had previously realized. Its inclusion in an overall rating yielded a more accurate representation of team performance than before available. Standardizing the statistic on a .000 to 1.000 scale also allowed me to compare and rank teams in Super Bowl history, learning new insights about success that anyone can enjoy and benefit from.

Understanding this new philosophy of team performance might require an open mind at first. It can be like watching the Super Bowl on a brand new 3D HDTV for the first time. The picture is crystal clear and shows reality much better than ever, but the glasses might feel a little strange on first wear. I did not change the great sport of football, just made it clearer and more interesting. Football experts gain a more accurate way to measure performance and encourage week to week improvement, and the psychological side of sports gains new respect.

Come along with me now as you meet some of the very interesting characters and situations shaping my life. Leaving many of you out was not intentional and I apologize, but I did not have time to make this a 1000 page book. Enjoy reading about some of the wild and fortuitous experiences that inspired me to become a sport psychologist. Jump into my time machine as we look back at all 44 Super Bowls from a slightly different, and more accurate, perspective that is a football lover's dream. Even if football was not your sport when you began reading, you just might fall in love with it by book's end. This was exciting to write, and you will hopefully be transformed, the way I was, by nothing short of the thrill of discovery.

Football Roots

Growing up in a Catholic South Florida family in the 1960s and '70s, watching or playing football seemed almost as important as attending Mass. Even our Parish Priest, at St. Joan of Arc in Boca Raton, ended Masses early praying for a Dolphins victory and allowing time to get home for the 1PM kickoff. My older sister and brother-in-law both attended Notre Dame, as did an uncle who joined Knute Rockne's team until he broke his leg and was forced to quit. I guess the spirit of Rudy in the famous movie best characterized him. (You will enjoy meeting another Rudy later in this chapter.) A second uncle was a former army chaplain and parish priest from Cleveland who visited two weeks a year to play golf all morning and watch football all afternoon. I played organized youth football for a few years with a first cousin whose son went on to become the most successful defensive end in Kent State football history just last year. A third cousin, as you will later read, has long been the most successful team president in the NFL. I'd heard his name and admired his accomplishments for years even though he selected the Colts Peyton Manning and the Bills Thurman Thomas to torture my local Dolphins, but I had no idea that we shared great grandparents until a few months ago. Even my father, a former Jesuit scholastic from Ohio, taught me to "follow the argument, and football, wherever it goes" and I soon pleaded with him to "throw me just one more long bomb" in the backyard. There was nothing in the world better than a fully outstretched, diving, over the head, finger-tip catch while flying over backyard bushes. Pursuing the greater glory of sports and football was both natural and exciting.

South Florida

The Super Bowl era kicked off on January 15, 1967, in the Los Angeles Memorial Coliseum as the Green Bay Packers dominated the Kansas City Chiefs in the first NFL-AFL World Championship Game, later called Super Bowl I. While LA may have hosted that first game, it was in my Miami backyard where the Super Bowl captured America's heart. Over the next four Super Bowls from 1968 to 1971 Miami hosted three, with the games in 1969 and 1970 so shocking American Football League victories that the leagues merged. The New York Jets and Kansas City Chiefs triumphed over the supposedly better National Football League Colts and Vikings, compelling the NFL to finally accept the innovative AFL upstarts and the NFL we have today became one in 1970.

While Pittsburgh produced legendary quarterbacks with names like Unitas, Namath, Montana, Marino, and Kelly, and Dallas later claimed to be "America's Team," Miami's warm winters spelled Super Bowl in January, and then the Dolphins glory years just added to the frenzy. Every year that I can remember America's obsession with the big game grew stronger. If my eyes were not already twirling spirals after three of four consecutive backyard Super Bowls when football was becoming America's number one sport and the next major team was 700 miles away in Atlanta, the real excitement was right around the corner.

This impressionable 8-year-old youngster would soon become transfixed by a Miami Dolphins team that nabbed Don Shula from Baltimore in 1970.

Don Shula

When I started following each Dolphins game closely local games were blacked out and we had no tickets. The play-by-play announcing of Rick Weaver on WIOD 610 radio shouting "Holy Toledo what a hit … Captain Crunch Mike Kolen just rappycaked him!"(With future media star Larry King's excellent color commentating on the sidelines) was a real blast of energy and emotion, but when Don Shula took over, a higher intelligence also arrived and my father could not contain himself. He excitedly proclaimed Shula a young and bright football mind who had attended John Carroll, a Jesuit university, while I had no earthly idea who or what John Carroll was or what he was talking about. I interpreted it as a simple truth that Shula would turn around our young team that had never won. My father explained that Jesuits were some of the toughest and brightest teachers in the world and that Shula was a class act and a winner because of his background. No wonder my two younger sisters and I later went to Loyola University of New Orleans, a Jesuit stronghold. My dad was right on about Shula, but who would have imagined the greatness he achieved that is now depicted in a bronze statue in front of Sun Life Stadium showing Shula carried off the field on the shoulders of players Al Jenkins and Nick Buoniconti after winning Super Bowl VII and completing a perfect season? Who would have imagined then that he would win the most games in NFL history?

For many parents having a son enter the Jesuits was perhaps the highest honor for a Catholic family in Ohio in the 1940s, and my dad became inspired by their message and entered the Society of Jesus at the Jesuit Novitiate at Milford, Ohio and proceeded to earn degrees in Latin and Greek, English Literature, and Philosophy; so, in addition to sports and football, academics and doing well in school were emphasized in my upbringing. My dad would stay in the Jesuits 12 years but left because he knew that becoming a priest was more his family's calling than his own, and he wanted a family of his own. Incidentally, he recently finished a book about his experience in the Jesuits called "All that is Seen and Unseen," both a gift to our family and a fascinating look back at an era that has long since passed. After he left the Order, he was hired by Time, Inc. in Chicago, which included Sports Illustrated among its other magazines. One of his first assignments for SI was to cover the US Olympic basketball team in Chicago as they returned from Australia in 1956 to play the Loyola Invitational tournament. There he met and befriended future basketball legend Bill Russell, got the scoop from Russell that he would join the Boston Celtics, and wrote an unsigned article on Russell "The New Pro" that appeared in a December, 1956 issue. I have the copy in my office.

Shula was more than everything he was cracked up to be. He brought to Miami an amazing work ethic, high standards, and real football smarts. Was this all just for the greater glory of a sport? I had heard about more accomplished coaches like Vince Lombardi in Green Bay and Hank Stram in Kansas City, but Shula was "The Don" in my young mind. Hanging onto every Shula word written or spoken in those early years and on the "Don Shula Show" which aired on television each Monday night during the season, I truly felt that I understood his psychology. His communication skills were exceptional. While he kept his message very simple, his schemes could be elaborate and complex to his opponents, such as the cross block that was the undoing of the Minnesota Vikings in Super Bowl VIII. He talked tough and appeared to instill a deep fear of overconfidence in the team when it won easily, and to be much more positive and supportive when the team struggled. Of course I was not a fly on the wall of those closed door meetings hearing the intensity and language that Dolphins defender Tim Foley told me about at the New Orleans Marriott Hotel in the early '80s, or that Joe Rose smiled about while we chatted as he was opening a nightclub in South Florida in the early '90s. In that same conversation, Rose also showed me his hands and told me they were raw hamburger from catching Marino's passes in practice. I'm sure my mother would have been appalled if her 9 year old son ever heard the locker room language in those days. Some things to motivate are best kept private. But listening to Shula's public statements and reading his comments in Dolphin Digest, were an education in sports psychology before the profession existed. I'd feel sorry for teams that did not have such a great leader. It was brilliant the way he pulled rabbits of success out of his hat time and time again.

First NFL Game

On Sunday November 15, 1970, I attended my first NFL game with my dad at the Miami Orange Bowl when the Dolphins faced the New Orleans Saints. Emerging from the innards of that stadium to see the field for the first time was like dying and going to heaven. How colorful, bright, large, and real everything looked compared with our fuzzy Zenith television. It was like emerging from the cave in Plato's Republic and having those dark shadows on the cave wall instantly transformed into a full color motion picture that I was part of.

Looking back, my dad's timing was mind-boggling to take me first to this particular game. There was much talk in the air about Tom Dempsey, the Saints kicker with only half a foot whom I studied with my binoculars. Just one week before this game Dempsey had kicked his team to victory on the longest field goal in history, 63 yards. His record still stands to this day, tied with Jason Elam of the Broncos who matched his feat in 1998. I wondered then and still do now how somebody with half a foot and a straight on style could drive a ball that far. "Was nothing impossible," I thought? Watch Dempsey's kick on YouTube, and you will be struck by how relaxed and calm his body remains as he slowly glides into the snap with perfect balance and rhythm. As he steps into his approach perfectly, he uncoils the most efficient and ferocious explosion of energy possible at just the right time. That kick has still not been surpassed in an NFL game. And what mental concentration!

Beyond Dempsey, however, this game was the true historical turning point of the Dolphins franchise. This game was the start of a dynasty almost as impressive as the Ming Dynasty in China. In the three games prior to the one I attended, the Dolphins had been shut out 35-0 by the Colts and 28-0 by the Browns, and then had lost 24-17 to the

Eagles the week before, so at 4-4 the playoffs weren't given much thought. I made a sign of support for the game that I was sure the players would study coming out of the huddle. We had tickets on the 30 yard line of this giant creaking erector set. Seats and cramped benches were more vertical than today, almost on top of the field like an opera house balcony, but the atmosphere admittedly had less decorum. We were so close to the field that you could feel the smashing hits and almost be splattered by flying sweat and blood. Miami fans routinely terrorized opposing quarterbacks with crowd noise that was as loud and as intense as the Gator swamp in the 1990s while UF played FSU or Tennessee. I was a part of that 12th and 13th man on the field going wild and waving white handkerchiefs, and quarterbacks often retreated to the huddle or complained to the officials who would then ask the crowd to be quiet. Of course that only incited us to swarm more violently and the enemy quarterback would eventually make a key mistake due to poor focus, or the increased crowd energy would lift the play of the Miami defense. I still love going to football games today, with a setting ten times more comfortable, but as a kid who wants comfort? Nothing matched the rumbling drum beats of pounding feet on rusty steel that the Orange Bowl epitomized. It created such incredible havoc, and I loved it all.

The first touchdown of this Saints game electrified the crowd when Miami's Lloyd Mumphord picked off Billy Kilmer and took it to the house on a 32 yard interception return. My homemade sign had worked and the Dolphins ended their losing streak with a 21-10 win, won their final 6 games to finish 10-4 and qualified for the playoffs for the first time ever. They lost a close one in the playoffs to the Oakland Raiders, but this only increased my interest. In 6 consecutive football seasons starting with 1970, the Dolphins only once lost two in a row! I was there for the beginning of something special. The team earned their first playoff appearance that year, won the AFC title in 1971, appeared in 3 straight Super Bowls from 1972 to 1974 and won the final two, achieved 17-0 perfection in 1972, and ultimately claimed Don Shula as coach with the most wins in NFL history.

Perfect Season

I knew that my thoughts about sports perfection had nothing to do with how teams did, but how could you not love what came next? I vividly remember where I was when I told my dad after the Dolphins lost Super Bowl VI to the Cowboys in January, 1972, that the Dolphins would win every game in 1972. He dismissed my thought as "crazy," asserting that "no team had done that before," and lectured that "on any given Sunday any team can win or lose." I firmly disagreed and said "just watch." We even made a $1 bet. When the 1972 team delivered by going 17-0 and winning Super Bowl VII over the Washington Redskins 14-7, he had to eat his words, and I was a dollar richer.

I've chatted with players from that team including quarterback Earl Morrall whom I met in 2009 at a Champs Sports event at the Hyatt Regency Sarasota. I was approaching the Hyatt garage when that unmistakable crew cut suddenly materialized. He looked great and I thanked him 37 years late for the "perfect season" and picked his brain for an article I was writing. He was very helpful. While he is mostly forgotten today outside of Miami or Baltimore, he only led the most successful team in history to more than 70% of their 1972 season wins! When Bob Griese went down with an injury, he stepped in and made it happen. I realize that offensive linemen Larry Little and Bob Kuechenberg moved mountains and there was less of a need to pass with Larry Csonka, Jim Kiick and Mercury Morris running the ball. My older sister Cathy, infatuated with Mercury, would go nuts when Morris electrified crowds with his jagged runs. We established a policy of waving our white handkerchief only when the team scored and later checking to see how wrinkled it had become as a measure of success. Morrall's veteran leadership and smart play had a crucial impact. He did not seek notoriety, and he would be awarded as "Unsung Hero" of the Dolphins in 2005. I hope you'll never again forget Earl Morrall when you think of the undefeated 1972 Miami Dolphins.

While perfection had supposedly been achieved and it inspired a future sports psychologist, MPI scores from the regular season and the Super Bowl win over Washington are very far from a perfect 1.0. As Oakland's owner Al Davis might say, however, "Just win baby!" Every slight advantage helps a team win, and the MPI (the Mental Performance Index I created) measures those advantages more precisely than before.

Success for the 1972 Perfect Team was earned moment by moment, the same way the MPI is scored. Success is rarely achieved by one big play and then checking out. It is not about being flashy, jumping around, or taunting the quarterback. It is not going helmet to helmet on a hit, or making one big play. Hitting and passion are important, and talented play is also needed, but mental mistakes wipe it all out in an instant.

MPI and team success is about taking care of each assignment, working extremely hard, staying focused and poised in the moment, executing properly, avoiding mistakes, playing smart, and so much more. To get there requires intelligent coaching, solid recruiting, resilience from injuries and pain tolerance, courage, blood, sweat, tears, and sacrifice. Success is not about being pretty or comfortable, and being number one is never easy or everyone would be tops. Winning goes to the team that refuses to lose, and this is accomplished by consistent execution and smart play over the entire game. When it all clicks it is very beautiful and you might end up with something like those rare 1972 Miami Dolphins.

Shula's teams annually committed the fewest penalties and the defense was so anonymous they were called "No-Names." They were very blue collar and so different from the flashy Marino-led teams in the 1980s and 90s. Yet they just kept winning the way the MPI rewards mental and physical performance. I remember late Los Angeles Times columnist Jim Murray (no relation) writing a story in the early 1970s titled "Who are the Miami Dolphins?" and poking fun at them for being so anonymous. We did not have the media options like we have today with the internet and Sports Center, but I enjoyed following every play as the perfect season unfolded. I even won a dollar from my dad. And as you will read later in the book, the Dolphins were much better in the Super Bowl the next year, and I think a much better team too, despite losing two games, but it was the perfect season that inspired me the most and the one we all remember.

Sea of Hands

Looking back it makes sense how I became obsessed with sports perfection, because it occurred and I actually believed it would. But this 5-year joyride ended one miserable night on what NFL Films dubbed the "Sea of Hands Play," on December 21, 1974. Boyhood dreams of athletic conquest vanished on a bizarre play in the first round of the playoffs. Miami had won back to back Super Bowls and a third title appeared inevitable until Oakland quarterback Kenny Stabler, with 24 seconds left, and falling down in Vern Den Herder's grip, shot-putted a lame duck into a sea of Dolphin defender's hands. Somehow Raider running back Clarence Davis caught it, and Oakland eliminated Miami from the playoffs 28-26. I was devastated, but five years of watching the best team ever could never be erased. Today as a sports psychologist in my 40s, I'm subconsciously trying to get back to one second before the Sea of Hands debacle, and someday I'll do my small part to help an NFL team win the Super Bowl. Like Julius Caesar crossing the Rubicon River and shouting out "The Die is Now Cast" in 49 BC, my passion for football and all sports at age 13 was fixed for life.

Crash

The "Sea of Hands" debacle was tough to stomach but there would soon be another "great" era for the Miami Dolphins that I enjoyed while in college. It began even before Dan Marino. Led by a "Killer B's" defense, resourceful offense, and smart coaching, the Dolphins won the AFC title and then lost to the Washington Redskins and John Riggins 27-17 in Super Bowl XVII. Two years later, the young Marino broke records all season long throwing rockets to Mark Duper and Mark Clayton, but Miami was beaten by one of the best ever in Super Bowl XIX, the San Francisco Forty-Niners.

One of my favorite players during these years and beyond was extremely tough and smart, and he later became a friend. He would play in both these last two Miami Dolphins Super Bowls and his name was Jim "Crash" Jensen. He embodied everything I try to instill in athletes today.

Many will not remember him because he was not a big household name, but he always produced and his love of the game was palpable. Originally brought in as a quarterback, that idea was not working with Dan Marino around, so he just adapted by playing almost every position on the field. He was known for his uncanny ability to make the big hit on special teams, convert third downs as both receiver and running back, force or recover the fumble, and he even threw touchdown passes! To me, Crash represented the ideal team player and we need more like him today. He would be named the 1988 "NFL Special Teams Player of the Year" and the Miami Dolphins "Unsung Hero" in 2006.

Baseball

When the Dolphins returned to earth I was playing a lot of first base on my youth all star team and playing tennis every day. My dad moved us to Coral Springs to be closer to a job he accepted at Nova University in Ft. Lauderdale. The nearest pro baseball was New York Yankees Spring Training in Fort Lauderdale, and I started following them in 1975. I remember clipping Yankee box scores into my notebook when they were 14 behind Boston one summer until they caught the Sox and won the division in one of the most exhilarating comebacks in history. I summarized each game. Sometimes it was a clutch home run or smart pitching change, while at other times it was an unnecessary error that made the difference (maybe the MPI for baseball is next!). Nothing was impossible. A team striving for success intoxicated me then and still does today.

Despite the positive ghosts of Ruth, DiMaggio and Mantle past, the Yankees had not won anything since the early 1960s. George Steinbrenner changed all that. Did I mention that leadership and money is important? First, they went to the World Series and lost to the Big Red Machine Reds in 1976. Then in 1977 and 1978 they won the World Series over the Dodgers. I remember my thrill as Reggie Jackson smacked 3 home runs on 3 pitches in game 6 of the 1977 series. I called my sister Cathy at Notre Dame each time he hit one, and we shouted wildly as we had during the years of Dolphins mania. It was similar to the feeling I had at a teenager friend Frank's home on April 8, 1974 when I recorded Hank Aaron's 715th career home run live off the television set. But there was even more incredible energy that night as if everyone just knew that Reggie was going to hit a home run on each pitch, and he did! His confidence was ridiculous. Look back at those clips if you want to see what confidence looks like. It was like Dempsey's 63 yard boot or Mohammed Ali's jabs. There was something that night beyond physical talent. It was on par with Wilt Chamberlain's 100 point game against the Knicks, or Michael Phelps' eight gold medals in at the 2008 Beijing Olympics. I still enjoy following the Yankees (and Marlins) today. A couple years ago I went on Fox national television to spar with host Neil Cavuto about the treatment of Yankee skipper Joe Torre. I admired Steinbrenner, but Torre deserved more respect for his accomplishments.

Twisting Time in Tulane Stadium

The ghosts of 3 Super Bowls past followed me to college at Loyola University New Orleans one moonless October night in 1979. Two buddies and I snuck into old Tulane Stadium, just a few long passes from my dorm, climbed over the fence with the "no trespassing" sign and jumped down to the stadium entrance. A 17-year-old freshman, I tasted the rewards of my delinquency by lumbering down to the same 50-yard-line of Poly Turf where Larry Csonka fumbled in Super Bowl VI against Dallas. "I thought you needed tickets to have this much fun," I reflected. I jogged over to where Hank Stram whooped it up wildly on NFL Films as his AFL Chiefs upset the favored Vikings in Super Bowl IV. Then I carefully looked back and imagined Franco Harris galloping 158 yards only four years earlier in the Steelers win over the Vikings in Super Bowl IX. While there was already a Salvador Dali with bending clocks of relativity in my Loyola dorm, this transport to a hallowed past was more surreal at night with fear of being caught. I still see and hear it all today. All those past echoes of football and media excitement, and the illusion of 80,985 fans screaming come back in an instant. Even long after wrecking crews demolished it all, the images are clearer than ever. It was an awesome evening and I hope you enjoy reading of the three Super Bowls played in Tulane Stadium in Chapter 3.

A little more than a year later on January 25, 1981, a stranger suddenly appeared at my ADG fraternity house residence only 45 minutes before the kickoff of Super Bowl XV, and sold me two tickets for $25 each. I quickly grabbed the first frat brother I could find, Farshid Amir from Iran, threw him into my Olds 98 station wagon, and gunned it over New Orleans pot holes and up onto the Louisiana Superdome parking ramp, somehow finding our way into the garage. When we emerged from the stairs, we realized that we were only a few feet from our 50-yard-line seats in the 15th row! Those seats would cost $7,500 a piece today. Going to an NFL game was never easier.

Huge success is often right around the corner to those who hang in there and believe a little more when all seems lost. I adopt this approach in my sport psychology work today because I realize that the difference between winning and losing is often tiny. People often beat themselves long before the opponent does. World number one tennis player at the time, Lindsay Davenport, is quoted on the cover of my book "Smart Tennis," saying "the game with yourself is often tougher than the battle against any opponent."

Raiders Coach Tom Flores, a former AFL star quarterback and Super Bowl back-up to Len Dawson, past Raiders offensive coordinator, and now head coach in Oakland in 1980, displayed this same kind of belief and support of a player. When his starting quarterback Dan Pastorini went down with a severe injury in the 5th game of the season, Flores called on back-up Jim Plunkett, a 1970 Heisman Trophy winner who never won anything in the NFL. I remember thinking "not Plunkett again" right before he threw 5 interceptions to lose to the Chiefs 31-17. "It's over for him," I barked, not knowing how completely wrong I would be! Tom Flores believed in Plunkett and he finished the year on an unexpected roll that took the Raiders all the way to this New Orleans Super Bowl. They shared a common background as rare Hispanic NFL quarterbacks and Plunkett benefited greatly from his mentorship.

I had been hitting tennis balls in my Loyola University field house earlier the week of the big game when suddenly green and white jerseys of the NFC Champion Philadelphia Eagles invaded for an unannounced practice. I briefly chatted with Eagles Coach Dick Vermeil, who greeted me with a "how you doing young man" pleasantry, then I watched him oversee quarterback Ron "Jaws" Jaworski's alley-oops to 6'8" wide receiver Harold Carmichael. I was told that the Eagles had been bussed immediately to practice after arriving in New Orleans, whereas it came out later that Flores allowed his players to let off a little steam on Bourbon Street before he imposed an 11 PM curfew on Tuesday. The Raiders ended up fresh and light while the Eagles appeared tight and nervous before the game. Not only had Flores grooved Plunkett back from desperation to glory that year, but he was also able to keep his team relaxed. Plunkett lit up the scoreboard with 3 touchdown passes in a 27-10 rout to earn MVP honors for Super Bowl XV. The Flores/Plunkett duo would strike again in Super Bowl XVIII when the Raiders destroyed the Redskins in Tampa 38-9. I don't have a vote, but if anyone is deserving of the Pro Football Hall of Fame, I would argue for both Tom Flores and Jim Plunkett. I can't believe I am writing this after the "Sea of Hands" play!

The Swamp

When I went back to graduate school after traveling the world in tennis for six years, I wondered if I could get involved with the big teams. Nothing is bigger in Gainesville, Florida than the Florida Gators football team, so I was naturally thrilled when they accepted my request to conduct my doctoral dissertation on the 1996 team. I studied the emotional adjustment to football injuries and how players cope in order to improve our overall understanding of sports injury rehabilitation. It was a good study merging more traditional psychological approaches toward stress and coping with the psychology of athletic injury. The team was coached by Steve Spurrier in 1996 and I went into the training room every week to speak with players and collect data. Trainers Chris Patrick and Mike Wasik were a big help and Mike and I became good friends and played a lot of tennis.

Unbelievably, the team I adopted for my dissertation in 1996 made it to the national championship game and won. "Here we go again," I thought. It was the first national championship in Gator football history, and they beat FSU in the Sugar Bowl 52-20. Did having a budding sports psychologist around all year hurt that team?

Amber Waves of Grain

The next year I was fortunate to secure perhaps the only authentic sports psychology internship in the country. It was the only one that was also a member of APPIC (an acronym for the Association of Psychology Postdoctoral and Internship Centers), which means it was approved by the American Psychological Association for providing the proper amount and type of clinical training, an important prerequisite to completing the doctorate at the University of Florida. APPIC member internships make it much easier to later get licensed as a psychologist because they have jumped through all the proper hoops in providing a planned training sequence with licensed psychologists providing supervision and a long list of other criteria evaluated by the APPIC Board for membership. APPIC publishes a fairly large 2 to 4 inch thick membership directory each year. To my amazement in 1997, there existed only one out of the many hundreds listed that even mentioned the word sport or the phrase sport psychology. It was an internship within the university counseling center at Washington State University and it also offered one intern the ability to work half their total time on sport psychology within the athletic department. Seizing this rare opportunity, I flew out to Washington for an early interview and told everyone there that they were far and away my top choice on national selection day. This is one tense day in the spring every year when fledgling psychologists wait for the phone to hopefully ring with an offer so that they will be able to acquire the final piece of graduate training needed to complete the doctorate. I even put this internship (located in the remote Palouse near Spokane) ahead of other attractive internships where I had interviewed including the University of Virginia that Thomas Jefferson made so famous (it was mostly medical psychology) and Nova University (near the Miami Dolphins training facility but with no training in sport psychology).

Needing to round out my training in an extremely rare area of specialization, I will forever appreciate that my wife of only one week, Charlotte, allowed me to drag her out to Pullman, Washington for a year that was to become the capstone of my training as both a clinical and sports psychologist. I also thank those at Washington State for offering me the position. It was a great year of supervised clinical experience with counseling center director Dr. Barbara Hammond and internship training director Dr. Rob Ragatz, among others, and the experience over in athletics where my real passion resided was fantastic too. Charlotte and I packed up the U-Haul and trekked across the country so that I could become a rare, but authentic, sport psychologist. I was still a lowly doctoral student intern, but getting paid to provide supervised sport psychology services to athletes and teams was a dream come true after five years of graduate study.

With my long ingrained passion for everything football (and also tennis where I worked quite extensively that year) I took every opportunity I could to learn and experience what top players and teams go through in order to help them. Over the course of that year, I spoke with many football players and coaches, whether formally or in brief chats in the training room, on the field, or on campus. Having just studied football injuries for my doctoral dissertation with the national champion Florida Gators, and still needing to defend my dissertation to get the PhD, I was particularly interested in knowing how the injured players at Washington State progressed. I enjoyed high-fiving players after their weekly wins, and the football culture of success was again contagious. If I did not notice the rolling wheat fields or small town lentil festivals, this could have easily been in 1972 Miami or 1996 Gainesville, because the football team was the real story again!

I was invited to observe football practices out on the field, and enjoyed the interactions between coaches, athletic staff, and players, and many hours of discussion with the university sports psychologist on the scene. It was emphasized in my training to be out on the field and in the natural sporting environment as much as possible in order to be visible to athletes and teams. This was natural for me because I had been a serious coach and athlete for years. I use that same approach in my work today and like to get out to a baseball game or tennis match or football practice whenever I can with a client, and I'll even dress more casually than the typical psychologist in a button down shirt and tie with slacks. It became ever more obvious just how important psychology is to helping a football team, or any team or athlete for that matter. I was learning by osmosis being around the football field and athletic department and then going to a variety of games. The university sport psychologist invited me to accompany him to every football team imagery/relaxation session on nights before all the home games at the team's regular hotel in nearby Moscow, Idaho. I had a lot of fun interacting with the guys before those sessions and it was amazing to watch imagery in action, and how players reacted all a little differently, before the big game. We'd first walk around the hotel and recruit 20 to 40 players to attend those evening imagery meetings after dinner and before lights were out and videogames were finished. Not all players attended, but it was always an impressive showing. I was soaking it all in and it was meaningful to be surrounded by and interacting with players in this total pursuit of excellence. I had already conducted imagery on my own, and I've done thousands of imagery sessions since those days in Pullman almost 15 years ago, but seeing a top college football team get ready and focused before the big game was a special treat as an intern and it made going all the way across the country worth it.

The Cougar football team was way off the radar, and ranked about 80 or 90 in the country with nothing special expected by media, but Coach Mike Price had done a great job getting the players all on the same page even before the season started and there was real talent. A few regulars in the imagery group went on to have NFL careers, and one is still a very famous player today. During one athletic retreat where we stayed overnight at a campground, and a number or football players attended, one of the monster defensive ends lifted me up and tossed me off the pier into the lake like a rag doll in much the same way he tossed opposing Pac-10 quarterbacks around. I experienced the reality of the sack without the hard ground! It was all in a fun spirit and I called it my initiation rite as a pre-doctoral sport psychology intern!

That WSU football team had not been to their conference bowl game, the Rose Bowl, in 67 years. As if football lightning had struck for the tenth time in my life, this team I grew to love went all the way to the Rose Bowl and fell just short of a national title. They lost in the Rose

Bowl to a Michigan team led by Brian Griese and Tom Brady. Success is certainly not just about talent, I thought. Hard work, resilience and focus were huge keys to success on that WSU team. Just as during the Perfect Season, there were many anonymous players with star attitudes and superior mentoring. They were talented and hungry players on a mission, clicking on all cylinders mentally, and each win in Pullman was just another blue collar step out of obscurity. Late in the season they were featured on the front page of USA Today Sports as a contender for #1 team in the nation. The year in Pullman, Washington, was like a repeat of the previous year in Gainesville but rather than being mired in a "swamp," we were rolling around "amber waves of grain" that geographic region sung about at the beginning of "America the Beautiful." Needless to say, these gifts I kept receiving of football inspiration only increased my love of the game and desire to make an impact somehow in football. I wanted to know more and more about what specific mindset contributes most to team success. While in the past I might have been a fan (and I know that "fan" was a dirty word for many athletes, at least in Gainesville and Pullman), I was now talking with and getting to know players in all sports and trying to help them however I could. Even if it were a small tip or a pep talk, I sincerely did what I could to try to help athletes and teams win. Come to think of it, I did some of the same things in Gainesville the previous year, but this year I was paid, had contact with athletes in many sports, and my work took place in more places than counseling center therapy rooms.

Later in the season during the UCLA game in Pullman, I sat in the training room shoulder to shoulder with WSU quarterback Ryan Leaf at halftime and observed firsthand what goes on at halftime during a heated and competitive football battle, and what they talked about. Nothing surprised me, but being there was special and made it all the more real and relevant in my training. I never worked with Leaf, but he was quite the shining star in Pullman that year with a bazooka for an arm. I mention this because he was one of the top two recruited quarterbacks entering the 1998 NFL draft along with Peyton Manning and everybody wondered who Colts President Bill Polian would select with the first draft pick for the Colts.

… Then he said, "Bill Polian is Your Cousin"

I had heard the name "Bill Polian" over the years with the same visceral reaction that Boston residents have to the phrase "New York Yankees," or mice have to "house cats," or perhaps Miami Dolphins players had when they heard about the Buffalo Bills in the early 1990s. My wife and I had only been dating one year when I took her to the Dolphins/Bills AFC championship game on January 17, 1993 in Miami. It was such fun to be at a home game just one win from the Dolphins first Super Bowl appearance since 1984. Unfortunately Bill Polian, in his work with Buffalo, had done his homework in picking players like Thurman Thomas and Jim Kelly, and those Bills routed Miami 29-10. In a football fun way, I must admit that I disliked everything about those Bills, and I despised Bill Polian for being so good as a talent evaluator that he received the NFL Executive of the Year award six times and built three Super Bowl teams in Buffalo, Carolina and Indianapolis. He even selected future Hall of Fame quarterback Peyton Manning to lead the Colts while passing on that guy Ryan Leaf who I sat next to at halftime of the UCLA/WSU game during that Rose Bowl run. Polian always seemed a step ahead of the competition, but to me he was just a name.

My mother last year asked me to solve a 90 year family mystery concerning her grandmother (my great grandmother) who had disappeared from our family tree without a trace. We just didn't know what happened to her. I was determined to solve this mystery and get my mother the information. I began by posting a quick note on an ancestry website and soon received an email and phone call from a bright law librarian in California who is my third cousin and who knew all. I told him all about my work with pro athletes and my appearance on the NFL Network and ESPN2. He loved football too and told me that Bill Polian is my grandmother's second cousin and my third cousin. My great grandmother apparently watched baseball for years and is buried in the Bronx not far from Yankee Stadium and had an uncle who took care of her who was a pro baseball player and is buried next to her. What fun! I did my homework and it's an indisputable fact, but I've still not met my third cousin the NFL genius! He'll receive some signed books to share with friends and family. The foreword writer in this book, Tom Flores, plays golf with Bill and admires him. He called us both crazy Irishmen! We share an obvious passion for athlete evaluation and development. We also share very Irish grandparents. I wonder what those ancestors think about us! Does life ever ceases to amaze?

Should Sport Psychologists Have Played in the NFL?

Like many kids at 8 or 9, I entertained rich delusions of quarterbacking the Dolphins to a Super Bowl title or batting 4th for the Yankees, but I was never gifted or narrowly focused enough as an athlete to realize those early dreams. I had far too many interests and distractions in high school and college and placed more importance on academics and social life. My former Jesuit scholastic father encouraged the classics and great books and my mother emphasized the need for higher education. I am told that I was the first in my family history to obtain a doctorate. I was tall and slender and ran down and caught anything thrown, quarterbacked my ADG fraternity football team and was even named their most valuable athlete one year, but my body was suited more for racket sports than combat sports.

So how can a sports psychologist without NFL playing experience create a new system to rate football performance? You will soon learn that football playing experience does not even seem to matter for NFL coaching success. Everything I've learned in football has come from working with clients, studying game tapes, reviewing summaries and statistics, and looking for the mental advantage. While I was a very good athlete, pro football resumes go into a special "freak talent" category that I have never been a part of.

I played and coached enough sports to know that the mind needs to be trained to exploit opponent weaknesses while remaining mentally strong. I won many tennis matches over more talented players physically, for example. I knew that mental performance is like a stealth weapon, and often more effective than blazing passing shots or a powerful serve. We rarely maximize our potential in sports, and I love challenging some of the greatest athletes in the world today to keep getting better. I help them solve performance problems, develop goals, build proper mindsets, instill confidence and correct focus to help them win more. And that is just the tip of the iceberg. It's also about relationship building and establishing trust.

My clients gain the benefits of one-stop-shopping as I can be there for more serious problems if needed. These may include anxiety, anger, depression, coach-player conflicts, personality disorders, and crises, because I took the time to become a licensed psychologist too. Since I knew I was going to ask my athletes to be the very best, how could I short-cut them by not going all the way in my own training? There was another motivating factor. Non-licensed mental coaches (or whatever title they use) are ethically required to refer their clients to a licensed psychologist when issues become serious or complex. But how can they do this without proper clinical training or awareness? I'm glad I went all the way in my training and education. While I'm always learning and hopefully never resting on my laurels, proper education and training enhances my confidence so that I can give confidence back to some of the rarest and most talented athletes in the world.

I start working with any client by developing rapport and assessing his or her overall profile which I clarify in a detailed 10 page report. With this blueprint in hand, I do whatever I can to help the client succeed. I love this dream job of helping others. Knock on wood, but I expect it to carry me to a much older age than any sports playing career could have.

I have all the respect in the world for those who have played in the NFL, but you might be surprised to learn that it doesn't even seem to matter much in later NFL coaching success. Todd Haley, head coach of the Kansas City Chiefs, never even played a down of organized football. He played college golf. Even great NFL coaches John Madden, Bill Belichick and Mike Shanahan never played a down in the NFL, and the immortal Al Davis of the Oakland Raiders went straight from an English degree to coaching. Over in basketball, Chuck Daly never played at all, but enjoyed a successful 14 year NBA coaching career and led the Detroit Pistons to consecutive NBA championships in 1989 and 1990. He also coached the Dream Team to the men's basketball Gold Medal at the 1992 Summer Olympic Games. If a coach doesn't need to play to have success, should a sports psychologist, even more removed from the physical and technical aspects of the game, need playing experience?

Columnist Martin Manley, on a mission to determine whether having played football was important to success as an NFL coach, did a fascinating recent study which he reported in an August, 2009 article in the Kansas City Star. Studying 145 NFL coaches with and without playing experience and separating them by the Top 30 and Bottom 30 in terms of winning, he found that "it doesn't appear to matter much whether the coach had been an NFL player or not." He added, "It would be easy to assume that you needed to have spent years in the locker room to understand how to treat players or how to motivate them, but I see no good evidence of that being the case."

As a clinical and sports psychologist, I have no interest in becoming a coach or interfering with coaching. I respect the coach as captain of the team ship and never try to interfere with his mission and plan unless I am asked. I retired from coaching 20 years ago and want to be there today to help the coach win games and make the players stronger. The above study that even NFL coaches don't need to have played to have success supports my belief that I'm not sure having played football at an elite level is even an advantage as a sports psychologist. In this age of specialization, I'm part of a much bigger support team and perfectly content remaining in my role. At the same time, I am confident that what I do professionally is greatly underutilized in football and other team sports. The NFL teams that have developed a serious professional mental training program with a qualified sport psychologist are few and far between, but those who do gain a distinct advantage in their quest for a Super Bowl title.

A Specialized Professional Service

Since I work with top athletes in all sports including football, I often begin sessions by informing my athletes that they are much better technical experts in their sport than I will ever be, and that is good. I never try to change a golf swing, blocking technique or fastball. That's what coaches are for. My clients are happy I stick to the mental game because that is why they came in. This even applies in tennis where I coached technique and strategy worldwide for years and even earned official coaching wins at the Australian Open, including one over former top 10 Russian superstar Igor Andreev. Technique and strategy evolve and I do not want to interfere. There is plenty to do in the world I live in with the mental game rather than cross over into technique. I let coaches coach and I do what I am best at in training minds.

Even while traveling and living on four continents, I still loved analyzing football plays with zeal, and would often go back and study games on video to understand the key to success on one play or another. Watching and analyzing so much football over the years has definitely helped in my work with NFL players. I'm called in from time to time to do mental coaching or counseling with players who are struggling, and I've had the honor of helping starting NFL quarterbacks perform better. A lot of our work involves helping players believe again, stay more relaxed, keep trusting, or remain focused, but it's rarely some trite saying or pat answer that helps. Each person is unique and the clinical experience I have gained over the years has taught me to take my time doing a solid evaluation before rushing to help a player. Everyone ticks so differently.

The Media Helps

In addition to helping athletes, the media has been a good friend in helping spread the mental coaching message. I've been privileged to appear on hundreds of television and radio shows to discuss football psychology including an "NFL Films Presents" episode filmed at my office in late 2009 on Love, Hate and Grief in the NFL with Steve Sabol that aired on ESPN2 and the NFL Network. It is always my hope that media, including this book, will inspire and inform those in high school, college, and NFL football programs. I would like coaches to see the value of using a wide array of techniques including the MPI to help their teams win more and play smarter football.

Have Racket and Will Travel

After college, my passion and experience in sports paid off in a 6-year international tennis coaching career that took me around the world a few times. I would later write columns for Tennis Magazine, Tennis Week, and Florida Tennis, author a best-selling mental skills book cover endorsed by the world's number one player at the time Lindsay Davenport ("Smart Tennis: How to Play and Win the Mental Game" published by Jossey-Bass/John Wiley), and fill in as a coach from time to time on the ATP Tour. I was fortunate to help reverse the biggest losing streak in pro tennis history. I also won a couple state titles as an amateur player in Florida.

From my years of playing and coaching I gained a tremendous amount of respect for the influence of proper thinking and discipline to achieve success. Players who lost focus lost points, games and matches. I realized that most of the battle was an inner quest to stay confident, focused, energized and emotionally even. But despite my sincere interest in promoting the mental game in the 1980s, it did not always go over as well as I would have liked. I certainly did not have the academic credentials or experience the way I do now. I survived and learned.

Manfred

My passion as a coach sometimes overflowed, and I once taught a tennis lesson to a man who introduced himself as "Manfred" while I was coaching at Hotel Stanglwirt in Tyrol, Austria, in the summer of 1988. I was quite frustrated that Manfred would not run faster or stay more focused during my drills. I became more and more animated in the German language with an American accent, barking out loud "Schnell" orders and pleading for him to concentrate more and not be so lazy. I knew how important mental skills were and I was going to show him, but he just wasn't willing to cooperate. "Why," I then asked myself, "are five clean cut men in bright yellow jackets with wire connecting to an earpiece taking such a close interest in this particular tennis lesson?" It wasn't until after the lesson was over and I walked past one of these guys that I noticed his automatic weapon under that jacket. This was no ordinary Manfred. He was a very well known face in Germany, Herr Manfred Woerner, seventh General Secretary of NATO (1988 – 1994) and former defense minister for West Germany between 1982 and 1988.

Later that night at a Munich newsstand, I bought a copy of Time Magazine, and right on the cover next to George Bush and Margaret Thatcher was Manfred Woerner. He later asked me to teach a lesson to him with his wife Elfie. I was as polite as I could possibly be in the German language to this nice couple!

Riyadh

Another time while coaching tennis in Riyadh, Saudi Arabia, in the mid 1980s, I was asked to teach a very quiet and strong man who only wanted to hit balls down the center of the court as hard as he could, without angles or movement, pure power without my instruction. He dressed half in traditional Saudi attire rather than the more fashionable Boris Becker or Stefan Edberg outfits of the day, and he brought two friends on the court, one on either side. They retrieved balls and handed them to my student in a formal way that I was not accustomed to.

My student was very polite and dignified, but this felt more like Wimbledon 1910 than the competitive sport I had played in high school or watched in Jimmy Connors' fiery tirades. My student's composure was much too refined for 1980s tennis and I only learned why when the pro shop receptionist informed me that this was no ordinary tennis student. He was the Crown Prince, and today his name is King Abdullah of Saudi Arabia. Thank goodness I kept my cool and patience with him!

Pursuing the Inner Game

These early experiences of backyard Super Bowls, Shula's wise press conferences, a perfect season, unreal success as a fan, cultural exposure, the chance to teach kings and world leaders, and so much more, taught me to be open minded and optimistic about human behavior. I was enlightened by the notion that nothing is impossible and that nobody should ever lack confidence or be intimidated. Whether a person is a king or pauper, and whether a team is losing or winning dreams are always possible if you put your mind to it. Yet while the mind was so important to success, it occurred to me that most athletes and teams were not even coming close to realizing their potential. To this day I am convinced that proper mental training is a huge key to team success. I was so inspired and I wanted to inspire others.

To make a living playing tennis, you have to be ranked in the top 100 in the world, and that was not likely to happen for me. Coaching tennis was great but I wanted to advance my education and impact people on a broader level. I began reading more and it soon dawned on me that the mental game was huge in sports and business. The mind, after all, is the captain of the ship. With a Bachelors degree in psychology, a sports career established, and inspiration from worldwide travel, I went back to graduate school to become a sports psychologist. I saw few limitations in human potential, wanted a bigger challenge, and imagined myself some day as the sport psychologist for a major pro sports franchise such as the Dolphins, Marlins, Panthers, or Heat, or even a pro team outside of Florida. Athletes in tennis and golf would need my help, but there was something special about sharing hard work and success as a team that appealed.

The mental game was alive and well in many popular magazine columns and I dove into graduate studies with vision and idealism. I was determined that one day every pro sports franchise would have a team psychologist on the payroll, just like a team physician, athletic trainer, or physical therapist and I wanted to prepare myself for one of those careers. While tennis was the sport that I had played and coached worldwide, it was impossible to escape my natural passion for everything football and I was determined to do something about it.

MPI Ponderings

In many ways, the MPI, the Mental Performance Index, represents that quest for the holy grail of perfection, in which each team always tries but never is able to realize a perfect score of 1.0. But in my system, the mental game and mental performance would count in the ratings too. It was not until graduate school where I fully studied sports psychology and mental skills as well as more traditional psychology, and then developed expertise in statistics, that I realized I was onto something very exciting with the MPI.

As a mental coach I needed to be able to know how well my teams had performed independent of outcome. "Teams can perform horribly and win," I thought, "or have their best performance ever and lose," and if you only look at outcome you are getting a very poor picture of performance. In a classic sports psychology cliché that is also good advice, I would tell my clients to place performance over winning because performance is something we control whereas outcome is not. Thinking about winning or losing also causes pressure and anxiety, and places focus on the future when it should be firmly in the present.

In a flash of insight that ultimately led to the MPI, I figured that if I were asking my athletes and teams to stay in the moment and to place performance over winning, then I needed a way to measure how well they performed independent of the outcome of the play or whether they had scored! In a second ah ha experience, I also realized that I needed to test whether focusing on performance over outcome actually works as assumed and leads to more success. If higher performance as measured on the MPI won more than lower performance, then I had my answer and the cliché about performance was true. Finally, I also had a hunch that mental skills were not being considered seriously in making betting lines. If this were true, then I should by definition have better data than companies making the line as well as the betting public, and should be able to show at least moderate success in beating the official spread before big games.

As a scientist, I could not live with myself if I rushed to judgment without testing my theories first. When it was all said and done, all three hunches appear to have been right on target. (1) The MPI did ultimately correlate highest with winning, (2) it helped me predict winning best, and (3) it helped me beat the official spread in a fun prediction 6 of 8 years before the Super Bowl. My early success had me being called the "Football Shrink" by a writer at the Sporting News, but I much preferred the Washington Post's description of me as the "Football Freud." This was fun!

I still don't think anyone knew what I was doing. My purpose was to see if my theory had teeth and if we could rely on the MPI to help coaches and teams win more. It was driven by my love of football, a permanent DNA alteration after the Perfect Team of 1972. Anyone could try to replicate what I had done, but the operative word is "try." They would probably only multiply complexity unnecessarily. One would have to know exactly what I do in rating games, know my many rules and exceptions, watch me rate games for many hours to have a clue, and then there would still be errors.

I never claim magical powers, but I do have one of the biggest advances in human history on my side. It is the same advantage that took men to the moon and back and has cured many diseases. It is called science. I was making hypotheses, measuring what needs to be measured, and then using statistics to test my hypotheses. Even the statisticians who helped me were impressed with how the data looked.

While these ideas simmered, it was not until I had a better grasp of statistics and the measurement of athletic performance, that I was really prepared to create the MPI. Two more specific events had to occur before I would be motivated to go on an 8 year mission in developing the MPI. One involved my new radio show where I reported on Miami Dolphins games, and the other involved an early experience working with an NFL quarterback to overcome a slump.

Dr. T

The person who first encouraged me to produce a radio show was Dr. Stephan Tchividjian, a psychologist in his 60s living in Coral Springs, FL. Born in Switzerland and ethnically Armenian, he was affectionately known as "Dr. T" on his South Florida talk radio show. I met Stephan in the summer of 2000 when he was a speaker at a seminar organized to help individuals manage their resources after coming upon sudden wealth through windfalls. Windfalls are notorious for being poorly managed by children when their parents die, so these seminars teach financial responsibly. My father spoke at this seminar on financial development and planned giving and thought the overall topic would be useful for my professional athlete clients, many who become targets for financial exploitation after going from poverty to wealth overnight. Newly signed NBA players, for instance, who couldn't afford shoes before a mega-year deal, are coerced into buying expensive jewelry, cars and boats at retail leading to massive losses.

I listened to Stephan speak and liked his honest and no nonsense demeanor. Having lived in Germany and Austria, I was intrigued by his accent because I was flying to Europe the next day with my wife for 3 weeks to conduct the "Smart Tennis Sport Psychology Tour 2000" to promote my new book in German at sport hotels throughout Switzerland, Germany and Austria. Stephan asked to have lunch when I returned and we did. His experience as a psychologist working within large fast food corporations like Burger King, Wendy's and Arby's, and his depth on business ethics issues intrigued me.

Going back some thirty years, Stephan's father had been the owner of a private school in Switzerland when the world's first televangelist and advisor to US presidents, Rev. Billy Graham, traveled through Europe and stayed as a guest in the Tchividjian home. Rev. Graham admired young Stephan so much that he came right out and declared that he had found Gigi, his oldest daughter, a husband. Rev. Graham would soon preside over the Tchividjian-Graham wedding and the rest is history and they now had a big family with at least 5 children. Stephan never uttered a negative word about Billy Graham, and admired him for his faith, integrity, energy and eloquence. We talked over many hours about leadership in developing a private psychology practice and expanding a new field. I shared my goals in the exciting and challenging field of sports psychology, and told him about my desire to help NFL teams and companies.

Stephan believed that social responsibility and ethics were the keys to both personal well being and success, but that many CEOs had made the mistake of selling themselves and their world short by greedily opting for short term profits despite personal or societal cost. He believed that the ultra wealthy or powerful leaders among us might appear content and secure, but may actually have the greatest needs clinically, and since their actions influenced so many it was important to offer them our services. As in the fable of the king with no clothes, he felt that CEOs and other top leaders weren't challenged enough when they steered off course, but that in their power they often found themselves isolated and lonely.

Stephan told me a story one day as we were having lunch at the Pete Rose Café in Boca Raton about how he walked into the office of his boss, a fortune 500 CEO, only to see him, head down on his desk, bawling in a flood of tears and remorse. When he gently asked what was wrong, the tearful leader replied that he deeply regretted wasting his entire life pursuing financial riches only to realize that his inner store was empty and that he really had nothing. He had no-one to love, no children who liked him, no real friends, and had lived out the truth of the following parable:

"For what will it profit a man if he gains the whole world and forfeits his soul?"
—Matthew 16:26

The next year, during a day tour of the Romantic Road during a business trip to Munich, Germany I imagined that this must have been how Mad King Ludwig of Bavaria felt as he looked down from his lonely Neuschwanstein Castle bedroom window shortly before he supposedly committed suicide in 1886. This is the castle that Disney copied for their Sleeping Beauty Castle, and I stood looking out that window down onto the lake below and pondered Ludwig's lonely reality some 105 years earlier and recalled the image Stephan had created of the lonely and tragic corporate executive. We were too late on the scene to be able to help out Ludwig, but there were many others I thought, and they did not even have to be kings.

These were the kind of discussions we had before forming a consulting firm together with the fictitious name "Corporate Executive Insight," talked about conducting seminars worldwide, and printed up letterhead and business cards. He was seeing clients in the Palm Beaches and rented office space from me one day a week. I could relate to the loneliness of the leaders that I had seen in my work in college and pro sports as many head NFL coaches, for example, face a similar tragic fate as they struggle with the loneliness of power and pressure to succeed without anyone to confide in. Stephan and I both saw a need to help leaders lead better by offering our services.

The "Tough Guys Talk" Initiative

Stephan and I had often discussed the misconception about talking to a psychologist or counselor that seemed to exist in our society, and especially in some of the more powerful quarters. It needed to change. The supposedly tough types that we often saw in business and pro sports, like the CEOs, NBA stars, or head NFL coaches had somehow learned to associate "toughness" with grueling schedules, physical pain tolerance and the hesitancy to open up about problems or seek counseling. But once they did open up it was clear that this repression had exacted a toll and they were filled with more needs than most. Examined closer, it just jumps out at you that what is really going on when an athletic or business culture fails to encourage help seeking, or when anyone avoids dealing with a serious issue, it is anything but "tough" and more accurately quite "weak!" Not meeting issues head on is actually rooted in deep fear and insecurity.

One example that was recently brought to my attention was when NFL hall of fame quarterback Warren Moon wrote a book in which he admitted that he was seeing a therapist for many years and sneaking in the back door of his therapist's office at night so that nobody would notice he was seeking help. Pro football hall of famer, Lesley Visser, who writes a beautiful epilogue in this book, called to tell me the news of Warren Moon's admission. I thanked her and told her that I would make sure to convey the message in this book that the toughest among us are those who when faced with problems and are not afraid to seek help, and I called it "tough guys talk." Warren Moon should be proud that he faced his issues, but societal pressure made it harder for him to share the benefits he was receiving with others until now.

I have a solution, and it starts with every top executive in major sports as a campaign to encourage star athletes to face problems head-on and talk with a counselor or sport psychologist when needed. Every senior executive and coach or manager in the NFL, MLB, NBA and NHL should institute a program and call it: "Tough Guys Talk" with a poster and just these words on top in bright bold lettering. It should be posted in every locker room listing some of the great players who won national championships while talking with a sports psychologist or counselor. The list would be most impressive because some great athletes do seek help but then don't talk about it because of the stigma that they will appear weak. Hogwash! These leaders would in one fell swoop begin to eradicate idiocy and allow more players to access care and be tough by talking rather than running like little children in fear of being ostracized.

The program I propose would start with just one team's GM. And since I am related to one of the greatest ever and feel that he can have an enormous impact like none other, I personally and cheerfully challenge Cousin Bill Polian to institute a "Tough Guys Talk" program with the Colts. When Mr. Polian or another top executive in sports does this he will establish himself even more as a visionary who cared enough for his people to allow them to develop and improve.

Producing a Radio Show

Stephan's weekly talk radio show was much better than Dr. Laura, giving thoughtful, patient, and informed advice absent the knee jerk solutions, quick judgments, or rude hang-ups. I was a guest a couple times on Dr. T's show, and he encouraged me to start my own show which I did in 2001, teaching people about the psychology of performance called "Mental Equipment" on WAXY 790 in Miami. It was during this broadcasting experience that I shared my historical enthusiasm for the Miami Dolphins and in talking about their recent performances I realized that I had the ideal platform to share my ideas about team mental performance.

I brought on many fascinating guests including wide receiver Ron Sellers who had played for the Boston Patriots before he played for both Tom Landry in Dallas and Don Shula in Miami, winning a Super Bowl ring with the 1973 team. I met Ron at a wedding at the introduction of my late mother-in-law Mary, who had taught Ron's children piano lessons.

Ron admired Mary for her work with his children and agreed to come on my show. He spoke about how Don Shula's practices in Miami were three times smarter and more intense than he had experienced in Boston. Because he was a legendary FSU receiver, we ribbed each other about the Gators/Seminoles rivalry and he told me that my MPI was a great idea to encourage improved mental performance which was so important to success.

Another guest, Vic Braden, was a legend in sports and media for years and talked about the nature of success and the need to provide kids a fun experience in coaching. He defined success as challenging ourselves without fear to try new things. It sounded just like the performance over outcome message emphasized with the MPI. I would catch up with Vic six years later in the Australian Open press lunchroom in 2007 where he introduced me to iconic broadcaster and ex-tennis star Tracy Austin, one of his favorite students.

Finally, Vince Spadea, the ATP Tour professional who had beaten players like Pete Sampras and Andre Aggasi and was once known as the "giant killer" for his record against the top 10 players came into my Boca Raton office studio to discuss some of our work together. He was in the process of coming back from the biggest losing streak of all time and presented the calm perspective that anything was possible with careful attention to the mental skills including hard work. He did it, rose to #18 in the world, and became an ATP Tour champion in Scottsdale.

The radio show forced me to conceptualize mental performance deeper than I had ever before. If I was reporting on the Miami Dolphins, I would need to interpret their mental performance more accurately and the MPI was the perfect way to do so. Moments after leaving the headquarters of an NFL team having worked with a starting quarterback, ESPN The Magazine called and asked to come out to my studio for a story about my radio show and the MPI. While the media found the MPI fascinating they could not have known it well since I did not give them much more than basics. The MPI was never intended to be a fun or interesting sidebar in some glossy magazine. It was a more reliable way to measure football team performance including the mental game. I wanted to help teams and coaches with the information and encourage them to see the value of the mental side more precisely. I wanted to quantify what I thought was really important.

Sadly, my friend and business partner Dr. Stephan Tchividjian suffered a heart attack not even a year after we formed our small consulting firm. He was forced to take a leave of absence from his radio show and counseling work and never resumed his show. He moved to a relative's home up the coast in Florida and eventually regained his health for a few years until he fell ill again, had a liver transplant, and passed away in January, 2010. Always ready to help others and deeper intellectually than most, Stephan was a very good man and a superb mentor to me, and his family should always be proud. He inspired me to do the right thing, get more into broadcasting, and continue following my passion in taking the mental game anywhere I could. It's too bad we never realized our dreams of helping more corporate executives and doing international workshops together, but great teachers are never really forgotten, and I shared the spirit of his message in my workshops and consulting work in such faraway places as China, Egypt, Turkey, England, Germany, and Australia. Rest in peace my good friend.

I began providing NFL game analyses pro bono to the head coach of an NFL team to give him added insight into his team's performances. I also sent him a couple CDs of my recent radio broadcasts in which I talked about ways his team could perform better mentally. I repeated this for college head coaches and was soon being paid weekly by a former Notre Dame national champion player and top NCAA Division I head coach who sent me game tapes of offense, defense and special teams for both his team and his upcoming opponents each week to analyze. This was repeated many times in college. Soon thereafter I also received a package from an NFL team headquarters from a head coach with a nice NFL t-shirt, business card with the head coach's phone number, and hand-written note of thanks on team stationary praising my work. This coach and I kept in touch and I offered to help him whenever he needed me.

Rudy

In addition to my background in sports psychology, I'm also a trained health/medical psychologist and my dissertation on football injuries overlapped nicely into both health/medical and sports psychology subspecialties. I've also had a fondness for the underdogs in life and sports like Rudy in that famous Notre Dame football movie. I gained an appreciation for the underdog at age 7 when my favorite cousin, a very successful man who often traveled and brought me back a gift from Switzerland or Germany, once brought me a close replica of the rope sling that David probably used to slay Goliath with a large rock. I would practice for hours with small rocks in my front yard until I finally broke a window and the sling mysteriously disappeared. I miss that sling. It was my favorite gift and I love the underdog even more today.

One day as an adult psychologist I was asked to talk with another underdog named Rudy in a rehabilitation hospital. Rudy was only in his 60s but in terrible health. He was by now a double amputee from complications of diabetes and vascular disease. He wanted to talk about end of life issues as he had no family and only about a month to live, but his mind was crystal clear. I hope I helped him with my counseling and you may be surprised when you hear about the influence a man named Rudy with no legs and 4 weeks to live can have on the NFL.

Rudy loved talking football and had played a lot in his youth. When I began seeing Rudy at his bedside, I had been trying to convince an NFL coach to let me help his quarterback who kept playing worse every week as the team kept sliding. He appeared to need mental coaching, but the quarterback kept telling the head coach that he did not need help. After a session one day at Rudy's bedside, I told him about my own situation without naming names or teams and asked for his advice in dealing with this NFL coach who was facing resistance from his quarterback. I said "Rudy, what do you think I should say to this coach?" after which there was a seven second pause until Rudy slowly and decisively lifted his head up, stared into my eyes and then said in a slow and deliberate manner, "you need to tell that coach that his quarterback needs a big scare, that if he is not scared into getting help he will take the whole ship down."

It then occurred to me "here I am with a double amputee and perhaps the least powerful man physically on the face of the earth and he is advising me to tell an NFL coach that he has been too soft and needs to scare his quarterback!" When I said that the mental game has no limitations I was not kidding! Rudy's mental game was on! Few would have asked him for advice on such an important matter, but I believe in the power of the human spirit coming from the least among us too. I always feel that I can learn from another human being because he or she has experiences totally different from my own and a different brain too. I thought back to Tom Dempsey and his physical limitations with only half a foot, and wondered if those limitations were relevant. Nobody has kicked a ball further in 41 years, but Rudy could kick it 73 yards mentally. If Rudy has no legs maybe his insight is even stronger than Dempsey's foot! I trusted his advice because it reminded me behaviorally of the principle of the quick slap on the rear BF Skinner might have recommended as punishment for a reckless child trying to cross a busy street of traffic without looking both ways.

That night I sent an email to the NFL coach and laid it out clearly. "Coach," I typed, "I think your quarterback needs a big scare. What you have tried has not worked and if the quarterback doesn't put the team first and get help your entire ship is going down." I ended with "call me if I can be of service." The next morning the head coach called and asked me to check my schedule. He wanted me to come down to team headquarters and talk with his starting quarterback. I came down and eventually broke through the quarterback's defenses. He finally listened, shared his unique concerns, completed the evaluation, and followed through on mental coaching exercises I gave him all week. He won the next two games in a row and performed incredibly well. He was a totally different quarterback after getting some mental training! If that coach and quarterback had only known what Rudy and I had to go through to get to them.

Rudy died a couple weeks later, so this was probably his last advice to anyone. As in the classic movie, Rudy got in the game by contributing mentally. That gutsy man's advice helped a starting NFL quarterback. Rudy and the head coach get the credit for this one. Never underestimate a person based on what he or she might not be able to do physically. The power of the mind is limitless.

NFL Resistance

Despite several of these early NFL experiences that helped players and teams, my efforts in the early 2000s of getting an NFL team to make sports psychology a regular part of a team's staff with office hours, even one or two days a week, were met with resistance. Comments from the head coach went like this: "I appreciate all you do and you might be the best at what you do and it has helped a lot, but I could not stand in front of the team now and tell them they have a sport psychologist." I could not believe my ears! Did all my efforts, passion, education, experience, and even success at the NFL level need to be hushed up and hidden like a dirty secret for those who are weak? Why couldn't coaches and teams be proud of mental coaching and sport psychology services as a great way to help players and teams perform better and win more?

Unbelievable, I thought! Had I forfeited a very fulfilling international tennis coaching career and gone to graduate school for 8 years to be treated like a disease? In coaching I was popular and my players wanted more and not less of what I offered. Leaving the United States to coach for six years followed by eight years of graduate study was like going into a time machine and traveling near the speed of light. According to Einstein's theory of relativity, the people who needed my services once I began my practice should have aged and become more advanced and prepared for sports psychology, but the reverse was actually true! Progressive Europe where I had lived in the 1980s was more forward thinking than NFL coaches appeared to be in the early 2000s. Had Einstein made a slight but critical miscalculation in his theory? I wanted to be the team psychologist for a major sports franchise, but now had to wonder if all the sacrifice and education had been worth it. Graduate school was far too expensive and I was all dressed up with nowhere to go in securing a position to match my training. Even though my rapport with players was excellent, there were great needs, and a proven track record, old ways of thinking about psychology were prevailing over common sense and need.

"How is success embarrassing," I thought? Are new doctors with the latest education silenced by hospital administrators because their expertise might lead to more accurate patient diagnoses? Do judges dismiss lawyers from the courtroom right when their knowledge of case law might convince the jury to acquit the defendant of murder charges? In my case, were years of education, experience, and hoop jumping to become a sports psychologist just for coaches to exploit and then hide so that other players or coaches could not take advantage of it and have greater success too? Is losing another game because the team was not as mentally prepared or tough as they could have been more desirable than winning and having to admit that a professional helped you after going to school forever?

Throughout history, outside-the-box vision and unconventional thinking have spurred inventions including advanced weaponry and military superiority. The same applies in sports. If you ignore the newest weapons of the mind and the best that an American program of graduate education can offer, you ignore science and miss progress. The history of psychology reminds some people about a darker past when the field treated only the mentally ill, or placed them in chains, but that was over 100 years ago! Sport psychology today is just the most suitable field for studying the mind and behavior in sports, and it is the profession that focuses on training athletes and teams to win more. The greatest athletes should feel privileged to gain this expertise and competitive advantage.

Chapter Two: Testing the Impact of the Mental Game

"All truth passes through three stages: First, it is ridiculed; Second, it is violently opposed; and Third, it is accepted as self-evident."

—Arthur Schopenhauer

Paradigm Shift

There are signs that a stubborn team sports world is finally changing and it is my hope that my relentless efforts in the national media, and in this book, will boost this quest to remove stigmas and ignorance about the mental side of sports and life even more. I want people to think of the MPI as a solid system of measuring performance differently and in many cases better than before. Think of it as advanced weaponry for victory. Does that sound weak? The real problems are ignorance, stupid stereotypes, and poor communication. The strongest and brightest among us achieve greater success, whatever it takes.

It was during NFL work and doing the radio show that I finally got it! I needed to take advantage of the fact that mental performance was not being measured even though it was critically important to success, and that if I could measure it effectively and then show the added impact of mental performance on winning or losing I would have made a discovery of sorts that would contribute to a paradigm shift in how we view sports. This is precisely what happened. The findings are so exciting, and I can't wait to share them with you.

In order to show the benefits of the mental game to stubborn traditionalists, I realized that I was in for a battle. I would need to objectively quantify mental performance. I would define it and give it a measurable value in the MPI. Then I would show how winning or losing is related to the MPI. I needed to be able to show that the costs of poor mental performance are far too high to ignore and that the benefits of extraordinary mental performance were greater than acquiring three number one draft picks. I had been an exhibitor at the American Football

Coaches Association in Louisville, Kentucky one year and had a feeling about how most of these football coaches go about their business. They were very conservative, but they did listen to success. If one coach wins a national championship many immediately copy him. Psychologically, I had to wake them up with a clear objective link to winning. I needed to scientifically establish the relationship between the MPI and on-field success. If it held up as I suspected because it was not being measured before, then I would have established a link between mental performance and winning that would force everyone to take the mental game more seriously. I laid out my theory and tested it multiple ways over 8 consecutive Super Bowls played between 2003 and 2010. The results will be shared after first giving some background in better understanding the basics of the MPI statistics.

An MPI Primer

While this is not intended to be a comprehensive explanation of MPI statistics, and it will all make sense more when it comes to life in the game reviews of Chapter 3, a brief description of the MPI at this point is warranted.

There are 14 main MPI statistics that I created to use in this book including:

(1) MPI Total (MPI-T) for overall team performance;

(2) MPI Offense (MPI-O) for offensive performance alone;

(3) MPI Defense (MPI-D) for defensive performance alone;

(4) MPI Special Teams (MPI-ST) for special teams performance alone;

(5) MPI Total Pressure (MPI-TP) for team performance in pressure situations;

(6) MPI Offense Pressure (MPI-OP) for offensive performance in pressure situations;

(7) MPI Defense Pressure (MPI-DP) for defensive performance in pressure situations.

The first 7 MPI statistics are expressed in terms of how a team performed in a game on a scale of .000 to 1.000 with .500 being roughly average performance. In addition to these 7 statistics that describe the performance of just one team, as much as possible a relatively pure measure of team performance, I also created MPI difference statistics by calculating the scores on these 7 MPI statistics of one team minus the opponent's corresponding MPI statistic. For example, the MPI Total Difference score is calculated by taking the MPI Total score of a team and subtracting the opponent's MPI Total score resulting in a statistic that shows "dominance," or how much better one team performed that day compared with their opponent. These additional 7 MPI statistics are as follows:

(8) MPI Total Difference (MPI-TD) for dominance of one team over another overall;

(9) MPI Offense Difference (MPI-OD) for offensive dominance over an opponent's defense;

(10) MPI Defense Difference (MPI-DD) for defensive dominance over an opponent's offense;

(11) MPI Special Teams Difference (MPI-STD) for special teams dominance;

(12) MPI Total Pressure Difference (MPI-TPD) = Total dominance in pressure;

(13) MPI Offense Pressure Difference (MPI-OPD) = Offensive dominance in pressure;

(14) MPI Defense Pressure Difference (MPI-DPD) for defensive dominance in pressure.

While there is no way to escape the fact that performance will always be somewhat relative in the sport of football since one team is always competing against another team on every play, and therefore performing better or worse is somewhat a function of relative skill level, mental skills, size, or motivation level of the opponent, this fact does not detract from our analysis at all for the following three reasons:

(1) Teams compete against one another at the same level. NFL teams only play other NFL teams. High school teams only play other high school teams.

(2) Coaches and sport psychologists still expect their players to perform their best regardless of the opposing team's record, reputation, or talent. Physical size differences, jet leg, and a thousand other potential excuses might be tried to explain poor performance or outcome, but it does not matter in rating performance. Poor or good performance simply exerts its effect and you still need to know what it was. There is no reason to create incentives for excuses. I tell my athletes to go way beyond the excuse even when there is a valid reason for one. I need to know how they performed because that is what I tell them to do and what counts. That approach also ensures the toughest and best performance. The MPI cannot measure what the coach had for breakfast or who is sick. It just shows performance in the moment even if the field is slick as ice. If that happens and MPI scores are low, I might write in my descriptive summary why scores were low, like high rounds on a bad weather day in golf, but players still need to bring it 100% regardless of conditions. To reduce excuses, a tough as nails approach works well. Does this psychology sound soft? An upset can happen any time, and setting goals to perform and be your absolute best every play is still the key. Being psyched out by a supposedly better team or coming in flat against a supposedly weaker team is not acceptable. The good coach or sport psychologist emphasizes performance over outcome moment by moment and play by play and the MPI measures precisely that.

(3) The third reason not to worry too much about relative performance in team ratings is that the difference score for that MPI statistic will also be reviewed and taken into account to see what happened. In looking at the total performance of one team against another team, for example,

both the MPI Total score and MPI Total Difference score will be reviewed and analyzed. The MPI Total Difference score will explicitly show how well one team dominated the other team!

The two main comprehensive performance statistics, the MPI Total score and the MPI Total Difference score each have their advantages and disadvantages. The beauty of the MPI Total score is that it just looks at how one team performed. A sharp or careless mental performance will raise or lower this statistic accordingly, and you get a good indication of how well that team performed over the entire game – period. This statistic is the purest single team performance measure and it is very important to look at and to track it from week to week. I do this for coaches. The MPI Total Difference score, by contrast, shows how the two teams compared relative to one another, and it is a great index of dominance. But if the two teams are very equal in performance level this value will be low, showing only slight dominance or none at all, and we will have no idea if both teams performed well or poorly. We will only know that they were close or far apart. That is why the MPI Total score is so critically important to take into account too.

Adding the two MPI Total scores together will produce a number that shows more or less the quality of the overall game in terms of performance. So if two teams performed at .532 and .529 respectively, the addition of these two numbers would equal 1.061 and we would say that it was a fairly high quality game with good performance on both sides (and probably reduced mental errors too) contributing to good scores. On the other hand, if the MPI Total scores were .465 to .413, their addition would result in a number less than 1, and in this case it would be .878, and we would say that the game was performed at a very low quality overall.

I had to look at all the MPI scores and three traditional statistics (Takeaways minus giveaways, penalties and turnovers, and time of possession) to determine which categories to place the Super Bowl games in. In a couple times when the scores were too close to call I looked at how the scores compared with the normative sample of all Super Bowl games, expressed in percentiles or z scores. So looking at where a team's MPI score fell on the normal curve or distribution of all 88 scores played tiebreaker in determining category as it revealed more than the MPI score alone. For example, determining which defensive unit had the best performance in a Super Bowl game was a challenge. The two best defensive units in Super Bowl history were the 1974 Steelers and 2000 Ravens teams, and they were both off the charts. I am confident that the MPI revealed the two top Super Bowl defenses easily, but you will have to read Chapter 3 to find out if you agree with my pick for best defense overall.

The MPI dominance statistics are especially important and accurate as they show what happened on both sides of the ball at once when the teams squared off. It showed which teams dominated their opponents on Super Bowl Sunday. But one team's large margin of dominance might occur against a team with much less talent, or a less impressive dominance might be against one of the better teams in history. The ramifications of these kinds of thoughts were a fun and deep challenge which I enjoyed in determining categories. Whether you agree or disagree with my rankings based on total performance, you will be impressed by the rich variety of performance categories produced by the MPI and the many "best" rankings later in this book.

That should be enough of a primer on the MPI as we now get into seeing what it all really means when it comes to the MPI and winning.

Testing the MPI - Winning Relationship

In order to understand the thinking behind testing the MPI – Winning relationship, first consider some of my basic assumptions.

It is clearly understood that: (a) as team performance improves, the probability of winning increases; (b) team performance consists of both physical performance & mental performance, but as stated, this mental performance was rarely if ever professionally measured until now with the MPI; and (c) no matter what happens with physical performance, as mental performance improves, the probability of winning increases, and as mental performance declines, probability of winning decreases.

Since the MPI is rare and unique in that it measures overall performance (both physical and mental performance together), any increase or decrease contributed to overall performance by mental performance will either raise or lower the MPI score. Thus, the probability of winning should increase as the MPI score improves, and the probability of winning should decrease as the MPI score declines. And the same logic applies for difference scores like the MPI Total Difference score. But here is the key: since the MPI finally, and more inclusively, measures performance in its entirety (both physical and mental) compared with past measures and statistics that ignored the subtle mental ingredients, by definition the MPI should be a more accurate and sensitive statistic that captures more accurately what really happened in a game! Greater knowledge is greater power.

As outlined below, I tested the MPI-Winning relationship three general different ways. All three results support my theory that mental performance matters and matters a whole lot in winning. The data also suggests that we are estimating team performance better than in the past using the MPI. Here is a brief summary of the results of the analyses:

(1) MPI scores from all 88 teams that played in 44 Super Bowl games consistently correlate positively and very strongly with winning and also have much stronger correlations than all other more traditional team statistics, and 37 statistics were examined in total. The greatest correlates of winning were as follows, as expressed in Pearson Product Moment correlations: MPI Total Difference (.82), MPI Offense Difference (.78), MPI Total (.77), MPI Defense (.76), and MPI Pressure Offense Difference (.67). Amazingly, these 5 MPI statistics were all more highly related to winning than even points scored or points given up (.66). While teams obviously need to score points and keep their opponents from scoring to win, and correlations like this must always be interpreted with caution, this data still shows that five MPI statistics had a stronger positive relationship with winning than points scored or defended against! This suggests that the key to winning a game is to perform well in both physical and mental areas (that which the MPI measures), or stated another way, scoring high on the MPI might be the primary

goal for a team that wants success, and it may give the team a more important target for improvement than scoring, in getting ready for an upcoming game. If you think about it, this is not strange at all. I have told my athletes and teams for years to place performance over outcome in order to have a better chance to win and that is precisely what this seems to show!

(2) Professional logistic regression analyses were performed by two impartial paid statistics experts with over 50 years of combined experience. I chose both professionals because they did not bring any biases since they did not understand American football. The first firm examined 37 variables involving all 88 teams, a total of 3,256 values. The analysis was replicated and shown to be accurate by a second firm that started with a Principal Components Analysis and followed-up with several multiple regression analyses. Both firms provided extensive support for the validity of the analyses and strength of the MPI variables over the traditional variables in how they relate to performance and outcome. Both firms sought to determine which of many variables combined in the most parsimonious way (not too many variables) to best predict outcome in the Super Bowl. By knowing this we would know where the MPI stood in terms of predicting to winning with other variables all combined. Analyzing traditional football variables combined with non-difference MPI variables determined that the best model of prediction involved 4 MPI variables and only 1 traditional variable. This model, in fact, was so good that it correctly predicted all the results in Super Bowl history except Super Bowl V. So 4 of 5 five variables that predicted the outcome of 43 of 44 Super Bowl games were MPI variables, and not more traditional variables such as net yards gained, turnover differential, or time of possession. Stated another way, if you were looking to see what the most important factors in winning were combined to pick a

winner, you would want to include 4 MPI factors and not some 32 other variables, many which are traditional team performance statistics. Here, as in number 1 above, we show a great positive relationship between winning and mental performance, which the MPI measures. I already suspected this, but the outside experts from two separate firms provided even further evidence. The second firm did a slightly different analysis, also valid, and also showing MPI variables as the greatest predictors of outcome in a logistic regression model. I suspected this already but I wanted some serious impartial views. The findings of these two firms both supported the overall theory of the importance of mental performance and the viability of using MPI variables in my work!

(3) What about an even more realistic and long-term test where I actually look at the MPI data derived from all NFL playoff games before each of eight consecutive Super Bowls and then put my neck on the line in the national and local media by saying what I think will happen based only on MPI data? That is exactly what I did! I was able to beat the official spread in 6 of 8 years doing this as I explain next.

"Statistical models of prediction are valuable, but what about actual prediction?" I was curious to see how rich the MPI data would be and if it was very rich and better than what others were getting (because, as I guessed, I had the mental factor and others did not) then I should do pretty well in estimating pre-Super Bowl performance, and from this information be able to have reasonable success in saying how the teams should match up in the Super Bowl. I studied each play over eight playoffs and crunched the numbers. Then I made my best attempt to say what I thought would happen publicly before the game on many radio and television shows including ESPN, CNN and Bloomberg Radio, and NBC and CBS television locally. Hundreds of publications including at least 20 major newspapers wrote about the MPI. I successfully beat the official spread 6 of 8 years including the first three in a row, creating a fun buzz that earned me the nickname "Freud of Football" by the Washington Post. When I got the winning team wrong, some thought the system was not accurate, but if they looked more closely they saw that when the numbers or teams were close, picking a winner is accomplished just as accurately by flipping a coin. But the fact is that this data allowed me to outperform the experts 6 of 8 years. I realize that 8 is a small sample size, but it did not disappoint and it provided additional real evidence that what I had was working well. Call me comprehensive, but this was my pilot test to see how the MPI would hold up.

From the three overall approaches to analyzing the MPI above (the second including several analyses from two separate firms) I must conclude that the MPI is a very accurate measure of what is going on in terms of performance in a football game, and I believe it is stronger than other statistics because it finally includes what should have been included all along, the forgotten but influential mental performance aspects. I always knew that mental performance mattered, and so do many, but I have now quantified what was ignored before.

I have improved the accuracy of measuring total team performance by measuring mental and physical performance together, perhaps for the first time. Because of this greater accuracy in measurement, teams now have the most accurate global index statistic possible in just a simple number between 0 and 1, like a baseball batting average. It will help in showing trends that coaches can exploit in preparing for games. Accuracy in measuring performance should also lead to greater accuracy in estimating outcome, and the data indicates that this is likely the case, but it would take a future book reporting results from hundreds of past games before I would ever boldly affirm that I have a stronger system of prediction than experts forming a betting line in Las Vegas. Sure, they could try to hire me to add to their overall improvement in prognostication, but that is not my goal. My goal is and has always been to advance our understanding of the mental game where I am an expert so that I can help NFL teams and teams in other major sports to win championships.

Summary of Findings

<u>Statement</u>: Mental performance was not being measured in traditional football team performance statistics even though it was widely believed that mental performance is critically important to performance and winning.

<u>Hypothesis</u>: If I could measure mental performance by creating an effective statistic that included mental performance in a total performance rating system, this statistic should yield higher correlations with winning than traditional statistics that don't have a mental component.

<u>Conclusion</u>: This I did by creating the MPI. It does correlate higher with winning than other variables.

Implications and Suggestions

The real question is what it all means and what to do now to improve your team's performance or your analysis of the game if you are in the media. This is what I now offer to football.

(1) Mental performance is unquestionably very important to winning in football. Regular professional services to coaches and players should now include a strong and regular mental training component to help teams maintain their highest performance, and have the best chance to win.

(2) Team performance assessment should now include a mental component. An accurate and reliable instrument like the Mental Performance Index (MPI) is needed to regularly and comprehensively measure the pulse of the team and upcoming opponents on both physical and mental performance.

(3) Regular tracking of team performance is critical and should be done in weekly reports to high school, college and NFL teams during or after games. Systems like the MPI are used to gather the data and provide this information throughout the season.

(4) Future studies are encouraged. I have discovered that mental performance was missing in team sports measurement. The MPI might be the only instrument available to do this accurately at present. I have scientifically produced data and analyses showing that mental performance is vital to team success. As with any good science, I encourage others in the field to attempt to replicate my finding that mental performance is crucial to winning and to develop reliable and valid measures that capture performance even better than I have.

I believe that I have provided objective evidence that football team success and mental performance go hand in hand. While I thought I knew this all along, I took the conservative and long-term approach to test my hypothesis empirically. I wanted to be confident in demonstrating this new discovery to others in sports. While no science is ever perfect, the extreme care and patience I used in establishing this will hopefully be understood more and valued over time as a significant contribution to tell the world that a new age in coaching and sports has arrived. It is an age that must no longer ignore the mental game and mental performance.

A Better Sports Medicine Staff

It is my hope that these findings eventually have a great impact on the advancement of football and other sports evaluation, coaching, and even performance. Placing mental experts such as highly qualified sport psychologists on staff to help prepare teams for success should become no less standard than having team athletic trainers, strength experts, massage therapists, dentists or physicians. This evolution in sports medicine will help eradicate ignorant stereotypes. Familiarity breeds liking and this is the case here too.

The greatest benefits to coaches, teams, and players will be in team performance and athlete well being. A new standard will be reached in training and teams not willing to adapt to the paradigm shift will find themselves behind the times. Echoing two-time Super Bowl champion head coach Tom Flores' foreword to this book, mental skills are as important as physical skills. They need to be learned and refined, practiced, rated, and tweaked to reach higher levels of success on the field. They are as important as running better pass routes or lifting for strength.

There should never again be any embarrassment in having a team strategist like myself help a coach accomplish his mission to get to the Super Bowl and win it. The national champion Florida Gators football team and trainers that I worked with (including Mike Wasik and Chris Patrick) in evaluating the mental side of injury throughout the 1996 season were not embarrassed by my presence in the training room or locker room, or by my finding that social support was very important in helping a player adjust to injury. Warren Moon's performance did not suffer from talking with a therapist even though he felt he needed to sneak in the back door and not be noticed. He became a Hall of Famer.

Help for Teams and Coaches

Teams can be evaluated better and then trained to improve using the MPI. I hope my efforts make general counseling more acceptable too. A player with depression or severe anxiety needs help, and may hurt the team if the issue is not resolved. Why should there be shame or stigma in seeking and receiving help? It benefits the athlete, the coach, and the team. Winning in sport is difficult enough not to have every advantage imaginable. Perfection may not be possible, but total excellence is.

Degree of perfection is measured on the MPI. A team that played at .560 overall is said to have performed at roughly 56% of perfection. And believe it or not, that is a very good team score that still shows lots of room improvement. In this case there is 44% percent room for improvement. Former New York Jets coach Herman Edwards' quote that "on every play in football somebody screws up" is so true!

My career after developing the MPI continues to evolve. I travel all over the world giving sports psychology seminars. The book "Smart Tennis" continues to sell as players are still discovering the benefits of applying a smarter approach that includes mental training. I have taken mental coaching beyond the traditional sports such as golf, tennis, football, baseball, basketball and hockey. I worked with a world title challenger at a major UFC event in Las Vegas, I worked with a USA judo champion who brought me with him to the 2008 Summer Olympic Games in Beijing, China, I work with polo players in Argentina and Palm Beach and show jumpers in my local area, and these are just a few of the many experiences.

The Biggest Comeback Ever

One of my most rewarding highlights was working with an American tennis pro who endured the biggest losing streak in tennis history and called for help. Twenty-one losses in a row is a streak in pro tennis history that might never be surpassed and Vince Spadea has never been ashamed of it because he faced it directly with true grit and mental toughness and overcame it. If the outcome were not success or if he did not encourage me to talk and write about this, it would never appear in this book. He was from Boca Raton and I had just opened an office there and kept reading the weekly accounts of his losing as the number kept going up, up, up. He had started at #19 in the world, but was slipping fast to almost #300!

Vince called me from Tokyo one day and asked for help. He was ready to quit, but eventually hung in there and made what I will argue is the biggest comeback in tennis history since it was the longest losing streak and still is. He would write a book "Break Point" and talk about our mental coaching work in it, and he also went on the Tennis Channel television show and talked about how sports psychology helped him turn it around. He would eventually return to #18 in the world and win his first title in Scottsdale, Arizona in 2004 after defeating James Blake, Andy Roddick, and Nicolas Kiefer for the title.

Measuring Success Needed for Advancement

As you can see by now, it was probably impossible for me not to get involved in the MPI or something like it that would measure and simplify our understanding of how close a team came to perfection and included mental factors. I had been raised in a rare Super Bowl and football Mecca and had followed a team that kept getting better every year with the winningest coach of all time who still owns the best season. In one fell swoop with the MPI I integrated years of football passion and knowledge, key sports psychology principles, and the wisdom and precision of statistics. Next I needed to refine my system so that it was extremely reliable and valid, come up with a way to report my findings, and then see if it all really worked. I played and toyed with it all year. I paid a computer programmer to put my system in a form on my computer so that with one key stroke I could update the scoring and get a running score throughout a game. I validated my measure with more traditional football statistics.

I could think of no better way than the baseball batting average to show in one number how a team performed. After rating Dolphins games all year and some other games too, I started to see that .500 was indeed going to correlate with roughly average team performance and those digits were very sensitive. Teams scoring at .540 or .550 were actually doing quite well and teams that scored over .600 never lost. To give you an example, you will see that no Super Bowl team has even come close to performing above .700 overall on the MPI Total score. That would equate to 70 percent of perfection and it just doesn't happen with 11 players on a team. Football is indeed a game of mistakes, and even a team winning a game decisively with a .600 MPI score failed 40 perfect of the time or were 40% short of perfection!

MPI Starts Strong

I rolled out the MPI during the 2002/2003 NFL playoffs and went on many radio and television shows to discuss my new system and give a fun pick for the upcoming Super Bowl game between the Oakland Raiders and Tampa Bay Buccaneers. True perfection was impossible to attain in football but you could still strive for it and you needed a way to quantify how close you came to it. The 0 to 1 scale would reveal each team's actual performance in the moment throughout the game – both the ugly and the beautiful. I said that Tampa Bay was performing much better than Oakland, a team that was favored heavily, but since my data showed that Tampa Bay was doing much better I went on Bloomberg Radio and told the host that the Bucs would blow out the Raiders by at least 2 touchdowns. The rest is history.

Scoreboard Points

Putting more points on the scoreboard than your opponent is usually how we think of winning a game. Teams win by scoring more points because those are the rules. But the way you score points is not by thinking about points, but by performing better in the moment on more plays than your opponent. So points alone are often a poor measure of performance. Just two blown assignments, for example, can produce 14 points and change a game to a win or a loss even when the losing team performed better. Still the focus has to be on performance first, and sports psychologists have been preaching to place performance over winning for years. Our finding that MPI scores (which measure overall performance including mental performance) relate more to winning than even points scored may appear shocking at first, but upon deeper thought it makes perfect sense that actually "doing" or "performing" is the real key to winning more and ultimately scoring more points too.

Chapter 3 examines every Super Bowl game played from the perspective of both on field fact and MPI analysis. Come with me now as we jump in the time machine and set the date to your favorite Super Bowl of all time!

Chapter Three: Biggest Super Bowl Ever

"Joy in looking and comprehending is nature's most beautiful gift"
—Albert Einstein

Introducing the MPI Bowl

If you are enjoying this book, we're just getting started. You now have a 50 yard line seat, as I did in Super Bowl XV, but to 44 games instead of just one. You are about to witness the biggest Super Bowl of all time, a huge battle pitting each one of these memorable teams against one another until only one is left standing. I've named this the MPI Bowl and it's going to be a lot of fun and we'll learn just as much too as you'll soon see.

The contestants from all 44 Super Bowls will be ranked on 17 different performance categories. The overall best performing team will be the champion and rise to the top as the winner of the MPI-Bowl. When the two teams square off for Super Bowl XLV in Cowboys Stadium February 6, 2011, they'll each have an opportunity to become the new overall champion, or best team ever, when their MPI scores are added to database.

Before paging ahead to see the winners of the first MPI Bowl, take a moment and write down your picks for the three best teams in Super Bowl history in terms of total performance. Later you can check how your picks match my data. What about the most dominant teams or teams that far outperformed their opponents? Best teams on defense, offense or in pressure moments of a game? "Best" is actually quite different from "dominant" in my system as you will discover. These are the kinds of questions I asked and answered by looking at each play with the MPI and then ranking all the teams in each of the categories.

Keep in mind that the MPI measures not only mental performance, but overall performance with mental performance as a contributing factor. The standard scale of .000 to 1.000 provides a simple and direct comparison of teams from any year on any variable. I admit that I stole the idea of a 0 to 1 rating from baseball! The numbers generated in this first MPI Bowl provide significant information for advancing football coaching and team performance training. I also wanted to stir up a little debate and give fans and media some off-season excitement in the agonizing wait until football starts up again.

The difference between the MPI Bowl and other less ambitious projects is immense. I even browsed a mythical Super Bowl tournament in the centerfold of a sports magazine recently, but just smiled and shook my head when I realized that it about 20% correct. The MPI Bowl stands alone as just one feature of this book, but it is the product of 8 years of serious research, planning and statistics with a reliable and valid team performance statistic. If you want an opinion in life, just ask your hairdresser or call the psychic friends network. You can also Google for anything you need, but be careful as everyone has an opinion. I will understand if you are upset if you learn that I did not pick your favorite team as best ever or rank it high enough, but at least give me credit for using a very thorough and advanced approach. My analysis, like the doctoral dissertation I did and even better, is the product of hard facts informed by the scientific method and a cutting edge tool subjected to years of refinement.

Now go get your Pepsi and nachos before the lines get too long. Kickoff to MPI Bowl I is less than thirty minutes away!

How this Book is Like a Giraffe

In Chapter 1, I shared my inspiration for becoming a sport psychologist and the resistance I later experienced in the professional sports world toward my chosen profession. Then one day a solution appeared to me when I was doing my radio show and it appeared almost out of the blue like a random idea. This is how most scientific discovery starts with a breakthrough of serendipity rather than a planned advancement. Huge gains are made in leaps and bounds with just one smart thought, and this process has repeated itself throughout history.

The evolution of ideas in human behavior follows the same course as biological evolution. A quirky genetic mutation in one generation suddenly provides a unique physical survival advantage, such as height, that is inherited and passed on to future generations who survive at a higher rate than those without this advantage. Longer survival of a generation (perhaps by reaching higher fruits during a drought) allows them to procreate at a higher rate, further passing on the height advantage until the stronger organism continues to makes the cut while the weaker or shorter one dies off. The shorter may need to adapt mentally, however, and the advantage humans received in their larger and more developed frontal lobes was decisive. It put us over the top with our greater ability to reason, plan, invent tools, and hide for instance, even if we were shorter than some animals and slower than most. Don't ever discount a mental advantage! It's what makes us who we are, and the MPI is just one of those tools.

Similar to the evolutionary height advantage of a giraffe, I believe that taking mental performance more seriously by measuring and training it is a human advance. There is no doubt that it provides an observable and measurable advantage in sports, and the same goes for any other area of life. But before I could rest on my hunch or insight, I still needed to test the MPI and my view of mental performance using a scientific approach. Talk about an evolutionary advantage! It was scientific thinking that gave the animals no chance against us for a long time. It allowed us to build a space program, develop MRI machines, and even Gatorade!

While I am not flying to the moon or curing cancer, those interested in sports and high performance in any endeavor should be excited about this book and the MPI. The professional service I offer has always been valuable and necessary, and there are years of scientific findings to back what I do to help athletes, but the idea of actually quantifying and measuring on field mental performance and then showing how important it was to success had not been done. I had to first have a hunch that something was missing. Then I had to pull out the big guns of science for 8 years, testing my theory with healthy skepticism. It held up well and now you are reading about it. I have translated my ideas into an objective and quantifiable system that measures what I was telling my clients to do all along. I supported the notion that training my star athletes to remain focused on performance really works, and it does. I needed a sledgehammer to show everyone something that was tangible and measurable.

Improving mentally can be viewed as esoteric or difficult to grasp if you are not careful. It is really quite physical and quite blatant, but I could not rave about my clients' success due to rules of confidentiality in the profession. I didn't need more eloquence! I needed the bull in the china shop approach to first wake up the sports community and then show them this data. I hope I have done a good job. I hope my message is well received by all the wonderful players, administrators, trainers, physicians, and, yes, even those great head coaches and senior executives of the football and sporting world. Call me somewhat aggressive or persistent if you wish in those early years of my practice, but at least I did something about it, turned to science, and now present you a gift.

A KR Tool

From my coaching and motor learning background, I remembered that "knowledge of results" or "KR" is crucial in learning, but mental performance was not being measured, so how could I give feedback to players and teams about their mental performances? It was not even measured by the media or fans and it did not exist in team performance statistics. There was a huge problem and I wanted to solve it. So I got creative and invented the MPI.

Coaches and sport psychologists share one important trait … we both want desperately to help our teams win! It is what keeps us in business. I would not be doing this for 12 years after graduate school if my athletes and teams got worse. The evidence on how it helps is overwhelming. Yet it was incredible that the mental factors so important to winning were not being measured and that mental skills needed to perform well were not being trained. My answer was to create something useful to teams and coaches as KR that it would capture "degree of perfection" with the mental component finally included. Then, as explained in Chapter 2, I tested and provided empirical support for the MPI and for my theory that mental performance greatly influences performance and outcome. The evidence was so overwhelming, this book was needed, and a paradigm shift has launched. A new respect for the mental game in sports has arrived for those who care about winning.

Pre-Game Program Describing a New Game

We better hurry back to our 50 yard line seats or we'll miss kickoff to a new game which reviews each of the previous Super Bowls from a perspective that allows mental performance its rightful place alongside physical performance. The MPI Bowl you are about to enjoy reveals both inner and outer strengths or flaws, mental and physical aspects of superb or sub-par performance, and so much more. You might be surprised at how some of the teams rank. This is because winning and performance is not always obvious at first glance.

In our new world, a winning team might maximize their mental performance but only possess average relative physical talent compared to their losing opponent with more attractive "show" or physical gifts. This physical powerhouse might be far inferior on mental performance, having lapses of concentration leading to repeated careless mistakes, less focused effort, or inconsistency, for instance. Both physical and mental aspects of performance are important to consider in the modern age.

You also find powerful teams physically that win despite making a lot of mental mistakes, and their MPI scores reflect that problem but they still win big on the scoreboard and the media anoints them as one of the greatest teams of all time. Were they really? They might have the potential to be, but they might not have been the greatest performing team of all time. The reality is that they could have won by far more without the mental flaws. Since they look flashy and talented, they might scare a lot of people, but remember this if you are an athlete or coach … these teams are the easiest to defeat with superior mental performance. They are upsets just waiting to happen and they don't even know it unless they look at their MPI scores and see how low they are really performing!

It's a shame when physical talent is wasted, and the team that puts it all together both physically and mentally is a rare breed. The top teams in the "Best Teams Ever" ranking usually have this ideal mix of both mental and physical superiority, but upsets make sports exciting and they happen almost as much as they do not. The 2007 New England Patriots, by all accounts, were poised to be crowned as the best football team ever assembled. They were supposed to match and even surpass the Miami Dolphins' perfect season by going undefeated, but it did not happen and we've almost forgotten that season. They succumbed to pressure whereas the New York Giants managed or even eliminated pressure. The David Tyree "helmet catch" perhaps best symbolized that game and the ability to stay focused and relaxed in the clutch. I predicted before the game that if the Giants could deal with pressure in that game they had a chance to win and they did. They found a way to win against all odds. It was perhaps the biggest upset in sports history. The Patriots could not close. I did not talk with the players after that game, but my guess is that they probably felt all the pressure in the world that game. I was hired to write an article for the official New England Patriots magazine before that game about how the Patriots could best cope with pressure, but my article fell on deaf ears and they lost anyway! I know what you are thinking. You're wondering if I subconsciously wrote a lousy article so that the Giants would win and the Dolphins would maintain on their perfect perch! I would like to think this is not the case, but if you read my first chapter you know that aqua and orange oozes out every time I cut myself shaving!

Winning the game is the overwhelming goal, but final score is often a terrible measure of performance. That is another reason the MPI is so needed. In the MPI, I look closely at what is needed for the team to do to have the best chance to win. Rather than give lip service to mental performance as we have done in the past, the MPI, by definition, ensures that mental performance get its day in court. If a team raises its MPI scores it enhances its chances of winning remarkably. Even so, there were four times when the lower performing team on the MPI Total score lost in the Super Bowl, and I will explain that later. For now it just goes to show that human performance is somewhat but never completely predictable and that sometimes teams even perform better and lose.

Form is Not Fundamental

I also include traditional statistics for our overall understanding. For example, you will read about quarterback Kurt Warner's three phenomenal passing achievements and see that shown in traditional statistics on passing yards. But Warner, as good as he was, led his team to only one Super Bowl win in three tries. Throwing for huge passing yards does not always win. Just ask Dan Marino. This "form" sometimes covers up a great deficiency in other areas of the game, or it can even lead other aspects of the game to become rusty if that is all you do in games and in practice. Competition is the great equalizer and balance is important to success. At the same time, there are so many different ways of winning and losing as you will see on all the various ranking categories. The Dolphins only threw the ball a combined 18 times with 14 completions in winning two Super Bowls. Efficiency, consistency, and first downs count a whole lot more to winning and performance on offense than form of play, color of jersey, or team mascots.

The choices that go into play calling from hundreds of possible variations are surely important to success and a part of coaching and on-field decision making, but even these choices are not always on the coach. Eddie Hill and Jim Jensen, both former Super Bowl players, told me a few days ago that the play they ran often changed from the one called by Don Shula. Play call is often dictated by field position, trends, and intuition, and frequently changed in the huddle or at the line of scrimmage. So rather than look at the form of the play, or why this or that worked, my MPI observations looked more for function, and to answer the question of whether it worked or not. I captured the equivalent of a getting a hit or not in baseball, not whether the pitcher threw a curve ball, slider, fastball, or knuckle ball, or whether the batter choked up on the bat or moved closer to home plate. The end product of how successful or not a play was, like a baseball hit or ground-out, told me a whole lot more of what I needed to know than the style, flavor, or form of performance. I chose to look at substance and functionality over form.

I'm Not a Mind Reader

I looked at what actually happened, whether good or bad and how good or bad, in a very fair, accurate and balanced system of analysis. I was already getting richer data by looking for mental performance and I made it even better by collecting much more data than any traditional measure could. I studied all the plays! And regardless of the play selected, I assumed some basic level of parity of talent and intelligence or the team would not be in the NFL, and would never have made it to the Super Bowl. Most every play has the chance to go for a touchdown, and I assumed that. Some error in measurement is assumed, but gross errors were not likely the way I kept it so simple. I understand statistics, football and mental performance, and it all came together in the MPI. I also know what a meaningful play is and is not and what field position means too. If horrible or extraordinary play calling or on-field decision making helps or hurts a team, the MPI will capture that.

I only measure and explain behavior. I do not read minds, but I do read plays. It's like the phrase "What you do will speak much louder than what you say." I look for what a team does, not what is said in a press conference or speech. I am a sport psychologist, so you might find it ironic that my system is not about talk. It is all about action. It is about action displayed on a play, pure and simple. And highly rated action on the MPI is much smarter and more efficient than action that is revealed to be careless and inefficient. There are so many more variables and I will not attempt to cover them in depth. It is more important that you get the essence of my message that mental performance is huge and must be included in the mix from now on. It has always won, it wins, and it will always win. Was that as subtle as a punch in the nose?

The Starting Lineup

I carefully placed each of the 44 Super Bowl games into one of 17 categories for review according to how the winning team performed and won on Super Bowl Sunday. For each team that won the Super Bowl, I wanted one category that best described their winning performance, and to have a place to review similar games together. I felt it would enhance our understanding and learning to clump games together in this way. Fourteen of the seventeen categories are based on an MPI score and represented by one single MPI statistic, and three more categories were created from traditional statistics that have a quantifiable mental component and are also very important in football. These were: (15) Takeaways minus Giveaways, (16) Time of Possession and (17) Fewest Turnovers and Penalties combined. So that is 17 categories with a mental component that can be captured quantitatively. An 18th category was created for the four teams that won the Super Bowl despite being outperformed on MPI-T, but this was just a category for reviewing these odd games with no number or ranking associated with it. The eight teams in that category (from 4 of the 44 Super Bowls) are still included in rankings on the other 17 quantitative categories. I kept the 18th category games together because they reveal the truth that no matter how hard we try, better performance will still lose at times. The final quantitative category contains the results of MPI Bowl I and represents the rankings of teams on the MPI-T or overall total performance. It is the global category that best represents the spirit of the MPI in emphasizing performance over outcome. Super Bowl teams on this final "Best Team Ever" list are presented from 1 to 32 in Chapter 4 along with top 25 rankings in all other areas. I computed the rankings of all 88 teams but for this book I decided to keep it simple and present the "best" in nature with this book's theme. Chapter 4 with the Top 25 rankings and final Top 32 should be fascinating to those who really want to study how games were played and won! Those who do not care for ranking lists can just skip it, but it is all there for those who want it.

At the top of each of the quantitative categories, you will see my ranking of just the best 3 teams in that category (or a few more in some cases) and a description of what the statistic measures. The Table at the end of the book further describes each of the 14 MPI statistics that were included, so there should be no confusion about what a statistic measures. You then enjoy a description of each game followed by a brief MPI graph showing 7 MPI statistics and then my interpretive summary. The summary explores how the game was won, including how mental performance contributed.

To place each Super Bowl contest into just one category, I persistently asked the question, "How did this team achieve success in the big game?" I let statistics and the normal curve guide me in making the decisions. It was done quantitatively and not subjectively. In the end, we all gain in better understanding the nature of high performance in one of the most competitive arenas in human history. Perhaps only the gladiators in the Roman coliseum faced a greater performance challenge, but that was also before the scrutiny of CBS, NBC and FOX.

Sponsor Stadium for Future MPI Bowls

I am writing this in a restaurant in West Palm Beach, Florida, with a nice large table, great holiday music and even better food and coffee, but I have not even tried to get a sponsor for this event. Willing companies are encouraged to contact me about sponsoring an upcoming MPI Bowl. I am proclaiming the most exciting Super Bowl in history now, even more exciting than any individual Super Bowl, so why should fantastic companies be shy about getting in on the thrill each year as this grows and generates more interest. If your company promotes football, other sports, success, health, food, learning, fun or any other smart concepts then you might be the perfect home for an upcoming MPI Bowl, and the win/win it all generates. Cities represented in the upcoming Super Bowl will be especially interested as their teams have the chance to stake their claim to "Best Team Ever" title in the MPI Bowl!

Referee Instructions

To the right of each category in parentheses find the abbreviation for the MPI statistic represented by that category and the actual value of the statistic. The year preceding each team (e.g., "1989" San Francisco 49ers) relates to the NFL season that team played before the Super Bowl game rather than the year in which the Super Bowl was played. For example, the team that won the Super Bowl on January 28, 1990 was the 1989 49ers. A guide to all 14 MPI statistics presented in chapters 3 and 4 can be found in The Table at the end of the book as needed too.

MPI Categories

The MPI-T is the most frequently reported MPI score as it shows overall total team performance. It is presented in parentheses for each team right after their points scored for each review.

LEGEND FOR CATEGORIES & GRAPHS

- #'s 1 to 3 (or more) rankings show the best in each category
  - Teams that best fit into that category are reviewed there
    - Teams reviewed in another category are noted

Each performance graph depicts 7 MPI statistics with a number (1-7) below the bar graph indicating the MPI statistic as follows:

(1) MPI-T; (2) MPI-O; (3) MPI-D; (4) MPI-ST;
(5) MPI-OP; (6) MPI-DP; (7) MPI-TP

Most Dominant Teams Overall (MPI-TD)

MPI-TD (Total Dominance) represents dominance of a team relative to its opponent in all three phases. It shows how much one team outperformed another. It is calculated as "MPI-T of team1" – "MPI-T of team 2"

#1--1985 Chicago Bears (.180)--Reviewed in "Best Teams Ever"
#2--1973 Miami Dolphins (.159)--Reviewed in "Best Teams Ever"
#3--1989 San Francisco 49ers (.158)--Reviewed in "Best Time of Possession"
#6 --1987 Washington Redskins (.129)

Super Bowl 22 – January 31, 1988 – Jack Murphy Stadium, San Diego, CA

Washington Redskins 42 (.548) Denver Broncos 10 (.419)

Brief Game Review

Super Bowl XXII followed a strike-shortened season causing each team to only play 15 regular season games. Coach Dan Reeves' AFC champion Denver Broncos were 3 point favorites who reached the Super Bowl after a 10-4-1 mark led by Hall of Fame quarterback John Elway. Elway had thrown for 3,198 yards and 19 touchdowns. The Broncos also had a very talented defense led by linebacker Karl Mecklenburg.

The NFC champion Washington Redskins had posted an 11-4 regular season record led by quarterback Doug Williams. Williams got a lot of attention as the first African American quarterback to start in a Super Bowl, and the day before the game he had a root canal. He also had an injured knee. Coach Joe Gibbs' Washington Redskins had a very strong defense led by players Charles Mann, Darrell Green, Barry Willburn, and Dexter Manley.

After the Redskins punted on their first drive, the Broncos scored on their first play when Elway connected with wide receiver Ricky Nattiel on a 56-yard touchdown pass and 7-0 lead. At the time it was the earliest touchdown in Super Bowl history. After Washington was forced to punt again, Elway drove Denver to the 6-yard line where Rich Karlis' field goal gave them a 10-0 lead. By the end of the 1st quarter, the Broncos had completely dominated Washington.

On the first play of the 2nd quarter Doug Williams rifled an 80 yard touchdown pass to Ricky Sanders, cutting Denver's lead to 10-7. The Broncos were forced to punt on their next possession, and Williams soon struck again on a 27 yard touchdown pass to Gary Clark for a 14-10 lead. Denver drove into field goal position but missed, and Washington soon took advantage when rookie running back Timmy Smith broke loose on a 58-yard touchdown run and the Redskins led 21-10 but did not stop. On their next possession Williams found Sanders again for a 50 yard touchdown pass and a 28-10 lead. When Denver got the ball back, the 2nd quarter horror show continued as Elway threw an interception to Barry Wiburn. Once again Washington drove all the way down the field and Williams threw an 8-yard touchdown pass to tight end Clint Didier to give the Redskins a 35-10 lead at the half.

Denver failed to make any sort of comeback and Washington's defense stayed strong, shutting out the Broncos the rest of the game. Washington would score another touchdown in the 4th quarter when Timmy Smith ran over from 4 yards out and the final score was 42-10. Washington set multiple Super Bowl records including most touchdowns in a quarter (5), most offensive yards in a quarter (356), most points in a quarter (35), most total yards (602), most rushing yards (280), and most touchdowns in a Super Bowl (6). Redskins quarterback Doug Williams was named Super Bowl Most Valuable Player after throwing for 340 yards and 4 touchdowns.

What Actually Happened?

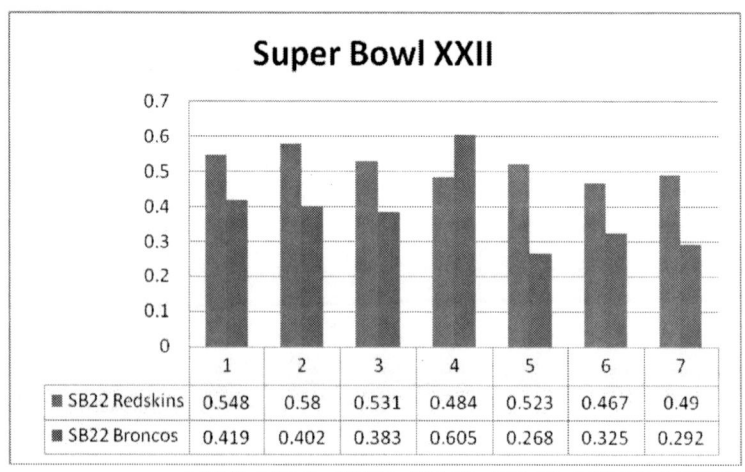

	MPI-T	MPI-O	MPI-D	MPI-ST	MPI-OP	MPI-DP	MPI-TP
SB22 Redskins	0.548	0.58	0.531	0.484	0.523	0.467	0.49
SB22 Broncos	0.419	0.402	0.383	0.605	0.268	0.325	0.292

The Super Bowl XXII Washington Redskins are easily one of the best overall teams in Super Bowl history. Let's examine the evidence. For one, they gained more net yards (602) and net yards rushing (280) than any other team in Super Bowl history. They were 3rd overall in net yards gained differential (275) and 10th overall in passing yards (322). They were also the 6th most dominant team overall (.129), 9th most dominant on offense (.197) and 11th most dominant on defense (.129). They scored the 6th most points (42), gave up the 5th least (10), and had the 4th best point differential (32). These number ones are hard to argue against. They are certainly not the best team overall but there is no doubt they are in the top 15.

The Denver Broncos' performance, aside from special teams play (MPI-ST=.605), which ranked 14th and special teams dominance (MPI-STD=.121), which ranked 13th overall, was quite embarrassing for a Super Bowl team. It was such an odd game as the Broncos were actually leading in the game 10-0 in the second quarter and one had the sense they might win in a blowout, but the reverse was the case.

Doug Williams earned the MVP and became the first quarterback to pass for 4 touchdowns in a single quarter, and throw 4 in a half, and he became the first African American quarterback to win the Super Bowl. He did this all the day after having a root canal and he had a knee injury.

Dr. John's Super Bowl 22 Lesson

"Stop making excuses and you start making history!"

Doug Williams had a daunting task ahead of him. He was to become the first African American quarterback to start in a Super Bowl. How would he handle that pressure? He had just had a root canal the day before and his knee had been surgically repaired and hurt from hyperextension. Did he make excuses? What pressure? What pain? He went out and threw for 602 yards. Nobody has matched him since. Go beyond the excuse and find reasons to win!

Best Performing Teams in Pressure Overall (MPI-TP)

MPI-TP (Total Pressure) represents performance of a team in two phases (offense and defense) in pressure situations only.

#1 --- 1966 Green Bay Packers (.716) --- Reviewed in "MPI-OP"
#2 --- 1976 Oakland Raiders (.700) --- Reviewed in "MPI-DP"
#3 --- 1985 Chicago Bears (.688) --- Reviewed in "Best Teams Ever"
#4 --- 1979 Pittsburgh Steelers (.675)

Super Bowl 14 – January 20, 1980 – Rose Bowl, Pasadena, CA

Pittsburgh Steelers 31 (.557) Los Angeles Rams 19 (.502)

Brief Game Review

Not many gave Coach Ray Malavasi's Los Angeles Rams and quarterback Vince Ferragamo a chance against Coach Chuck Noll's 11 ½ point favored Pittsburgh Steelers and quarterback Terry Bradshaw. The Steelers had already collected three Super Bowl titles by 1980. Even an article in Sports Illustrated called the NFC Championship contest before the Super Bowl "a game for losers by losers trying to earn a right for slaughter in Pasadena" in the Rose Bowl where the big game would be played..

The Steelers had posted a 12-4 record in 1979 en route to a second straight Super Bowl appearance and fourth in six years. They dominated on both sides of the ball, leading the league in both total yards gained and points scored. Their "Steel Curtain" defense finished the regular season with the top rated defense in the AFC, allowing only 4,621 yards of offense the entire season. Their defense was so good that it limited the Seattle Seahawks to negative seven yards of total offense and just one first down during a regular season game.

Unlike the Steelers, the Los Angeles Rams were excited to make the playoffs for the first time in almost a decade despite going 9-7. They were the first team ever with 9 wins or fewer to reach a Super Bowl, but they were actually better than their record showed. They had a strong defense and second ranked offense in total yards led by running back Wendell Tyler who rushed for over 1,000 yards in the regular season.

The Steelers jumped out to an early 3-0 lead on a 41-yard field goal by Matt Bahr after stopping the first Rams drive, but the Rams soon drove down the field for a touchdown to take a 7-3 lead. On the next drive the Steelers marched 53 yards in 9 plays culminating in a 1-yard touchdown run by Franco Harris to take the lead back 10-7. This see-saw battle continued as the Rams drove 67 yards in 10 plays, before settling for a 31-yard field goal to tie the game at 10. Before halftime the Rams added one more field goal to go into the locker room with a 13-10 lead, and whoever was not watching this game by halftime would soon tune in.

On the opening drive of the second half Pittsburgh took the lead back when quarterback Terry Bradshaw found Lynn Swan on a 47-yard touchdown pass to go up 17-13. On the Rams next possession, running back Lawrence McCutcheon hit Ron Smith for a 24-yard touchdown pass and 19-17 lead after missing an extra point. At this stage Pittsburgh almost lost the game. Bradshaw, in a late game slide, threw two interceptions and almost a third that would have been run back for a touchdown by Nolan Cromwell and given the Rams a 9 point lead.

As would happen so many times in Super Bowl history, the resilient Steeler defense held enough for the offense to do its part. Early in the 4th quarter with the Steelers, facing 3rd and 8 on their own 27 and still down in score, Bradshaw heaved a huge bomb to the outstretched arms of John Stallworth running right down the middle for a 73-yard touchdown that gave Pittsburgh the lead for good 24-19. Franco Harris' one yard touchdown run was icing on the cake of a 31-19 victory in a game in which the lead changed 7 times.

Steeler's quarterback Terry Bradshaw was named the MVP of the game despite throwing three interceptions.

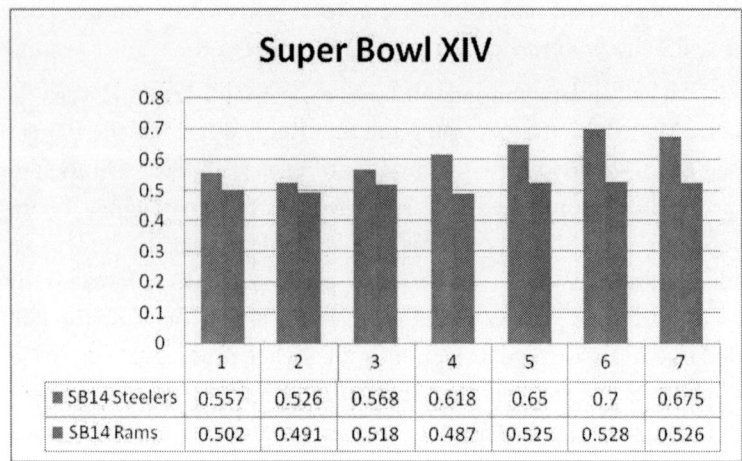

	1	2	3	4	5	6	7
■ SB14 Steelers	0.557	0.526	0.568	0.618	0.65	0.7	0.675
■ SB14 Rams	0.502	0.491	0.518	0.487	0.525	0.528	0.526

MPI-T MPI-O MPI-D MPI-ST MPI-OP MPI-DP MPI-TP

Despite 4 overall interceptions including 3 by Bradshaw, this was actually a relatively high quality game in terms of performance shown in the classic see-saw battle with effective offensive and both teams over .500 on MPI-T. It almost looks as if the Steelers high performance raised the performance of the inexperienced Rams team, but it was still a decisive Steelers victory as you can tell by looking at the blue bar graph and its dominance over the Rams red graph on all 7 primary MPI scores.

The Rams played clean football with only 2 penalties and no fumbles but failed to make the big play when it counted. The Steelers lived up to their pre-game billing as a great team as they posted the 7th best overall performance making it even more impressive that the Rams still had a good chance to win in the 4th quarter. The Rams might have won if not for an easy interception that was dropped, Bradshaw's resilience, and the Rams' inability to double cover John Stallworth on the game clinching bomb.

It is also clear the extent to which the Steelers defense (MPI-D = .568) outplayed the Rams offense (MPI-O = 491), but it was in pressure situations of this game that we saw the decisive Steelers forte. The Steelers were at 70% of perfection in defensive pressure situations (.700 on MPI-DP) and almost as good in overall pressure situations (MPI-TP = .675).

The MPI-TP score was the 4th best in Super Bowl history. This was a fun game for the fan.

Dr. John's Super Bowl 14 Lesson

"Never let your last mistake spoil your next achievement!"

Quarterback Terry Bradshaw threw three interceptions and still won the MVP award for coming through when it counted. This is what I call short-term memory and resilience in action.

Most Dominant Teams in Pressure Overall (MPI-TPD)

MPI-TPD (Total Pressure Dominance) represents relative dominance of a team over its opponent in pressure situations only. It is calculated as "MPI-TP of team 1" – "MPI-TP of team 2."

#1--1966 Green Bay Packers (.368)--Reviewed in "MPI-OP"
#2--1969 Kansas City Chiefs (.363)
#3--1985 Chicago Bears (.363)--Reviewed in "Best Teams Ever"

Super Bowl 4 – January 11, 1970 – Tulane Stadium, New Orleans, LA

Kansas City Chiefs 23 (.549) Minnesota Vikings 7 (.409)

Brief Game Review

Super Bowl IV matched up Coach Bud Grant's Minnesota Vikings of the NFL, and Coach Hank Stram's Kansas City Chiefs of the AFL. It was also the last Super Bowl officially named the AFL-NFL World Championship Game. Soon after this game, the NFL and AFL would merge into one league.

The supposedly much better NFL Minnesota Vikings entered the game as 13 point favorites. The Vikings reached the Super Bowl after finishing with an NFL best 12-2 regular season record. The Vikings "Purple People Eaters" defense was considered the most frightening in pro football and so intimidating that it allowed the fewest points and yards all season. On offense Minnesota was led by quarterback Joe Kapp who was not just a throwing quarterback but also had great running and scrambling ability. Minnesota's offense led the league in total points scored with 379.

The Kansas City Chiefs had a much less successful 1969 regular season, finishing in second place in their own division, but they would go on to beat the Oakland Raiders 17-7 in the AFL Championship Game. The Chiefs were led by a defense which allowed the fewest points in the AFL that season with 177. On offense Kansas City's main strength was their running game led by running back Mike Garret who rushed for 6 touchdowns and a total of 732 yards. Garret ran behind a fantastic offensive line headed by AFL All-Stars Jim Tyrer and Ed Budde.

After Minnesota opened the game on their first drive with a punt, Kansas City drove 42 yards in 8 plays to set up a 48 yard field goal by kicker Jan Stenerud. It was a Super Bowl record at the time. After the Vikings were forced to punt again on their next drive, the Chiefs and quarterback Len Dawson got the ball and drove all the way to the Vikings 25-yard line but would have to settle for another field goal and a 6-0 lead. Minnesota failed to do anything offensively and Kansas City got another successful field goal (25 yards) from Stenerud to give the Chiefs a 9-0 lead. On the ensuing kickoff, Vikings return man Charlie West fumbled and Kansas City took over at the Vikings 19-yard line. Kansas City capitalized by scoring the first touchdown of the game on a Mike Garrett 5 yard touchdown run. The score gave the Chiefs a 16-0 halftime lead.

Late in the third quarter the Vikings finally got on the scoreboard with a 10 play 69 yard drive that ended on fullback Dave Osborn's 4-yard touchdown run. Kansas City would respond immediately though on their next drive of 82 yards in 6 plays, scoring on a 46-yard strike from Len Dawson to Otis Taylor. The Kansas City 23-7 lead held up as the final score as both defenses dominated in the fourth quarter. The 80,562 attendance was a Super Bowl record. "The Super Bowl" had become more and more popular.

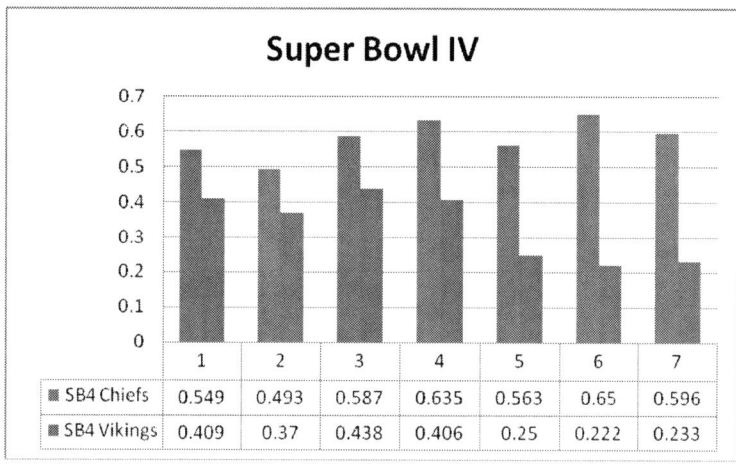

	1	2	3	4	5	6	7
SB4 Chiefs	0.549	0.493	0.587	0.635	0.563	0.65	0.596
SB4 Vikings	0.409	0.37	0.438	0.406	0.25	0.222	0.233

MPI-T MPI-O MPI-D MPI-ST MPI-OP MPI-DP MPI-TP

The domination displayed on the above graph almost speaks more than words or on-field hits ever could! The Chiefs dominance over the Vikings was the second overall most dominant performance in pressure situations in Super Bowl history as is visually represented in the number 7 box above showing the discrepancy on the MPI-TP scores between the Chiefs and Vikings (.596 to .233). If you look closer at box 6 you will also see that the dominance in this game came on both sides of the ball and on special teams, but especially with the Chief's defense almost pushing around Joe Kapp and his Viking's offense around at will (MPI-DP = .650 to .222).

As Tom Flores, backup quarterback to Len Dawson for Kansas City, would say after the game "Our defensive line just overpowered their offensive line." It should be noted that the Kansas City Chief's defense in this game was the 5th overall best performance by a defense in Super Bowl history (MPI-D = .587). Offense did not disappoint either, as the Chiefs in offensive pressure situations were 4th best in history in their domination of the Viking's defense (MPI-OPD=.341). By contrast the Chiefs were just average (MPI-O = .493) in overall offensive performance, so this shows the extent that they performed when it mattered.

Dr. John's Super Bowl 4 Lesson

"The reputation of your opponent is meaningless. History is filled with inferior teams that dominate and great teams that wither"

The Kansas City Chiefs proved once again that winning is achieved in the trenches, and when it counts most, not on paper or in the media.

Best Performing Offenses (MPI-O)

MPI-O (Offense) represents performance of a team's offense and aims to be independent of how the opponent's defense performed.

#1 -- 1984 San Francisco 49ers (.646)--Reviewed in "MPI-OD"

#2 -- 1994 San Francisco 49ers (.641)

#3 -- 1973 Miami Dolphins (.630)--Reviewed in "Best Teams Ever"

#5 -- 1998 Denver Broncos (.615)

#18--1997 Denver Broncos (.566)

Super Bowl 29 – January 29, 1995 – Joe Robbie Stadium, Miami, FL

San Francisco 49ers 49 (.563) San Diego Chargers 26 (.448)

Brief Game Review

Coach George Seifert's San Francisco 49ers entered an 18 ½ point favorite after finishing the regular season with a league best record of 13-3. Quarterback Steve Young led their powerful offense. The 49ers' 505 points in 1994 led the league. Young also broke the league record for passer rating throughout an entire season with an outstanding number of 112.8. He threw for 3,969 yards and 35 touchdowns and was awarded the NFL Most Valuable Player.

Coach Bobby Ross' San Diego Chargers made their way to the Super Bowl with an 11-5 record and #2 seed in the AFC playoffs.

Quarterback Stan Humphries operated a powerful rushing attack led by running back Natrone Means who ran for 1,350 yards and 12 touchdowns and was selected to the pro bowl.

As predicted, the 49ers dominated from start to finish. On the first drive of the game, Steve Young connected with wide receiver Jerry Rice for a 44-yard touchdown, setting a new Super Bowl record for quickest touchdown. After forcing San Diego to punt, San Francisco drove again 79 yards in 4 plays and scored on a 51-yard touchdown pass to Ricky Waters to take a 14-0 lead. The Chargers responded by driving 78 yards in 13 plays, and Means' 1 yard touchdown run cut the lead to 14-7. San Francisco's 70 yard drive in 10 plays ended with Steve Young finding William Floyd and a 21-7 lead, and they would add to it before halftime and a 28-10 lead.

The second half just got worse for the Chargers as two scoring drives later the 49ers led 42-10 and the rout was on. The 49ers and Chargers exchanged scores and the game ended 49-26 in favor of the 49ers. Steve Young was awarded Super Bowl MVP after throwing for a Super Bowl record 6 touchdown passes.

What Actually Happened?

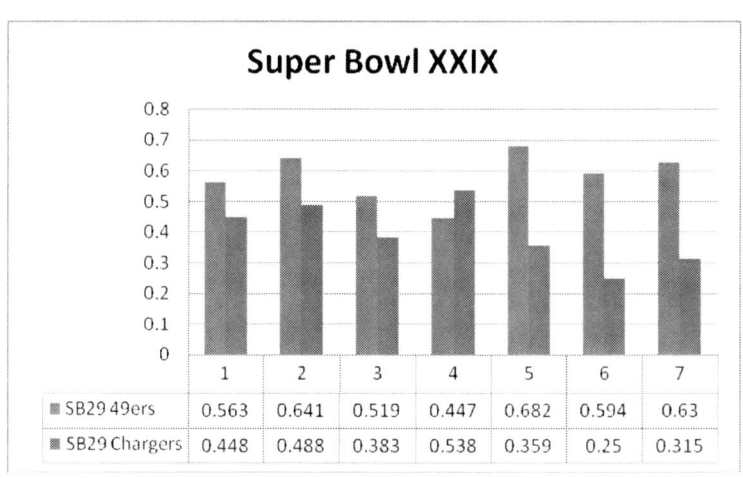

Super Bowl XXIX

	1	2	3	4	5	6	7
■ SB29 49ers	0.563	0.641	0.519	0.447	0.682	0.594	0.63
■ SB29 Chargers	0.448	0.488	0.383	0.538	0.359	0.25	0.315

MPI-T   MPI-O   MPI-D   MPI-ST   MPI-OP   MPI-DP   MPI-TP

It can easily be argued that the San Francisco 49ers offense in Super Bowl XXIX was the best and most well oiled unit ever assembled. Only the 49ers team ten years earlier can make a stronger argument and the MPI statistics would support either view. The numbers indicate that this was the second best pure offense (MPI-O=.641), second most dominating offense (MPI-OD=.258), second most dominating offense in pressure situations (MPI-OPD=.432), and third best pure offense in pressure (MPI-OP=.682).

Considering that we are comparing 88 teams, these numbers should astound the reader. Even a Rolex watch might not accurately symbolize this 49ers offense, but a new Patek Philippe tuned well might. Good arguments can be made that you had the best all around quarterback in Steve Young (6 TDs, 0 interceptions) throwing to the best all around receiver in Jerry Rice (10 receptions, 3 TDs). No doubt smart play and intelligence played a huge role in this juggernaut. Overall, San Francisco was the 6th best performing team ever (MPI-T=.563) and the Chargers really had no chance the way the 49ers performed.

Only 19 of the 88 teams in Super Bowl history passed for more yards than the Chargers in this game, so it was not the 49ers best defense and the Chargers could definitely move the ball. Only 18 teams dominated their opponent more on special teams than San Diego too. But these footnotes pale in comparison to the outstanding performance of the 1994 San Francisco 49ers and their offense on this day in Miami.

Dr. John's Super Bowl 29 Lesson

"Give credit where due. After you've tried everything, it's ok at the end to admit that a higher force reigned supreme."

Only a handful of players in history have had the talent and smarts of Jerry Rice or Steve Young. To have had to face them together when they were in sync with one another was a challenge almost too great to overcome, and better to appreciate.

Super Bowl 33 – January 31, 1999 – Pro Player Stadium, Miami, FL

Denver Broncos 34 (.531) Atlanta Falcons 19 (.506)

Brief Game Review

Coach Mike Shanahan's defending Super Bowl champion Denver Broncos were led by 38-year-old quarterback John Elway. They entered the game as 7 ½ point favorites after cruising through the regular season with an AFC best 14-2 record. There was even some talk of a "perfect season" after they won their first 13 games. The Broncos offense ranked 2nd in the NFL in most points scored (501) and were ranked third in yards gained (6,276). Adding the powerful running of Terrell Davis to the Pro Bowl leadership of Elway was almost too much for any defense to handle. Davis amassed 2,008 yards and 23 touchdowns and won both the Offensive MVP award and the NFL Most Valuable Player Award.

Coach Dan Reeves' Atlanta Falcons were more of a surprise in 1998. Their own 14-2 record was viewed as the result of overachievement rather than of pure talent. They pulled a huge upset in the NFC Championship after being 10 point underdogs against the Minnesota Vikings. Atlanta was led by their Pro Bowl quarterback, Chris Chandler, who threw for 3,154 yards and 25 touchdowns. Their defense was 4th in the league in allowing points, 8th in yards given up, and 2nd in fewest rushing yards allowed.

There was more pre-game hype than usual this year. Atlanta coach Dan Reeves who previously coached the Broncos made it public the he believed Elway and new Broncos head coach Mike Shanahan conspired to have him fired while he was the coach of Denver. Shanahan denied these allegations and claimed that he was angered and hurt by Reeves' comments. Another story questioned whether this would be Elway's last game.

The Falcons received the opening kickoff and drove to the Broncos 15-yard line before settling for a 32-yard field goal and the 3-0 lead. The Broncos responded by driving 80 yards down the field and scoring on a 1-yard touchdown run by Howard Griffith for a 7-3 lead. Early in the 2nd quarter Denver got to the Falcons 8-yard line but had to settle for a field goal and a 10-3 lead. The Falcons replied with their own long drive but Atlanta kicker, Gary Anderson, missed a 26-yard field goal. Denver soon struck again as Elway connected with wide receiver Rod Smith for an 80-yard touchdown pass and a 17-3 lead. Atlanta would add a late field goal to cut the lead to 17-6 at halftime.

Denver missed two golden opportunities to pad their lead at the beginning of the third quarter, driving to the 20 yard line before Jason Elam missed wide right. The Broncos again drove to the Falcons 29-yard line, but Elam missed again. Atlanta appeared to be coming back and reached Denver's 21-yard line before Chandler was picked off by Broncos cornerback Darrien Gordon who returned the ball to the Atlanta 24. Denver finally converted five plays later to take a 24-6 lead on yet another one yard Griffith run. After Atlanta moved the ball well, Gordon again intercepted Chandler and the Broncos clinched their second straight Super Bowl title win when Elway ran it in from 3. The remaining scoring was academic and John Elway became the oldest player selected to win the Super Bowl MVP.

<u>What Actually Happened?</u>

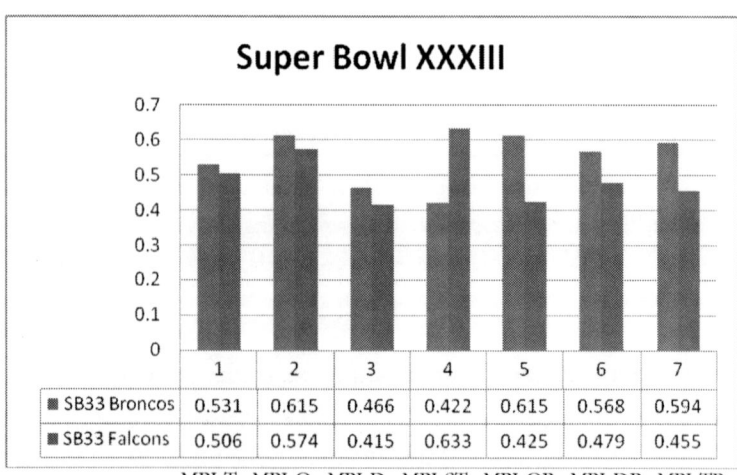

	1	2	3	4	5	6	7
■ SB33 Broncos	0.531	0.615	0.466	0.422	0.615	0.568	0.594
■ SB33 Falcons	0.506	0.574	0.415	0.633	0.425	0.479	0.455

MPI-T MPI-O MPI-D MPI-ST MPI-OP MPI-DP MPI-TP

This was clearly John Elway's special day and his performance was far superior to his first Super Bowl win the previous year over the Green Bay Packers. It was a fine display of passing efficiency supplemented by another 100+ yards rushing game by star running back Terrell Davis. While not nearly as much could be said of the defense (MPI-DD was ranked 83!), this offense was stellar, achieving a 5th overall pure offensive performance (MPI-O=.615), 5th net yards gained (457), 6th overall passing yardage (336), and 8th overall offensive dominance (MPI-OD=.200). Only the 2009 Saints, 1973 Dolphins, and two strong 49ers teams of 1984 and 1994 played offense closer to perfection than this second Elway title team.

The Falcons were not without strengths. Their special teams play was the 8th overall (MPI-ST=.633) in terms of pure play, and 6th in dominance (MPI-STD=.211), and their offense was 16th in total performance (MPI-O=.574). Despite these particular advantages, the defense overall was poor at best, but it must have been made worse playing against one of the best quarterback/running back tandems in the Elway/Davis machine.

Not only was John Elway smart (his team's performance advantage in pressure moments was also decisive), but he was a quarterback on a mission to do everything possible to leave on his own terms. Many would later write about his work ethic on the practice field and in the gym. He was talent infused with work ethic minus age. Without a strong running game provided by the offensive line and Terrell Davis, however, it is doubtful that his career would have ended so well.

<u>Dr. John's Super Bowl 33 Lesson</u>

"To upset a superior opponent you first need to get your own house in order. Start by reducing distractions and mistakes."

The Atlanta Falcons did neither. They made themselves vulnerable to Elway & Davis with off-field controversy and on-field turnovers. The Broncos even failed to clinch the game several times, but the weakened Falcons never posed a threat.

Super Bowl 32 – January 25, 1998 – Qualcomm Stadium, San Diego, CA

Denver Broncos 31 (.509) Green Bay Packers 24 (.479)

Brief Game Review

Super Bowl XXXII pitted the heavily favored defending champion Green Bay Packers coached by Mike Holmgren against Mike Shanahan's new kid on the block Denver Broncos who got there with a 12-4 record but only second place finish in the AFC West. With a potent offense that led the league in both total yards (5,872) and points scored (472), Denver running back, Terrell David, was named to the pro bowl after rushing for 1,750 yards and 15 touchdowns. At quarterback the Broncos were led by ageless veteran John Elway who had posted a pro bowl season himself. The Packers were looking to repeat after a 13-3 regular season record and NFC Central division title. They were led by Pro Bowl quarterback, Brett Favre, who led the league in passing touchdowns (35), while winning his 3rd MVP award of his career.

Green Bay struck first as Favre rifled to Antonio Freeman on the first drive for a 22 yard touchdown pass and a quick 7-0 lead. Denver bounced right back as Elway engineered a 10-play, 58 yard drive capped by a 1-yard touchdown run by Terrell Davis to tie the game at seven. On the Packers next series, Favre was intercepted at Green Bay's 45 and Denver cashed in after a drive and Elway's 1-yard touchdown run to give the Broncos a 14-7 lead. Denver would add a field goal to go up 17-7, but midway through the second quarter Green Bay marched 95 yards in 17 plays to close the gap to 17-14 at halftime.

Early in the second half, Green Bay tied the game at 17 as more and more fans across the world tuned in. Denver impressed with a 92-yard drive during which John Elway demonstrated how tough a field general he really was, with no fear of personal pain or injury. In a play for the ages that gave the Broncos added confidence, Elway dove high into the air on a 3rd and 6 from the Green Bay 12. Damning all torpedoes and absorbing big hits by safeties Le Roy Butler and Mike Prior, Elway twirled completely around and returned to earth for a first down at the 4 yard line. Denver had their moral advantage as Davis took it in from 1 yard out. Rather than giving a concession speech, Green Bay showed never-say-die resilience of their own in moving the ball 85 yards in 4 plays and scoring on a 13 yard touchdown pass to Antonio Freeman.

With the game tied at 24, defensives stiffened, offenses stalled, and the punters got into the action four times in a row. Costly penalties against tackle Ron Verba hurt Green Bay, and after a punt Denver found themselves with the ball at the Packer's 49-yard line with 3:27 remaining. A 15-yard facemask penalty and 23 yard pass from Elway to Howard Griffith, moved Denver to the 11. Davis plowed in from 1-yard out to give the Broncos a 31-24 lead with 1:45 left. The Packers comeback attempt fell short and the Broncos were improbable world champions.

Denver running back, Terrell Davis was named Super Bowl MVP with 157 yards rushing even though he had left the game for most of the second quarter after a kick to the head. What made it even more special for Davis, was that he was a San Diego native playing in front of his hometown.

What Actually Happened?

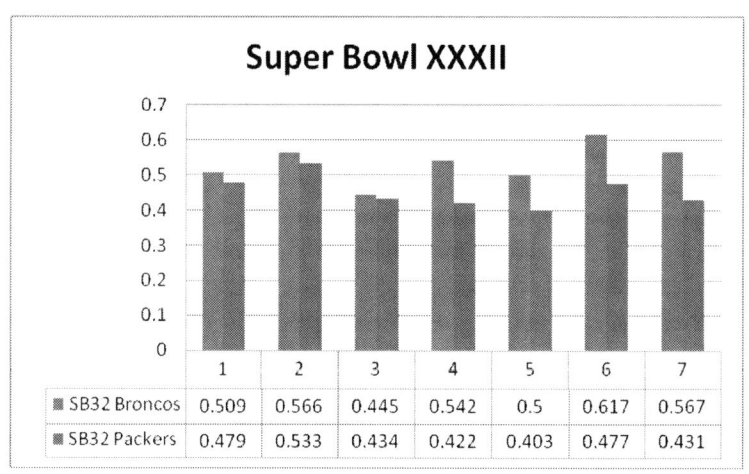

	1	2	3	4	5	6	7
■ SB32 Broncos	0.509	0.566	0.445	0.542	0.5	0.617	0.567
■ SB32 Packers	0.479	0.533	0.434	0.422	0.403	0.477	0.431

MPI-T MPI-O MPI-D MPI-ST MPI-OP MPI-DP MPI-TP

This Broncos victory involved two relative strengths in the areas of pure offensive performance (MPI-O=.566) and offensive dominance of the Packers defense (MPI-OD=.132), but each was only ranked 18th in Super Bowl history. Net rushing yards of 179 for Denver was a more impressive performance that was overall 12th best and this clearly justifies Terrell Davis receiving the MVP award.

This victory should be attributed to efforts of the offensive line, Terrell Davis' 157 yards rushing despite injury, and John Elway's risk taking and courage. Elway's brave dive for a first down was a dive for the entire team that symbolized the start of back to back championships for the Broncos. It was almost unheard of career success in his final two seasons for Elway, reminiscent of Jim Plunkett a decade before. Elway's leap is what many players said inspired them after the game.

The Green Bay Packers showed great resilience in coming back in this game but also helped the Broncos repeatedly with too many costly mistakes (including 4th highest penalties in Super Bowl history) to be crowned champions. It was a distant cry from the Packers teams of the 1960s who rarely made these errors. In fact it was a sloppy game overall with 16 penalties and 5 turnovers that contributed to overall reduced MPI-T scores of .509 to .479.

In sum, this was a rare and sloppy game where statistics revealed nothing extraordinary. It was mostly the accomplishments of star running back Terrell Davis, who gained 157 yards despite being kept out of almost a full quarter of play, and Hall of Fame quarterback John Elway, who disregarded injury to achieve team success, that carried the Broncos to glory.

Dr. John's Super Bowl 32 Lesson

"Be Courageous! Just one act of selfless courage in a critical moment of battle inspires your team 10 times more than talent"

John Elway flung himself fearlessly into the air for a first down. Terrell Davis played well after being hurt. The inspiration of courage spread wildly and paid off well as the Broncos become champions.

Most Dominant Offenses (MPI-OD)

MPI-OD (Offensive Dominance) represents relative dominance of a team's offense over its opponent's defense. It is calculated as "MPI-O of team 1" – "MPI-D of team 2."

#1 -- 1984 San Francisco 49ers (.297)
#2 -- 1994 San Francisco 49ers (.258)--Reviewed in "MPI-O"
#3 -- 1973 Miami Dolphins (.255)--Reviewed in "Best Teams Ever"
#7 -- 1986 New York Giants (.203)

Super Bowl 19 – January 20, 1985 – Stanford Stadium, Stanford, CA

San Francisco 49ers 38 (.586) Miami 16 (.446)

Brief Game Review

Coach Bill Walsh brought his San Francisco 49ers to the Super Bowl after they had become the first NFL team to win 15 regular season games. Its offense bragged 5 pro bowlers including star and future Hall of Famer quarterback Joe Montana. Its defense led the league in fewest points allowed, 227. Four of their defensive backs were selected to the pro bowl.

Coach Don Shula's Miami Dolphins had reached the Super Bowl after a 14-2 regular season record. They had even crushed the Pittsburgh Steelers 45-28 in the AFC Championship game. Quarterback Dan Marino's famed passing accuracy featured a quick release rarely seen before. With it he had set many regular season and personal best records. Imagine 5,084 yards passing, 48 touchdown passes, a 64.2 completion percentage, and a 108.9 passer rating! With a combined 33-3 record after the Playoffs for teams heading into the Super Bowl, it is still the best combined record for two teams in Super Bowl history.

But the Marino/Montana epic struggle fizzled. What was supposed to be a shootout ended up a one sided affair as the 49ers moved the ball at will and Miami struggled to advance the ball, especially on the ground. Miami set a Super Bowl record with fewest rushing attempts, 9, and gained only 25 yards rushing. The Dolphins got out to a 3-0 lead as the initially over-hyped 49ers missed tackles, failed to move the ball and dropped passes. However, that was only for starters. The 49rs soon kicked into fourth and fifth gear and scored on their next six drives. On the 49ers second possession, they drove 78 yards in 8 plays and scored on a 33 yard touchdown pass from Joe Montana to Carl Monroe. The Dolphins responded on their next drive and with 45 seconds left in the first quarter scored on a touchdown pass from Marino to Dan Johnson. The entire football world for a brief moment thought this was still the game for the ages. In the second quarter the 49ers offense clicked smoothly on Joe Montana's sharp decision making and accuracy, and Roger Craig's nimble legs and soft hands, and took a 14-10 lead with an 8 yard Montana to Craig pass. The 49ers kept their lead for the rest of the game, scoring two more touchdowns before half to go up 28-10, but the Dolphins did not quit. They first scored on a hurry up drive and field goal, and then Jim "Crash" Jensen recovered an onside kick at the 49ers 12 yard line with 4 seconds left and Uwe Von Schamann kicked another field goal. Suddenly it was 28-16 and Miami had some hope again going into the locker room.

But in the second half, it was all San Francisco as their defense stepped up strong and as the offense kept playing well. The 49ers added an early field goal to go up 31-16 then added a touchdown when Montana again found Roger Craig for a 16 yard touchdown pass to take a 38-16 lead that held up for the rest of the game. Montana was named Super Bowl MVP, completing 24 out of 35 passes for a Super Bowl record 331 yards, 3 touchdowns, and a 127.2 passer rating. He even gained 59 yards rushing which was the most by a quarterback at the time. Montana admitted after the game that "it was pretty close to the best I've ever played." He added, "I didn't throw anything I didn't have confidence in" and stated that the confidence had carried over to the defense and back to the offense. "It's a snowball kind of thing," stated Montana.

This Walsh over Shula, Montana over Marino Super Bowl had been essentially a home game for the 49ers. San Francisco was just about 30 miles away from Stanford! It was also the first time a president participated in the Super Bowl coin toss as President Ronald Reagan called the toss from the White House via satellite.

What Actually Happened?

Super Bowl XIX

	MPI-T	MPI-O	MPI-D	MPI-ST	MPI-OP	MPI-DP	MPI-TP
SB19 49ers	0.586	0.646	0.536	0.474	0.472	0.75	0.618
SB19 Dolphins	0.446	0.504	0.349	0.636	0.275	0.528	0.395

There is no question that the 49ers offensive display in Stanford Stadium on this day was the single most dominant in Super Bowl history (MPI-OD=.297). This is almost a 30 percent difference between the 49ers offense and the Dolphins defense, an astounding difference that would have probably led to 14 more points without the two fumbles. This was also the second best pure performance overall (MPI-T=.586), best pure offense (MPI-O = .646), and 2nd most net yards gained (537). While the 49ers defense was 17th overall in ranking, their defense in pressure situations (MPI-DP=.750) ranked a very impressive 3rd overall, coming up with big plays when it counted.

Miami, to their credit, was 5th overall in special teams (MPI-ST=.636), better than 83 other teams to play the big game. And characteristic of Don Shula teams, this team only committed one penalty.

Historians might forget how really good San Francisco's defense was in this game because their offense was the best ever and led by perhaps the best quarterback in history. Marino's record breaking passing offense and effective running and short passes were reduced to an average

"48th ranked" performance overall (MPI-O=.504) as the 49ers thoroughly dismantled Miami by game's end. Coach Bill Walsh would later say, "It was a nearly perfect game for us."

An extra comment is needed here to emphasize that this 1984 San Francisco 49ers team is unquestionably one of the 5-best Super Bowl teams of all time. Tune in later to see where they actually rank.

Dr. John's Super Bowl 19 Lesson

"Diversify your weapons. A balanced attack with multiple ways to win defeats a one-dimensional foe."

The 49ers crushed one of the best offenses assembled with a more diverse attack that would produce 4 NFL titles in 11 seasons. Miami, lacking as balanced an attack, never returned to the Super Bowl.

Super Bowl 21 – January 25, 1987 – Rose Bowl, Pasadena, CA

New York Giants 39 (.545) Denver Broncos 20 (.467)

Brief Game Review

Coach Bill Parcell's 9 ½ point favorite New York Giants finished the regular season 14-2 with a powerful offense led by quarterback Phil Simms, who during the regular season threw for 3,482 yards and 21 touchdowns. The Giants running game was even stronger as Joe Morris set a franchise record with 1,516 yards rushing and 14 touchdowns. New York also had a very good defense nicknamed "Big Blue Wrecking Crew" led by Hall of Fame linebacker Lawrence Taylor who would win both the NFL Defensive Player of the Year Award and the NFL MVP award with a league leading 20 ½ sacks. Taylor was only the second defense player ever to receive this latter award.

Dan Reeves' Denver Broncos made it to Pasadena after finishing the regular season 11-5 led on offense by fourth year quarterback, John Elway. During the regular season Elway threw for 3,480 yards and 19 touchdowns. Denver also had a very strong defense which led the AFC with fewest rushing yards allowed with 1,651.

Denver drew first blood on a 48 yard field goal to take a 3-0 lead, but the Giants drove back 78 yards in 9 plays as Simms found tight end Zeke Mowatt on a 6 yard pass for a 7-3 lead. Late in the first quarter Denver went up 10-7 on a 4-yard John Elway scamper. On the Broncos first drive of the second quarter, they moved well and got to the 1-yard line before they were stopped and had to settle for a 23-yard field goal attempt. When Rich Karlis missed, it was the shortest miss in Super Bowl history.

With just under three minutes left in the first half and Denver backed up to their own goal-line, New York defensive end George Martin sacked Elway in the end zone for a safety to cut Denver's lead to 10-9. Right before halftime, Denver drove again inside New York's 20-yard line but once again Karlis missed and the score remained 10-9 going into half. Karlis admitted after the game that those two missed field goals were demoralizing. "Both times I didn't get my hips all the way through the kicks. I was steering the ball, and I know better than that. I felt the team unravel after that. I really hurt them."

On the opening possession of the third quarter, the Giants executed a perfect fake punt, snapping directly to assistant quarterback Jeff Rutledge for a key first down. Simms later found tight end Mark Bavaro for a 13-yard touchdown and a 16-10 lead. The Giants again drove the field after stopping Denver and kicked another field goal for a 19-10 lead. The Broncos continued to falter on offense and the Giants punished them further for a 26-10 lead on Joe Morris' 1-yard touchdown run. The teams exchange scores from here, but the game was never again in doubt. The Giants 30 points in the 2nd half set a new Super Bowl record for most points in a half. Phil Simms was awarded the Super Bowl Most Valuable Player after throwing for 268 yards and 3 touchdowns, and his 22 of 25 88% completion percentage and 150.9 passer rating made him the most accurate passer in NFL playoff history. After the game,

Simms would say that he never once came close to having a negative thought. Bill Parcells called it "the best game a quarterback has played."

<u>What Actually Happened?</u>

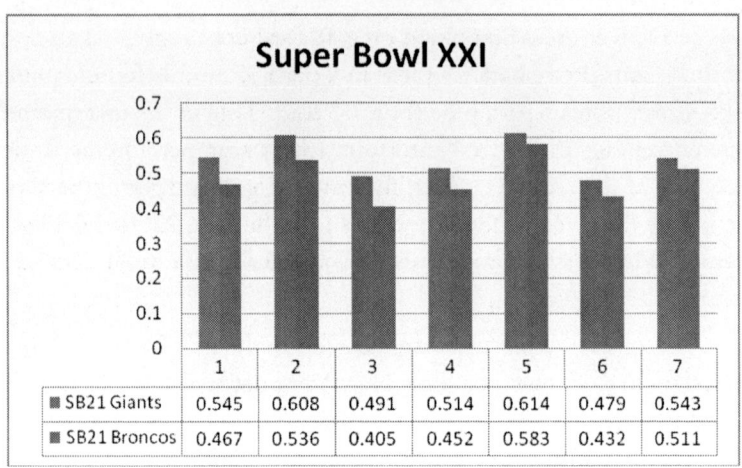

Super Bowl XXI

	1	2	3	4	5	6	7
■ SB21 Giants	0.545	0.608	0.491	0.514	0.614	0.479	0.543
■ SB21 Broncos	0.467	0.536	0.405	0.452	0.583	0.432	0.511

MPI-T MPI-O MPI-D MPI-ST MPI-OP MPI-DP MPI-TP

The Giants executed the 7th best pure offense (MPI-O=.608) and 7th best offensive dominance (MPI-OD=.203) in Super Bowl history. Phil Simms' clean and error free record performance was unquestionably the deciding factor. The team also played a solid game in not turning the ball over, but did commit 6 penalties. The Broncos were 11th best in net passing yards (320) and 16th in offensive performance under pressure (MPI-OP=.583), both tributes to John Elway but not enough for victory.

The Broncos failed to score in key moments and then had to settle for field goals which they missed. While Rich Karlis appropriately admitted that his misses let the team down, and the team's special team's performance left a lot to be desired ranked 72nd overall and 40% of perfection (MPI-ST=.405), there are better explanations for this outcome. The Giants red zone defense and the Bronco's inability to score in close should probably count even more than a couple missed three pointers. It was still refreshing to hear Karlis admit that he did not execute in the most basic way and this is exactly what the pressure of a big game can do to a player. On the other side of the ball, the Giants came up with the big plays in a fake punt and a key safety, and this all provided momentum and confidence.

One of the touchdown catches, by Giants wide receiver Phil McConkey, was featured in a recent episode of NFL Films Presents (Love, Hate & Grief in the NFL, 2009) in which McConkey recalled years of dreaming of making a touchdown in the Super Bowl, and then actually realizing his dream on a deflected catch in the fourth quarter. While McConkey's catch can hardly be said to have originated in his mind, players who practice mental imagery regularly put themselves in the best frame of mind to seize advantages when they appear. McConkey was an overachiever like Jim "Crash" Jensen was, and it's interesting that they both talk about mentally rehearsing good performances in advance. It was on this same episode that I discussed mental differences between offense and defense and how emotions affect performance.

Dr. John's Super Bowl 21 Lesson

"Nothing limits how good you become when you eliminate negative thinking"

For one day Phil Simms only entertained positive thoughts, and he almost achieved perfection. It was plenty enough to lead his team to a Super Bowl title.

Best Performing Offenses in Pressure (MPI-OP)

MPI-OP (Offensive Pressure) represents performance of a team's offense in pressure situations and aims to be independent of how the opponent's defense performed.

#1 -- 1966 Green Bay Packers (.775)
#2 -- 1981 San Francisco 49ers (.731)
#3 -- 1994 San Francisco 49ers (.682)--Reviewed in "MPI-O"
#11--2007 New York Giants (.625)

Super Bowl 1 – January 15, 1967 – Memorial Coliseum, Los Angeles, CA

Green Bay Packers 35 (.548) Kansas City Chiefs 10 (.464)

Brief Game Review

Super Bowl I was originally known as "the first AFL-NFL World Championship Game." It was the first championship game between the two leagues and many newspapers referred to it as a "Super-Game." Coach Hank Stram's Kansas City Chiefs made it there with an 11-2-1 regular season record led by their league leading offense which had 2,274 total yards and 448 points. Three of their running backs ranked in the top ten in rushing in the AFL and quarterback Len Dawson had the top AFL passer rating. The team placed 11 players on the All-AFL team. Coach Vince Lombardi's Green Bay Packers got to the Super Bowl after finishing the NFL regular season with a 12-2 record led by their all-star quarterback Bart Starr who was the top rated quarterback in the NFL and league MVP. During the season he threw for 2,257 yards, 14 touchdowns and only 3 interceptions.

There was pressure on both teams to represent their league well. The NFL wanted to prove that the AFL was inferior and the AFL wanted to belong. The pressure might have been greatest on Packers head coach Vince Lombardi and the rest of the Packers to beat the Chiefs. The entire NFL was counting on them not just to win, but to win big.

As for the game, both teams punted on their first possessions of the game. When the Packers got the ball back for the second time they marched 80 yards in 6 plays ending the drive on Bart Starr's 39-yard touchdown pass to Max McGee for a 7-0 lead. The Chiefs had a chance to cut the lead on their next drive, but Mike Mercer missed a 40-yard field goal. Early in the second quarter Kansas City drove 66 yards in 6 plays and Len Dawson's 31-yard touchdown pass to Otis Taylor tied the game at 7. The Packers wasted no time in a 73 yard drive ending on a 14-yard run from fullback Jim Taylor to put Green Bay ahead 14-7. With under a minute to go in the Half, the Chiefs brought it closer on a 31-yard field goal that made it 14-10 at halftime.

Lombardi's halftime behavior was calm as he slightly adjusted the defense to be more aggressive by blitzing more. The result? The Packers ended with six sacks. They completely dominated from start to finish in the second half on both sides of the ball. The defense repeatedly forced punts and the Chiefs offense crossed mid-field only once in that second half. Kansas City was limited to 12 yards in the third quarter while the Packers would add three more touchdowns and move at will. They scored twice on short runs by Elijah Pitts and once on a second touchdown pass of 13 yards to Max McGee. The game turned out as most expected with a 35-10 final score. Packers quarterback Bart Starr was awarded the MVP for the game after throwing for 250 yards and two touchdowns.

<u>What Actually Happened?</u>

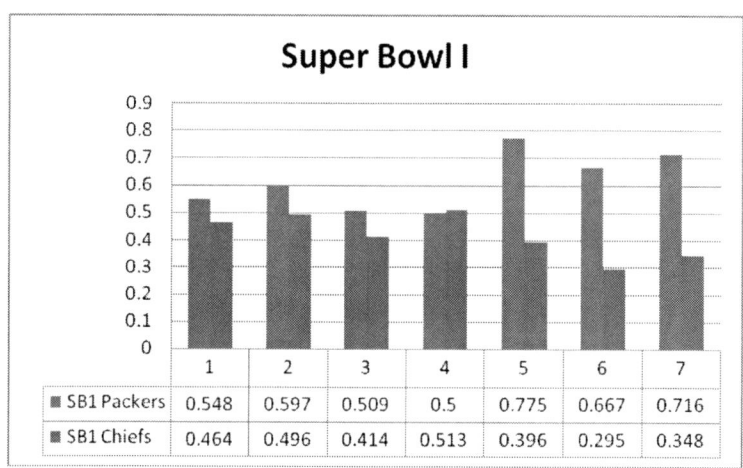

	1	2	3	4	5	6	7
■ SB1 Packers	0.548	0.597	0.509	0.5	0.775	0.667	0.716
■ SB1 Chiefs	0.464	0.496	0.414	0.513	0.396	0.295	0.348

MPI-T MPI-O MPI-D MPI-ST MPI-OP MPI-DP MPI-TP

Effective would be an insult in describing Green Bay's offense in critical 3rd downs and other important moments of this game. The offense is still ranked number one in two categories (MPI-OP=.667, MPI-OPD= .480) and the entire team is still the best overall performing team in pressure (MPI-TP=.716) and most dominant team in pressure (MPI-TPD=.368) too! They certainly did it when they needed to. They were the

10th ranked offense of all time (MPI-O=.597), 12th in yards allowed (239), and the overall 14th best performing team of all time (MPI-T=.548).

Kansas City might have been led to false confidence after being down by only 4 points at halftime, but all great coaches make adjustments and Lombardi was among the best. The one area that the Chiefs showed a slight edge was on special teams (MPI-ST=.513 compared with the Packers score of .500), but other than that this game was a clear, decisive, and precise performance by the Packers, especially on offense and they actually did much better in critical moments of the game than overall.

Dr. John's Super Bowl 1 Lesson

"Get away, relax and come back … then have fun and attack!"

When Max McGee didn't think he would play he could not over-think or get tight. He took his mind off football the night before and inadvertently prepared for a career performance. When facing pressure, get away for a few minutes or hours, then come back to compete like never before.

Super Bowl 16 – January 24, 1982 – Pontiac Silverdome, Pontiac, MI

San Francisco 49ers 26 (.538) Cincinnati Bengals 21 (.490)

Brief Game Review

This was the only Super Bowl up to then (1982) featuring two teams with losing records the previous season. Each was 6-10 the year earlier. Coach Bill Walsh's San Francisco 49ers got to the Super Bowl by finishing the regular season a league best 13-3 led by their very young but talented quarterback Joe Montana. Montana threw for 3,565 yards and 19 touchdowns during the regular season. Coach Forrest Gregg's Cincinnati Bengals also made it there with a league best 12-4 on the arm of quarterback Ken Anderson who threw for 3,754 yards and 29 touchdowns. Anderson won both the NFL Comeback Player of the Year and MVP awards. The Bengals had a stingy defense which did not give up more than 30 points in a game all season.

In the beginning, the Bengals offense drove nearly the length of the field before Anderson was intercepted at the 49ers 5 and the ball was returned 27 yards to the 32. Montana and the 49ers took over and drove 68 yards with San Francisco scoring on Montana's 1-yard quarterback sneak to end the first quarter. To begin the second quarter the Bengals again threatened to score, but wide receiver Cris Collinsworth fumbled at the 5-yard line and San Francisco recovered at the 8. From there, the 49ers drove 92 yards, finishing on a 10-yard touchdown pass from Montana to fullback Earl Cooper for a 14-0 lead. Before the half was over, San Francisco would add two more field goals to take a commanding 20-0 lead into the half.

The Bengals received the second half kickoff and drove 83 yards in 9 plays to cut the deficit to 20-7. That touchdown inspired the Bengals defense who then shut down the 49ers. Late in the 3rd quarter, Cincinnati had the ball on 2nd and goal from the 1. The 49ers defense stuffed them for three straight plays and took over on downs! Early in the fourth the Bengals assembled a 7 play 53 yard drive to grow closer 20-14, but then San Francisco added two more field goals to put the game out of reach 26-14. Cincinnati added a touchdown with 20 seconds left to make it look close at 26-21, but it was too little too late.

Joe Montana, who completed 14 of 22 passes for 157 yards and a touchdown, earned the MVP. Cincinnati hindered themselves repeatedly with five turnovers. This was the first time in Super Bowl history that a team gaining more yards on offense and scoring more touchdowns lost the game.

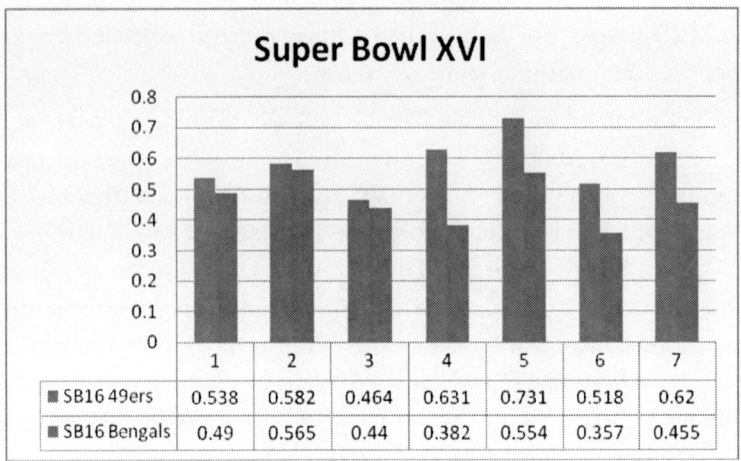

Super Bowl XVI

	1	2	3	4	5	6	7
▪ SB16 49ers	0.538	0.582	0.464	0.631	0.731	0.518	0.62
▪ SB16 Bengals	0.49	0.565	0.44	0.382	0.554	0.357	0.455

MPI-T MPI-O MPI-D MPI-ST MPI-OP MPI-DP MPI-TP

The 49ers offense led by young Joe Montana was by far at its best in pressure moments of this game and ranked 2nd overall on MPI-OP (.731) and 3rd on offensive dominance in pressure situations (MPI-OPD=.374). Special teams dominance was also stellar for San Francisco and it ranked 4th overall in Super Bowl history (MPI-STD=.249). Considering that this 49ers team was only an above average winning Super Bowl champion on total performance (MPI-T=.538), their performance when it counted most really stood out! If there is ever an argument for the importance of mental performance, it is shown in these critical times and how some teams improve, like Montana's did so many times in history, and how others fold.

By contrast, the Bengals were killed by turnovers and a failure to close the deal when they were near the goal line. By all means credit the 49ers for making a goal line stand when it counted. The Bengals best performance was on offense which ranked 19th overall (MPI-O=.565) and Ken Anderson's 95.2 passer rating was just below Montana's rating of 100 in this game. The special teams play of the Bengals was a horrendous 83rd overall (MPI-ST=.382).

Super Bowl XVI showcased the production of the San Francisco offense in key pressure moments which at 73 percent of perfection was better than any other team in Super Bowl history with the exception of Bart Starr's Packers in Super Bowl I (MPI-OP=.775). Joe Montana aptly earned the MVP award as he led that offense. Few at the time knew how many defensive coordinators Montana would terrorize for a decade to come with his calm demeanor and ability to find the open receiver when so many others would not.

Dr. John's Super Bowl 16 Lesson

"Looks are deceiving! Calm execution in pressure looks natural to the unaware eye, but is earned with hard work and great effort"

What is missing in the final product of a great clutch performance are the hundreds of hours of work, imagery, review, and planning. Joe Montana and his team worked so that they could execute more easily when it counted.

Super Bowl 42 – February 3, 2008 – U. of Phoenix Stadium, Glendale, AZ

New York Giants 17 (.538) New England Patriots 14 (.490)

Brief Game Review

This game will be remembered for two things. First, it was the biggest upset in Super Bowl History. Coach Bill Belichick's New England Patriots entered the game 18-0 (16-0 regular season, 2-0 playoffs) and were looking to become the first team in NFL history to go 19-0. Coach Tom Coughlin's New York Giants, 13 to 14 point underdogs, snuck into the playoffs with a wild-card and won three straight road games to even get to the Super Bowl. The second thing people will recall this game for is "the helmet catch" by David Tyree. Tyree made one of the most amazing catches ever in Super Bowl history in the 4th quarter of the game when he caught a pass from Quarterback Eli Manning that kept a drive alive and eventually helped the Giants become Super Bowl Champs.

Even though the Patriots were lofty favorites, many believed the Giants could pull the upset because they had played New England very close in week 17 (won by New England 38-35). Coach Tom Coughlin told his players "everything would be positives, there would be no negatives." The confidence from that game carried the Giants all the way through the playoffs knowing that they could compete with one of the best teams ever. The Giants also surprised people when arriving in Arizona for the Super Bowl. Both teams were supposed to arrive on Sunday January 27th, which the Patriots did. Instead, the Giants choose to wait and not come until Monday. They stayed at their own home facility and worked on their game plan. By doing this, the Giants were following the same tactic that the last two Super Bowl champions (Colts and Steelers) had used.

The Giants opened the game with the longest opening drive in Super Bowl History, consuming nearly 10 minutes and went 77 yards on 16 plays before settling for three. The rest of the game was a hard-nosed defensive battle with the Patriots only leading 7-3 entering the fourth quarter.

In the fourth quarter Eli Manning found David Tyree for a five yard touchdown pass with 11:05 remaining to go up 10-7. New England regained the lead with 2:42 left when Quarterback Tom Brady threw to wide open Randy Moss in the end zone. With only 2:39 left, Eli Manning drove the Giants down the field with help of David Tyree's amazing catch when Tyree was forced to pin the ball with his right hand up against his helmet as he was falling to the ground to preserve the drive. With just 35 seconds left Manning hooked up with Plaxico Burress in the end zone for the game winning score.

With Manning's two fourth quarter touchdowns, he was named Super Bowl MVP. Also, Giants punter Jeff Feagles became the oldest player in Super Bowl history to win a Super Bowl at the age of 41. With the victory the New York Giants won their third Super Bowl overall and became the first NFC wild card team to win a Super Bowl.

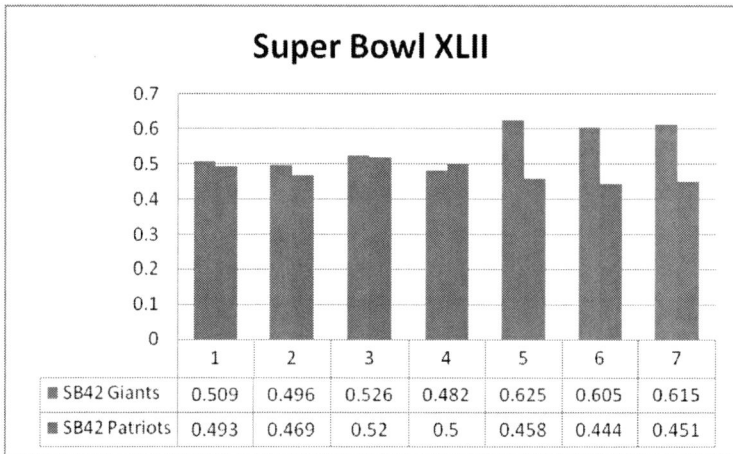

Super Bowl XLII

	1	2	3	4	5	6	7
■ SB42 Giants	0.509	0.496	0.526	0.482	0.625	0.605	0.615
■ SB42 Patriots	0.493	0.469	0.52	0.5	0.458	0.444	0.451

MPI-T MPI-O MPI-D MPI-ST MPI-OP MPI-DP MPI-TP

This was a game for the ages, and one that the Giants won for one primary reason – they handled pressure better than the Patriots, especially on offense (MPI-OP=.625) which ranked 11th in history, and they were 15th overall in total pressure performance (MPI-TP=.615). This contrasts sharply with the Patriots performance in similar situations as can be seen clearly on boxes 5, 6 and 7 above on the graph in red. This great pressure play of the Giants was perfectly symbolized by the Tyree helmet catch and Eli Manning's performance when he needed it. The Giants defensive line also stuffed the Patriots strong running attack.

The only key area where the Patriots outperformed the Giants was on special teams (.500 to .482). This game tells us again how really hard it is to go undefeated. When a team has won all their games there is nowhere to go but down. The Giants were more loose and aggressive in pursuing their dreams while the Patriots 45% of perfection performance in pressure situations, and subdued performance throughout the game, shows that they did a very poor job of removing the burden of having to win. Placed so high on a pedestal, their crash was that much louder when they came back to earth.

The fact that so many believed the Patriots would win this one, but they did not, really emphasizes how truly close competition in sports is. This is why high mental performance is needed. Just one slight lack or gain of confidence, or one slip in attention, and the entire history of pro football changes! The Patriots were primed to become the best team ever assembled. Nobody believed they would lose except the Giants. Now they are a mere 49th ranked team in terms of total performance in Super Bowl history (MPI-T=.493) and there is still only one undefeated team, the 1972 Miami Dolphins. They might have had a great 18-0 run but they will unfortunately be remembered for the 19th loss.

Dr. John's Super Bowl 42 Lesson

"When others say you'll win, prepare as if you need a 110% effort to stay in the game."

When others say you'll lose, smile knowing you have nothing to lose and will play the game of your life. Victory occurs on the field, in the moment, and one helmet catch at a time.

Most Dominant Offenses in Pressure (MPI-OPD)

MPI-OPD (Offensive Pressure Dominance) represents relative dominance of a team's offense over its opponent's defense in pressure situations. It is calculated as: "MPI-OP of team 1" – "MPI-DP" of team 2."

#1 -- 1966 Green Bay Packers (.480)--Reviewed in "MPI-OP"
#2 -- 1994 San Francisco 49ers (.432)--Reviewed in "MPI-O"
#3 -- 1981 San Francisco 49ers (.374)--Reviewed in "MPI-OP"
#7--- 1978 Pittsburgh Steelers (.289)
#24--1988 San Francisco 49ers (.073)

Super Bowl 13 – January 21, 1979 – Orange Bowl, Miami, Florida

Pittsburgh Steelers 35 (.538) Dallas Cowboys 31 (.490)

Brief Game Review

These were two of the best football teams of all time according to the media. Pittsburgh quarterback Terry Bradshaw had the best season of his career, completing 207 of 368 passes for 2,915 yards and 28 touchdowns and leading his team to a 14-2 regular season record while winning the NFL Most Valuable Player Award. Wide receivers Lynn Swann and John Stallworth provided a great deep threat. Franco Harris was the team's leading rusher for the 7th consecutive season, recording 1,082 yards and 8 touchdowns, while also catching 22 passes for another 144 yards. Fullback Rocky Bleier had 633 rushing yards and 5 touchdowns. The Steelers' stellar offensive line was anchored by future hall of fame center Mike Webster. Pittsburgh's defense finished No. 1 in fewest points allowed (195) second in the league against the run (allowing 107.8 yards per game) and ranked third in fewest total yards allowed (4,529). This was the team that Pittsburgh Steeler Coach Chuck Noll brought to Miami to face Coach Tom Landry's Dallas Cowboys in Super Bowl 13.

Coach Landry's defending champion Cowboys had finished 12-4 during the season and become the first team to appear in five Super Bowls. Dallas led the league in scoring (384) and was No. 2 in total yards gained (5959). The Cowboys were again led by quarterback Roger Staubach who finished the season as the top rated passer in the NFL, throwing for 3,190 yards and 25 touchdowns. Wide receivers Drew Pearson and Tony Hill provided the deep passing threats and running back Tony Dorsett had another fine season, recording a total of 1703 combined rushing and receiving yards. The Cowboys' Defense finished the season as the top ranked defense in the league against the run by only allowing 107.6 yards per game, 2nd overall (4009), 3rd in points allowed (208).

The game was on! On their opening drive, the Cowboys advanced to the Pittsburgh 38-yard line before fumbling on a reverse pass play recovered by Pittsburgh on the 47 yard line. Bradshaw then moved the ball with passes of 12 and 28 yards to John Stallworth, the second going for a touchdown and putting the Steelers on top 7-0. The Cowboys responded well but were stopped by two sacks and forced to punt before the Steelers mounted their own drive which ended when linebacker D. D. Lewis intercepted a pass intended for Stallworth.

After a Bradshaw fumble later in the period, Cowboy quarterback Staubach threw a 39-yard touchdown strike to Tony Hill, tying the game at 7. On the next series for Pittsburgh, Mike Hegman ran a fumble back 37 yards for a touchdown and a 14-7 Cowboys lead, but on the third play of Pittsburgh's ensuing possession, Stallworth caught a pass from Bradshaw at the Steelers 35-yard line then broke a tackle and outraced every other defender to the end zone, turning a simple 10-yard pass into a 75-yard touchdown completion to tie the score at 14–14.

Pittsburgh's "Steel Curtain" defense then dominated the Dallas offense and forced a punt. The Steelers began with Bradshaw's 26-yard completion to Swann, and Pittsburgh eventually missed a field goal. With less than two minutes in the half, Dallas advanced to the Pittsburgh 32-yard line, but Pittsburgh defensive back Mel Blount intercepted. With time running out, Bradshaw completed 2 passes to Swann for gains of 29 and 21 yards, then later completed a 7-yard touchdown pass to fullback Rocky Bleier, giving the Steelers a 21–14 lead at halftime.

Defense prevailed in the third quarter, but Dorsett running helped the Cowboys drive to the Steelers 10-yard line. Staubach then spotted 38-year old reserve tight end Jackie Smith wide open in the end zone and threw him the ball. The pass was a little behind Smith, but was catchable. Smith dropped the pass and the Cowboys had to settle for a field goal cutting their deficit to 21–17. Though Smith played 16 years in the league and is now enshrined in the Pro Football Hall of Fame, he is perhaps best known for his embarrassing blunder on the sport's biggest stage.

The Steelers scored 14 unanswered points after some controversial plays and led 35-17 with less than 7 minutes left in the game. Some of the Steelers were already celebrating victory, but the Cowboys refused to give up. Dallas drove 89 yards in 8 plays to score on Staubach's 7-yard touchdown pass to Billy Joe Dupree. Then after Dallas' Dennis Thurman recovered an onside kick at 2:19, Drew Pearson caught 2 passes for gains of 22 and 25 yards as the Cowboys drove 52 yards in 9 plays to score on Staubach's 4-yard touchdown pass to Butch Johnson. With the ensuing extra point, the score was cut to 35–31 with just 0:22 left in the game. But the Cowboys' second onside kick attempt was unsuccessful. Bleier recovered the ball and the Steelers were able to run out the clock to win the game. Terry Bradshaw was named Super Bowl MVP for the first of two years in a row.

<u>What Actually Happened?</u>

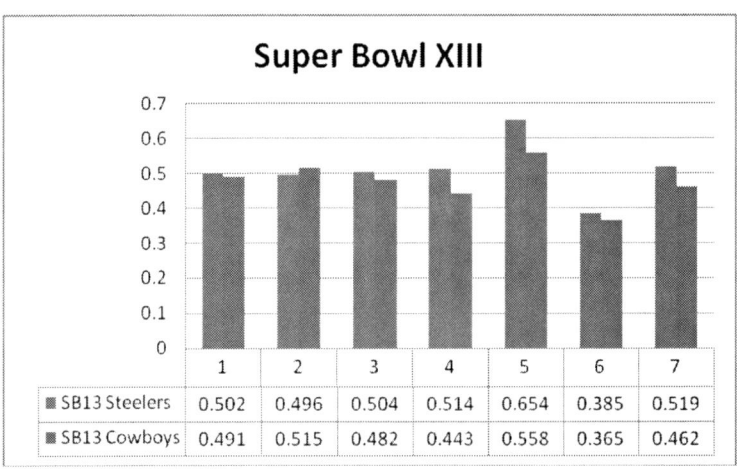

	1	2	3	4	5	6	7
■ SB13 Steelers	0.502	0.496	0.504	0.514	0.654	0.385	0.519
■ SB13 Cowboys	0.491	0.515	0.482	0.443	0.558	0.365	0.462

MPI-T   MPI-O   MPI-D   MPI-ST   MPI-OP   MPI-DP   MPI-TP

This was an extremely close game in terms of overall performance as can been seen on the MPI-T bar graphs above (.502 to .491 advantage for Steelers). The Cowboys offense actually had a better overall day, but not a more dominant day compared with the Steelers' offensive dominance over the Cowboys' defense. This indicates a very strong defense that was able to do enough to slow down the high powered Cowboys.

The real difference in this game, however, was in pressure situations on offense for Pittsburgh (MPI-OP=.654) which ranked 7th in Super Bowl history, and in offensive dominance in pressure (MPI-OPD=.289) which also ranked 7th. This indicates that Terry Bradshaw was brilliant when it counted in important situations, and so were his receivers Swann and Stallworth. That passing unit was phenomenal in key moments. Bradshaw is a winner and quite deserving of the Super Bowl

MVP he received for his 4 touchdowns against only 1 interception performance and a passer rating of 119.2.

The Cowboys were able to exert their will some on offense in key pressure moments and had the 15th overall offensive dominance in pressure situations (MPI-OPD=.173). Staubach had a 100.4 passer rating but he was outclassed by Bradshaw on this day.

Dr. John's Super Bowl 13 Lesson

"When two great teams collide, the one that takes the pressure better is left standing"

These were two very fine teams, but Terry Bradshaw, Lynn Swann and John Stallworth made more plays in key pressure moments of the game, and the Steelers became champions.

Super Bowl 23 – January 22, 1989 – Joe Robbie Stadium, Miami, FL

San Francisco 49ers 20 (.521) Cincinnati Bengals 16 (.460)

Brief Game Review

Bill Walsh had assembled a powerful team but not as strong as one that had won the Super Bowl 4 years before against Miami. The 49ers finished the season 10-6 and mixed it up at quarterback between Steve Young and Joe Montana. Montana led the team to the playoffs with 2,981 yards passing and 18 touchdowns. His target was Jerry Rice who caught 64 passes for 1,306 yards and 9 touchdowns. Roger Craig had earned NFL Offensive Player of the Year for his rushing and receiving skills.

The Cincinnati Bengals were led by head coach Sam Wyche, and quarterback Boomer Esiason who tossed for 3,572 yards and 28 touchdown passes. Esiason had a number of pro bowl teammates on offense including receivers Eddie Brown and Tim McGee and tight end Rodney Holman. Ickey Woods was their top rusher with 1066 yards and

15 touchdowns. The Bengals had a great defensive line but were average overall in terms of performance, ranking 17th in the league.

The 49ers Mike Wilson dropped a pass at the Bengals' 2, where the 49ers had to settle for a field goal, and then Roger Craig fumbled. The Bengals had been outplayed but the score was only 3-3 at the half and the Bengals even led the game 6-3 toward the end of the third quarter. After Bill Romanowski tipped and intercepted Esiason's pass the 49ers tied it on a field goal. On the ensuing kickoff the Bengals' Stanford Jennings ran it back for a touchdown and in the 4th quarter the Bengals led 13-6! The 49ers got the ball back and Montana and his receivers connected well until Rice caught one for a touchdown to tie the game. Montana almost blew it when he threw a pass right to defender Lewis Billups who dropped it. Later Cincinnati kicked a field goal to go up 16-13 and set the stage for the most memorable drive in Super Bowl history. Montana and the 49ers started on their own 8 yard line with just over 3 minutes in the game. Unleashing years of refined skill, passing accuracy, smart decision making and the wisdom of Bill Walsh, the 49ers drove the field and won it on a 10 yard pass to John Taylor. Jerry Rice was the MVP as he had 11 catches for 215 yards and a touchdown. Tune into Lesley Visser's epilogue where she specifically discusses this drive and the genius behind Bill Walsh in achieving it and so many other Super Bowl accomplishments.

<u>What Actually Happened?</u>

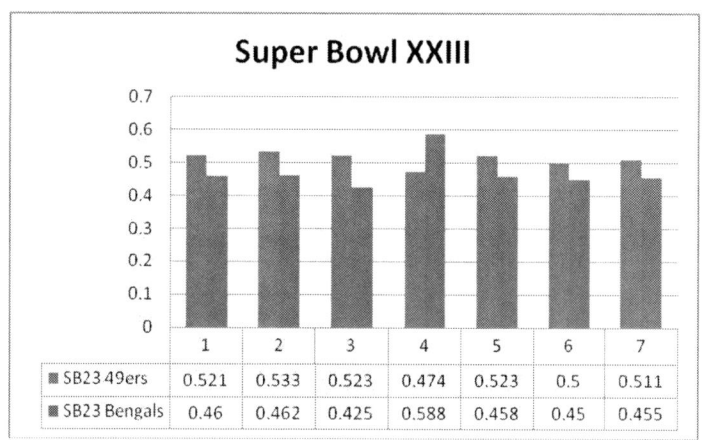

	1	2	3	4	5	6	7
■ SB23 49ers	0.521	0.533	0.523	0.474	0.523	0.5	0.511
■ SB23 Bengals	0.46	0.462	0.425	0.588	0.458	0.45	0.455

MPI-T MPI-O MPI-D MPI-ST MPI-OP MPI-DP MPI-TP

San Francisco performed decisively better than Cincinnati in 6 of 7 major categories as seen in the above graph. The only area where the Bengals were better was on special teams (MPI-ST=.588 to .474) which was ranked 16th in Super Bowl history.

The 49ers posted the 7th best mark in net yards gained and 4th best ever in passing yards in this game and would have done even better without the misses. The defense had the 18th best dominance ever over the Bengal's offense (MPI-DD=.061).

This game is categorized as a dominant offensive team performance in pressure situations but not because of the entire game, but only for the final now famous drive in which Joe Montana stared down nerves and played even more relaxed that he was accustomed to.

Dr. John's Super Bowl 23 Lesson

"Joe Montana"
Need I say any more?

Best Performing Defenses (MPI-D)

MPI-D (Defense) represents performance of a team's defense and aims to be independent of how the opponent's offense performed.

#1 -- 1974 Pittsburgh Steelers (.653)
#2 -- 2000 Baltimore Ravens (.637)
#3 -- 1985 Chicago Bears (.622)--Reviewed in "Best Teams Ever"
#7--- 2002 Tampa Bay Buccaneers (.585)

Super Bowl 9 – January 12, 1975 – Tulane Stadium, New Orleans, LA

Pittsburgh Steelers 16 (.539) Minnesota Vikings 6 (.453)

Brief Game Review

Coach Chuck Noll's Pittsburgh defense dubbed "the Steel Curtain" clashed in Super Bowl 9 with Coach Bud Grant's "Purple People Eaters" of Minnesota. There was no question about the defenses. Add to that the presence of two outstanding quarterbacks, Steeler Terry Bradshaw and Viking Fran Tarkenton and you could sense a war was on.

Pittsburgh came to their first Super Bowl playing for a league championship for the first time in team history. Their 73-year old owner Art Rooney founded the Steelers as a 1933 NFL expansion team, but suffered through losing seasons for most of its 42-year history and had never made it to an NFL championship game or a Super Bowl. But in 1969, Rooney hired Chuck Noll to be the team's head coach and its fortunes started to turn following a disastrous 1-13 first year under the future Hall of Fame coach. Quarterback Terry Bradshaw led the team to a 10-3-1 regular season record, but the Steelers main offensive weapon was running, as Franco Harris rushed for 1,006 yards and five touchdowns. The Steelers' main strength during the season was their staunch defense, which led the league with the fewest total yards allowed (3,074) and the fewest passing yards allowed (1,466). "Mean" Joe Greene won the NFL Defensive Player of the Year Award for the second time in the previous three seasons.

The Vikings came into the season trying to redeem themselves after a one sided Super Bowl loss to the Dolphins the previous year as they became the first team ever to lose two Super Bowls. Minnesota's powerful offense was still led by veteran quarterback Fran Tarkenton who had passed for 2,598 yards and 17 touchdowns. The Vikings' primary offensive weapon was running back Chuck Foreman, who led the team in receptions and rushing. Aided by a defense featuring future hall of fame defensive linemen Carol Eller and Alan Page, and future hall of fame safety Paul Krause, the Vikings won the NFC Central for the 6th time in the previous seven seasons.

The game statistics catalog the Steelers' overwhelming performance. The Vikings were limited to only nine first downs, 119 yards of total offense, and 17 rushing yards. They had only two rushing first downs and only five passing first downs. Jack Lambert tied for most tackles and was later quoted as saying "the game rewards the ones that hit the hardest." Tarkenton completed only 11 of 26 passes for 102 passing yards, no touchdown passes, and tied a then Super Bowl record with three interceptions. His quarterback rating was 14.1. Furthermore, Pittsburgh became the second Super Bowl team after the Miami Dolphins in Super Bowl VII to hold their opponents' offense scoreless. Minnesota's only score came on a blocked punt, and they would miss the extra point attempt.

Meanwhile, Pittsburgh accumulated 333 yards of total offense and scored their final touchdown on a 4 yard Bradshaw to Larry Brown pass. Franco Harris had run for a 9 yard touchdown in the third quarter to put the Steelers up 9-0.

Steelers running back Franco Harris, who ran for a Super Bowl record 158 yards (more than the entire Minnesota offense) and a touchdown, was named the Super Bowl's Most Valuable Player. The final score: Pittsburg 16, Minnesota 6.

What Actually Happened?

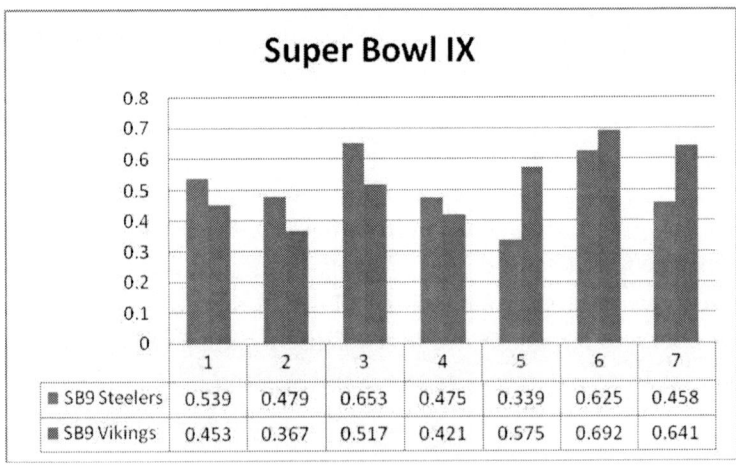

	1	2	3	4	5	6	7
■ SB9 Steelers	0.539	0.479	0.653	0.475	0.339	0.625	0.458
■ SB9 Vikings	0.453	0.367	0.517	0.421	0.575	0.692	0.641

MPI-T MPI-O MPI-D MPI-ST MPI-OP MPI-DP MPI-TP

This Steeler's defense displayed the best single performance in Super Bowl history (MPI-D=.653) and its dominance over the Viking's offense was the 2nd ranked overall (MPI-DD=.286) only behind the Super Bowl XXXV Ravens. They were also the best defense in total net yards allowed (119). A strong argument could be made that this was the best defensive unit ever assembled in the Super Bowl era. On offense, the Steelers posted the 5th best net rushing yards despite having a poorer than average offense overall (MPI-O=.479). This is both a credit to the Vikings pass defense and to Franco Harris and the entire offensive line. Bradshaw was extremely efficient too at quarterback with a 108.0 passer rating.

The Vikings played very well on defense in pressure moments of this game and ranked 12th overall (MPI-DP=.625). This kept the Steelers from scoring more points. On offense, however, they were ranked 85th (MPI-O=.367) and this is a credit to the Steelers' defense.

In sum, the best performing defense in Super Bowl history easily won a slugfest against a very solid Vikings defense.

Dr. John's Super Bowl 9 Lesson

Super Bowl Jeopardy

Answer: *"NICKNAME FOR A DEFENSE THAT ALLOWED ONLY 17 YARDS ON 21 CARRIES IN A SUPER BOWL*

Question: "WHAT IS THE *STEEL CURTAIN?"*

In this coming out party for the Pittsburgh Steelers, the future most successful franchise in Super Bowl history set the standard for how tough, mean and hard hitting defense should be played. The Vikings averaged .8 yards per rush.

Super Bowl 35 – January 28, 2001 – Raymond James Stadium, Tampa, FL

Baltimore Ravens 34 (.549) New York Giants 7 (.421)

Brief Game Review

Coach Brian Billick's Baltimore Ravens led by quarterback Trent Dilfer entered the game with the second best defense and fewest rushing yards allowed during the regular season. However, the Ravens offense had trouble scoring and was considered only average at best and ranked only 13th in the league. The Ravens had won their last seven regular season games to finish 12-4, but entered the playoffs as a wild-card team.

Coach Jim Fassel's New York Giants led by quarterback Kerry Collins entered the Super Bowl with a 12-4 NFC record after acquiring running back Ron Dayne in their offseason to compliment wide receiver Tiki Barber's speed. The two were known as the "Giants' Thunder and Lightning." Collins' favorite passing targets in addition to Barber were wide receivers Amani Toomer and Ike Hilliard.

Defense ruled the first quarter with the first five possessions ending in punts. Two plays later, Dilfer connected with wide receiver Brandon Stokley for a 38 yard touchdown pass and the Ravens led 7-0. The second quarter continued to be a defensive battle until Dilfer found his receiver Qadry Ismail on a 44 yard pass late in the second quarter and a couple plays later the Ravens made it 10-0 on a field goal.

In the second half, the Giants forced the Ravens to punt on the opening drive. A few plays later, the Ravens safety Kim Herring intercepted a Collins pass. The Ravens were stopped and missed a 41 yard field goal. After exchanging punts the game broke open in a most astounding way. First Duane Starks intercepted a Collins pass and ran it back 40 yards to put the Ravens ahead 17-0. On the ensuing kickoff Giants' Ron Dixon answered by running it back for a 97 yard touchdown and the score was 17-7. Unbelievably on the following kickoff, Jemaine Lewis ran the kick back 84 yards for a touchdown and the Ravens lead was 24-7. This was an unheard of three touchdowns in a row in 36 seconds and was probably the most exciting 3 play sequence in NFL history, not to mention Super Bowl history!

Futility set in for the Giants who only achieved one first down in their next four possessions and were never able to move into the Ravens' territory. Meanwhile the Ravens mowed over the favored New York Giants adding 10 more points and winning the game with a final of 34-7.

<u>What Actually Happened?</u>

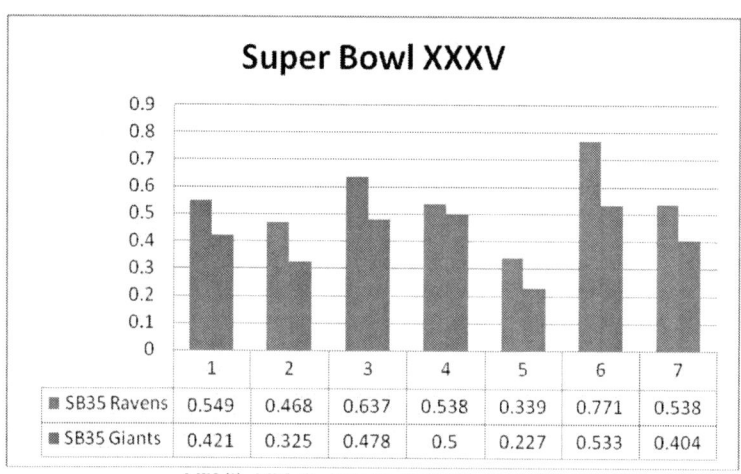

	1	2	3	4	5	6	7
■ SB35 Ravens	0.549	0.468	0.637	0.538	0.339	0.771	0.538
■ SB35 Giants	0.421	0.325	0.478	0.5	0.227	0.533	0.404

MPI-T MPI-O MPI-D MPI-ST MPI-OP MPI-DP MPI-TP

The dominance of the Baltimore Ravens defense in this game was extraordinary and stands out as the single best in Super Bowl history (MPI-DD=.312) whereas their offense ranked 68th overall (MPI-O=.468), so this was a most unusual team that thrived on their defense almost exclusively in this game. Other performances of note included a #2 ranking in Super Bowl history in the following areas: pure defense (MPI-D=.637), pressure defense (MPI-DP=.771), defensive dominance in pressure (MPI-DPD=.544), and a #3 ranking in T-G (5), points allowed (7) and net yards allowed (152).

The Giants had no chance because they could not move the ball. Kerry Collins' quarterback rating was 7.1! The one glimmer of hope following Ron Dixon's touchdown runback was immediately snatched back by Jermaine Lewis' runback. Statistically, the Giants' best unit performance came on defense where they limited the Ravens to 244 net yards gained (14th ranking).

Dr. John's Super Bowl 35 Lesson

"Who needs offense?"
-Coach Billick's parrot

Every so often one side develops a weapon so superior to its rivals that nothing else matters. The 2000 Baltimore Ravens defense was one of those weapons ... like cannons against bows and arrows!

Super Bowl 37 – January 26, 2003 – Qualcomm Stadium, San Diego, CA

Tampa Bay Buccaneers 48 (.550) Oakland Raiders 21 (.453)

Brief Game Review

Tampa Bay coach John Gruden was facing the Oakland Raiders whom he had coached from 1998 to 2001. After the 2001 season, the Raiders traded Gruden to the Bucs for 8 million dollars and four draft picks. It would be the first time that the league's number one defense (Bucs) and number one offense (Coach Bill Callahan's Raiders) would face one another in a Super Bowl. A huge story leading up to the game was the disappearance of Raiders Pro Bowl center Barret Robbins who was eventually found a few days before the game in a hospital where he was being treated for bipolar disorder. The Raiders had to play without him.

The Raiders opened by driving to the Bucs 23 yard line and settling for a field goal and 3-0 lead. The Bucs followed suit with their own drive and field goal, then added another one in the second quarter to take a 6-3 lead. Before the half was over, Tampa Bay began moving the ball at will and Oakland missed a couple of big chances for turnovers. Quarterback Brad Johnson and his Bucs added two touchdowns to go up 20-3 before the half. The second half only got worse for the Raiders as the Buccaneers dominated the line and Brad Johnson's 8 yard touchdown pass to Keenan McCardell increased the lead to 27-3. Then just two plays into the Raiders next drive, Raiders quarterback Rich Gannon threw an interception which Dwight Smith returned 44 yards for a touchdown and the rout was on 34-3.

The Raiders made a noble comeback effort with a blocked punt returned for a touchdown and a 48 yard touchdown pass to cut the lead to 34-21. Tampa Bay finished off Oakland in the fourth quarter, however, with two interceptions returned for touchdowns. This was the first time in Super Bowl history that one team scored three defensive touchdowns. Gruden's prior knowledge of the Raiders was seen as the key. Gruden even played quarterback for the scout team in practice so his defense could see what the Raiders would do. Bucs safety John Lynch later said that almost all the plays run by the Raiders offense were plays Gruden told them to anticipate. Bucs safety Dexter Jackson won the MVP award for two interceptions. He became only the third defensive back to win it.

<u>What Actually Happened?</u>

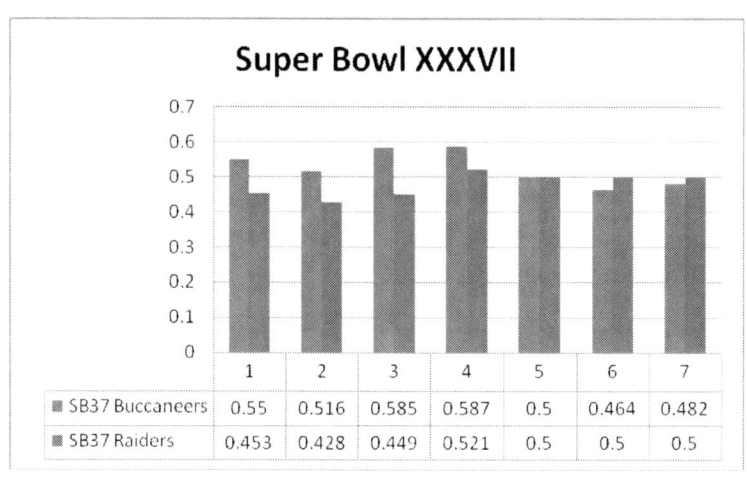

	1	2	3	4	5	6	7
SB37 Buccaneers	0.55	0.516	0.585	0.587	0.5	0.464	0.482
SB37 Raiders	0.453	0.428	0.449	0.521	0.5	0.5	0.5

MPI-T MPI-O MPI-D MPI-ST MPI-OP MPI-DP MPI-TP

Tampa Bay performed exceptionally well as the 7th best pure defense in Super Bowl history (MPI-D-.585) in taking care of the offense hurt by the disappearance of Barret Robbins. The IQ advantage in having Coach Jon Gruden's knowledge of his former Raider's offense had to help too. The Buc's +4 on Takeaways minus Giveaways ranked them 4th overall. What we might forget in all this defensive excellence, however, is that the Bucs actually moved the ball well and scored two touchdowns before the defense really got into the act. Their time of possession statistic was 9th ranked overall, a very solid contributing factor to team success. Overall the Bucs had the 11th best performing team in the Super Bowl (MPI-T=.550).

Oakland had chances early on to make big plays on defense, but missed a couple easy interceptions as Tampa Bay breathed a sigh of relief. Could all the pre-game distractions have exacted their toll on Oakland's focus? It is possible. The Raiders did not play well as their overall performance was ranked 74th (MPI-T=.453) in history when they were supposed to win this game. Their best relative efforts came on offense in pressure situations, ranking 28th which only looks good in comparison to how bad they performed in other areas. This day will always belong to the Tampa Bay defense.

Dr. John's Super Bowl 37 Lesson

*"Win the psychological war beforehand and your chances
in battle improve remarkably"*

Oakland knew nothing about one of their own starting players. Tampa Bay knew everything about all of Oakland's players. While Oakland came in distracted and confused, Tampa Bay was mentally quick and two steps ahead with intelligence briefings all week by the perfect spy … an ex head coach!

Most Dominant Defenses (MPI-DD)

MPI-DD (Defensive Dominance) represents relative dominance of a team's defense over its opponent's offense. It is calculated as "MPI-D of team 1" – "MPI-O of team 2."

#1--2000 Baltimore Ravens (.312)--Reviewed in "MPI-D"
#2--1974 Pittsburgh Steelers (.286)--Reviewed in "MPI-D"
#3--1985 Chicago Bears (.260)--Reviewed in "Best Teams Ever"

Best Performing Defenses in Pressure (MPI-DP)

MPI-DP (Defensive Pressure) represents performance of a team's defense in pressure situations and aims to be independent of how the opponent's offense performed.

#1--1976 Oakland Raiders (.825)
#2--2000 Baltimore Ravens (.771)--Reviewed in "MPI-D"
#3--1971 Dallas Cowboys (.750) tie
#3--1972 Miami Dolphins (.750) tie
#3--1984 San Francisco 49ers (.750) tie--Reviewed in "MPI-OD"
#3--1985 Chicago Bears (.750) tie--Reviewed in "Best Teams Ever"
#3--1990 New York Giants (.750) tie--Reviewed in "Time of Possession"
#4--2006 Indianapolis Colts (.700) tie
#4--1979 Pittsburgh Steelers (.700) tie--Reviewed in "MPI-TP"

Super Bowl 11 – January 9, 1977 – Rose Bowl, Pasadena, CA

Oakland Raiders 32 (.550) Minnesota Vikings 14 (.453)

Brief Game Review

Super Bowl 11 became the first Super Bowl matching top seeds from each conference. It was also the last Super Bowl finished during daylight hours and the earliest played in the calendar year, on January 9.

Coach John Madden's Oakland Raiders had won their final 10 games of the 1976 season and finished with a league best record of 13-1. NFL teams dreaded their defense. Safeties Jack Tatum and George Atkinson had a reputation for violently punishing opposing receivers. Linebacker Ted Hendricks' speed, not to mention his 6'7" shadow alone, intimidated offensive runners and receivers. After some injuries, John Madden's defense adopted a 3-4 scheme and it worked as he had designed it. Quarterback Ken Stabler, the AFC's top-rated passer and star receiver Fred Biletnikoff who just seemed to catch everything even remotely close to him, led a well-oiled offense.

Coach Bud Grant's Minnesota Vikings got to the Super Bowl by winning the NFC Central their eighth time in nine years with an 11-2-1 record. They led the NFC in allowing only 176 points, the fewest during the regular season. They were led by legendary quarterback Fran Tarkenton and power runner Chuck Foreman as well as some of the biggest NFL names on any defensive line including Carl Eller, Alan Page and Jim Marshall.

The first quarter was scoreless, but Minnesota had its chances early by blocking a Ray Guy punt and getting the ball on Oakland's 3 yard line before fumbling it back to the Raiders two plays later. Early in the second quarter Oakland went up 3-0 on a 24 yard field goal, got the ball back, and drove 64 yards in 10 plays capped by a 1 yard touchdown pass to Dave Casper for a 10-0 advantage. They made it 16-0 before halftime after a nifty Neal Colzie punt return, 35 yard drive, and 1 yard touchdown run by Pete Banaszak. They missed the extra point.

Early in the second half, Oakland reached the 23 yard line but had to settle for a field goal and 19-0 lead. The Vikings finally scored on an 8 yard touchdown pass from Fran Tarkenton to Sammy White but the comeback was short-lived when cornerback Willie Brown intercepted Tarkenton and ran it back 75 yards for the touchdown. The Raiders led 32-7 after a missed extra point and the Vikings scored once more but it was too little too late and Oakland won 32-14.

The Raiders gained the most yards in a Super Bowl until that time with 429, and Oakland wide receiver Fred Biletnikoff was named Super Bowl MVP with only four catches for 79 yards.

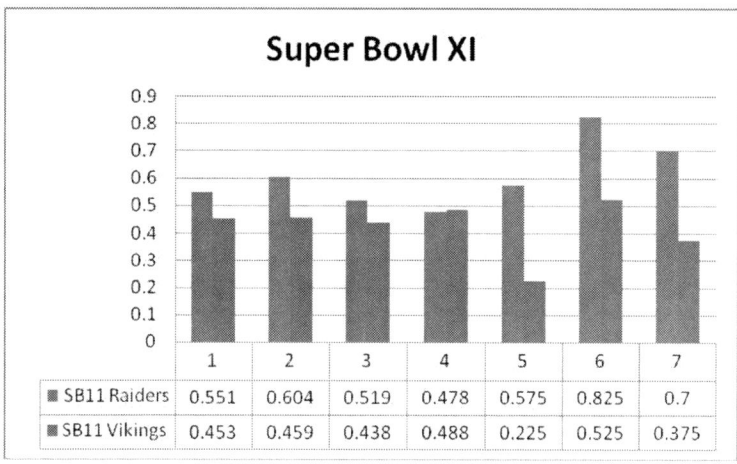

	1	2	3	4	5	6	7
■ SB11 Raiders	0.551	0.604	0.519	0.478	0.575	0.825	0.7
■ SB11 Vikings	0.453	0.459	0.438	0.488	0.225	0.525	0.375

MPI-T MPI-O MPI-D MPI-ST MPI-OP MPI-DP MPI-TP

While the yards gained and passes caught were impressive, the real strength on this day was the Raiders defense. They were almost flawless in defensive pressure situations (MPI-DP=.825) and they ranked 1st overall in both defensive pressure performance and defensive pressure dominance (MPI-DPD=.600). Being best among 88 Super Bowl teams in those two categories and 60% better than the Vikings in pressure situations is so good it needs repeating! The Raiders also ranked 2nd overall in total pressure performance (MPI-TP=.700), were tied for best in turnovers (0), and were 3rd best in net rushing yards (266).

In looking at the performance discrepancy in this game, the Vikings did not even belong on the same field as the Raiders. The decisive score does not even do this game justice. The Vikings did slightly outperform the Raiders on special teams if that is any concession (MPI-ST.488 for Vikings and .478 for the Raiders), but based on performance the score should have been more like 50-7.

```
┌─────────────────────────────────────────────────────────────┐
│              Dr. John's Super Bowl 11 Lesson                 │
│                                                             │
│   "Be offensive on defense! Instill fear with toughness and │
│   aggression and make hits hurt."                           │
│                                                             │
│   The 1976 Oakland Raiders had a habit of playing nasty,    │
│   aggressive and violent defense.  It paid off against the  │
│   Vikings and to this day still remains the toughest, best, │
│   and most dominant defense in key moments of a Super Bowl. │
└─────────────────────────────────────────────────────────────┘
```

Super Bowl 6 – January 16, 1972 – Tulane Stadium, New Orleans, LA

Dallas Cowboys 24 (.538) Miami Dolphins 3 (.445)

Brief Game Review

Dallas Cowboys Coach Tom Landry's Cowboys were six point favorites. They had finished the regular season 11-3 on the arm of quarterback Roger Staubach, the NFL's top rated passer. Running backs Duane Thomas, Walt Garrison, and Calvin Hill had combined for 1,690 yards rushing and 14 touchdowns. As good as the offense was, the Dallas "Doomsday Defense" only gave up one touchdown in their last 25 quarters leading up to the Super Bowl! The flex defense was advanced for its time and allowed Dallas to stuff running games by bringing up safety Cliff Harris.

Miami Dolphins Coach Don Shula got this team to the Super Bowl for the first time after finishing the regular season 10-3-1 including a streak of eight straight wins. Quarterback Bob Griese who was the AFC's Most Valuable Player had led the league in passing for 2,089 yards and 19 touchdowns. Brutal fullback Larry Csonka (1,051 yards) and deft halfback Jim Kiick (738 yards) led a powerful rushing attack. Did they fumble often? Only one time all year.

But Super Bowl games are not regular season games. After exchanging punts Dallas forced a Larry Csonka fumble for the first time all season and Chuck Howley recovered the ball at the Dallas 48. Dallas drove down to the 2 yard-line but settled for a field to go up 3-0. Towards the end of the 2nd quarter Dallas put together a 9 play, 76 yard drive ended on a 7 yard touchdown pass from Staubach to wide receiver Lance Alworth, and the Cowboys led 10-0. Miami drove late in the 2nd quarter to set up a Garo Yepremian 31-yard field goal as time expired. On their way to the locker rooms, the scoreboard showed Dallas 10, Miami 3.

Dallas opened up the 2nd half with an impressive 8 play, 71- yard drive that ended on a Duane Thomas 3 yard touchdown run to give the Cowboys a 17-3 lead. The Cowboys would dominate the rest of the game as Miami's offense sputtered to a total halt. Early in the 4th quarter Staubach connected with tight end Mike Ditka for a 7-yard touchdown pass and a 24-3 lead that would be the final score. Staubach was named Super Bowl MVP after throwing for 119 yards and two touchdowns.

<u>What Actually Happened?</u>

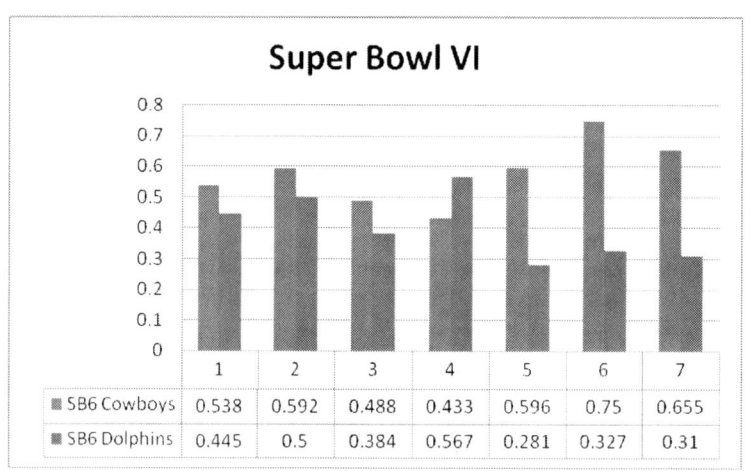

	1	2	3	4	5	6	7
SB6 Cowboys	0.538	0.592	0.488	0.433	0.596	0.75	0.655
SB6 Dolphins	0.445	0.5	0.384	0.567	0.281	0.327	0.31

MPI-T MPI-O MPI-D MPI-ST MPI-OP MPI-DP MPI-TP

Reviewing the statistics of this game, it becomes even clearer how totally the Dallas Cowboys dominated, and especially in key pressure moments on defense (see the blue bar above in section 6). They were best in history at points allowed (3), and that was achieved in large part to their extreme forte in the area of defensive performance in pressure (MPI-DP=.750) which was tied for 3rd best in Super Bowl history. The defensive dominance in pressure over Miami's offense was 6th best overall (MPI-DPD=.469) and tied with the 1985 Chicago Bears in that category. Overall dominance in pressure was 4th best (MPI-TPD=.345). Amazingly, the Cowboys offense was almost as good. They were the 4th best in rushing yards (252), 4th best in time of possession (39:12 to 20:48), and the 6th best dominating offense (MPI-OD=.208).

Miami won a couple more minor battles with zero penalties (tied for best) and 11th best special teams dominance score (.134) but it was no match for the loaded and high performing Cowboys on this day. It was a total Cowboys performance and victory.

Dr. John's Super Bowl 6 Lesson

"Remove your opponent's top weapon and everything falls into place"

The Miami Dolphins were a powerful running team. The Cowboys neutralized it with a flex defense that gave Dallas another man on the defensive line. With no big running game to rely upon, the Dolphins were forced out of their comfort zone and the more experienced Cowboys prevailed.

Super Bowl 7 – January 14, 1973 – Memorial Coliseum, Los Angeles, CA

Miami Dolphins 14 (.511) Washington Redskins 7 (.485)

Brief Game Review

Coach Don Shula's Miami Dolphins went undefeated during the season, despite losing their starting quarterback when Bob Griese fractured his right leg and dislocated his ankle in the 5th game. In his place, 38-year-old quarterback Earl Morrall led Miami to victory in their nine remaining regular season games, and was the 1972 NFL Comeback Player of the Year. Miami had the same core of young players who helped the team advance to the previous year's Super Bowl VI and the team still had a powerful running attack, spearheaded by running backs Larry Csonka, Jim Kiick, and Eugene "Mercury" Morris. Morris, who in previous seasons had been used primarily as a kick returner, took over the starting halfback position from Kiick. Csonka led the team with 1,117 yards and six touchdowns and Miami set a record with 2,960 total rushing yards during the regular season, and became the first team ever to have two players rush for 1,000 yards in one season (Csonka and Morris) and Miami led the NFL in points scored (385). Receiver Paul Warfield provided an effective deep threat option, and Miami's offensive line, led by future hall of famers Jim Langer and Larry Little, was also a key factor for the Dolphins' offensive production. And Miami's "No-Name Defense" (a nickname inspired by Dallas Cowboys head coach Tom Landry when he could not recall the names of any Dolphins defenders just before Super Bowl VI), were led by future hall of fame linebacker Nick Buoniconti.

Coach George Allen's Washington Redskins, in contrast to young Miami, were the oldest team in the NFL. They had earned the nickname "The Over the Hill Gang." The team finished the 1972 season with an NFC-best 11-3 record. The Redskins were led by 33-year old quarterback Billy Kilmer, who threw for 1,648 yards and a league leading 19 touchdowns during the regular season, with only 11 interceptions, giving him an NFL best 84.8 passer rating. Their powerful rushing attack featured Larry Brown who gained 1,216 yards (first in the NFC and second in the NFL) and caught 32 passes for 473 yards, and scored 12 touchdowns, earning him both the NFL Most Valuable Player Award and the NFL Offensive Player of the Year Award. Washington also had a solid defense led by linebacker Chris Hanburger and cornerbacks Pat Fischer and Mike Bass.

The Dolphins' "No-Name Defense" dominated the game, allowing Washington to cross midfield only once in the first half and only four times overall. Miami drew first blood on a 28 yard pass from Griese to Howard Twilley in the first quarter. In the second quarter Jim Kick went over from the 1 and Miami led 14-0 at the half.

Both teams' defenses played well in the second half, but Miami played better and appeared on the verge of kicking a field goal late in the game so that their 17-0 season would match a 17-0 game score. Then Miami's placekicker, Garo Yepremian, grabbed his blocked field goal try, and tried to throw a forward pass. Washington cornerback, Mike Bass, caught it and returned it 49 yards for a touchdown. It was the longest period in a Super Bowl to date for one team to be shut out, as Washington had been held scoreless until 2:07 remained in the fourth quarter. Final score: Miami 14, Washington 7.

Dolphins' safety Jake Scott was named Most Valuable Player. He snatched two Billy Kilmer passes, one of which he intercepted in the end zone in the fourth quarter and returned 56 yards to end a Redskin's threat.

<u>What Actually Happened?</u>

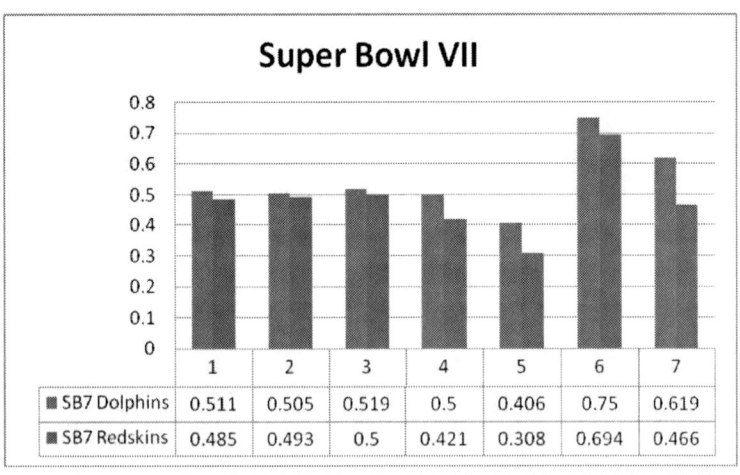

	1	2	3	4	5	6	7
■ SB7 Dolphins	0.511	0.505	0.519	0.5	0.406	0.75	0.619
■ SB7 Redskins	0.485	0.493	0.5	0.421	0.308	0.694	0.466

MPI-T MPI-O MPI-D MPI-ST MPI-OP MPI-DP MPI-TP

The "perfect team" dominated in every category on the MPI but especially in pressure situations on defense where they were tied for 3rd best of all time (MPI-DP=.750). The team was not, however, anywhere near a perfect performance in this game as can be seen on their overall performance score (MPI-T=.511) which only ranks 35th. The Redskins did not threaten to score much, but when they did the Dolphins rose to the challenge each time. There are analogies to this Dolphins team and the Patriots teams of the 2000s in how well they performed when it mattered most and the Dolphins used to call their defense a "bend but do not break defense." So overall performance scores might look lower than expected, but in this case the pressure score on defense tells the story. Miami was also 9th in net yards allowed (228).

Also give credit to Washington's defense which held the "perfect team" to 14 points and was best in pressure situations on defense, ranking 12th overall (MPI-DP=.694). Still, the Dolphins were never threatened in this game and would have probably won this game by 17 rather than 7 if not for that one bizarre play in which Miami's Garo Yepremian tried to throw a blocked field goal which Mike Bass returned for a touchdown.

Jake Scott received the MVP for his two interceptions, and he played well with one interception that really hurt Washington, but our data suggests that left defensive tackle Manny Fernandez should have received the MVP instead. He was a much bigger factor in this high octane 3rd best overall pressure defense and he also led the defense in tackles.

Dr. John's Super Bowl 7 Lesson

"A perfect team is far from perfect"

Even though the 1972 Miami Dolphins achieved a perfect season record, they did not even come close to a perfect performance against the Redskins. They dominated this game, but 34 teams performed better on Super Sunday. To show how fragile perfection is, one fluke play by the Redskins could have tied this game, and two could have won it. Still … the Dolphins achieved what no other team has ever achieved, and they deserve the accolades!

Super Bowl 41 – February 4, 2007 – Dolphin Stadium, Miami, FL

Indianapolis Colts 29 (.550) Chicago Bears 17 (.453)

Brief Game Review

An improved Indianapolis Colts defense and ever powerful offense led by one of the best quarterbacks ever in Peyton Manning went 12-4 in 2006 and came back from an 18 point deficit to beat Tom Brady and the Patriots in the 2006 AFC Championship game, one of the most memorable games ever. It was a major breakthrough for Manning and the Colts who had for too long lived in the shadow of Patriot's success. The Chicago Bears led by Coach Lovie Smith and 30-year old quarterback Rex Grossman, finished the season with an NFC best record of 13-3 to advance to their second Super Bowl in franchise history. The Bears excelled on defense, ranking third in fewest points allowed and second in fewest points allowed per drive. The game featured the two closest NFL cities, a short 3 plus hours down I-65, so many called this the I-65 Super Bowl.

The rain was continuous throughout the game, but that did not hinder Bears' return man Devin Hester from running back the opening kickoff 92 yards for a touchdown for the earliest lead in Super Bowl history. On the Colts' first drive of the game, defensive back Chris Harris intercepted a deep third-down pass from Manning and returned it to the Bears' 35 yard line. Chicago was stuffed on their ensuing possession and forced to punt. After several short runs and passes, the Colts scored on a 53 yard touchdown pass from Manning to Reggie Wayne cutting the Bears lead to 7-6 after the extra point snap was dropped. The Bears then scored on a Grossman pass to Muhsin Muhammed after a 57 yard drive set up by a Colts fumble. The big play on the drive was a 52 yard run by Thomas Jones, a thrill which gave the Bears a 14-6 lead. The Colts inched back with a field goal to make it 14-9, and moved the ball well again to take a 16-14 lead into the half on a 1 yard run by Dominic Rhodes.

The Bears were unconventionally sloppy in the second half with fumbles, a missed snap, and an 11 yard loss on a sack as the Colts' defense applied more pressure. The Colts added two field goals and the Bears one, putting the Colts ahead 22-17 entering the fourth quarter. The Bears got the ball back with about thirteen minutes to play and Grossman threw one nice completion before Kelvin Hayden intercepted a pass and returned it 56 yards to the end zone for a 29-17 final score. Bob Sanders intercepted an errant Grossman pass in the rain and this game was in the books.

With this win, Colts coach, Tony Dungy, became the first African-American coach ever to win a Super Bowl.

What Actually Happened?

Super Bowl XLI

	1	2	3	4	5	6	7
SB41 Colts	0.525	0.512	0.54	0.543	0.559	0.7	0.611
SB41 Bears	0.48	0.462	0.49	0.487	0.275	0.547	0.442

MPI-T MPI-O MPI-D MPI-ST MPI-OP MPI-DP MPI-TP

Did you think this Super Bowl winning Colts team won, as usual, with their prolific passing attack? After all, Peyton Manning got the MVP. Think again. He did play much better in the second half, but it was solid defensive play in pressure situations that carried the day for the Colts (MPI-DP=.700) and ranked tied for 4th overall in Super Bowl history!

Time of possession ranked 8th overall (38:04 to 21:56) and net yards rushing ranked 9th (191) for the Colts, so they were effective running and once again the value of balance in winning a Super Bowl is

147

retold like an oft repeated and necessary bedtime story. While having Manning throw for 247 yards and maintain possession helped, passing yards ranked below average for a Super Bowl winner at 35th overall. Overall offensive performance only ranked 41st (MPI-T=.525), so it was not the offense but the defense that got it done best.

The Bears remained true to form in posting a relative strength on defense (MPI-D=.490) which ranked 39th of 88 teams, but as you can see from the above graph, the Colts dominated in every one of the 7 main categories and should have probably won this game more easily. Even though the game seemed close in score until the 4th quarter, the Colts won most of the battles and never seemed to lose confidence. It was amazing that not one Colts player on defense was selected to the Pro Bowl, but they certainly got the job done in 41.

Dr. John's Super Bowl 41 Lesson

"Keep a low profile and just Win"

The Colts were long known for their big passing game, and it led them back from an 18 point deficit to beat the Patriots to reach the Super Bowl, but it was a relatively unknown group of defensive players who really made the difference in winning this Super Bowl. Credit the coaching leadership of Tony Dungy and the personnel moves of Bill Polian, but credit mostly a defense that decided to make a name for themselves with a championship rather than individual awards.

Most Dominant Defenses in Pressure (MPI-DPD)

MPI-DPD (Defensive Pressure Dominance) represents relative dominance of a team's defense over its opponent's offense in pressure situations. It is calculated as: "MPI-DP of team 1" – "MPI-OP of team 2."

#1--1976 Oakland Raiders (.600)--Reviewed in "MPI-DP"
#2--2000 Baltimore Ravens (.544)--Reviewed in "MPI-D"
#3--1990 New York Giants (.531)--Reviewed in "Best Time of Possession"

<u>Best Performing Special Teams Unit (MPI-ST)</u>

MPI-ST (Special Teams) represents performance of a team's special teams and aims to be independent of how the opponent's special teams performed.

#1--1992 Dallas Cowboys (.708)
#2--2009 New Orleans Saints (.703)
#3--1973 Miami Dolphins (.673)--Reviewed in "Best Teams Ever"
#4--1993 Dallas Cowboys (.671)

Super Bowl 27 – January 31, 1993 – Rose Bowl, Pasadena, CA

Dallas Cowboys 52 (.548) Buffalo Bills 17 (.472)

<u>Brief Game Review</u>

Coach Jimmy Johnson's Dallas Cowboys were a powerful team in 1992 led by quarterback Troy Aikman who was hottest that year with 3,445 yards passing and 23 touchdowns. Emmitt Smith was spectacular as a runner, leading the league with 1,713 yards rushing while Michael Irvin was the star wide receiver who caught 78 passes for 1,396 yards and 7 touchdowns. The team finished the season 13-3 and seemed poised to win their first Super Bowl in years. Defense was also strong, but there were many unheralded players who had not yet made a name for themselves.

The Buffalo Bills had a chip on their shoulder, having lost the previous two Super Bowls to the Redskins and the Giants. They were a very talented team with 12 players making the Pro Bowl. Their offense led by quarterback Jim Kelly and running back Thurman Thomas was number two in the league and tops in rushing. Frank Reich, however, would get most of the snaps at quarterback for the Bills as Kelly was injured. Defense was very solid led by lineman Bruce Smith, who terrorized opposing quarterbacks, and nose tackle Jeff Wright.

The Bills started strong as Thomas scored on a 2 yard run to take an early 7-0 lead after a Steve Tasker blocked punt. After Dallas was forced to punt Jim Kelly was intercepted by James Washington. Dallas drove and scored on an Aikman touchdown pass to Jay Novacek to tie it at 7. Dallas would continue forcing turnovers, scoring on a fumble return to go up 14-7 and then forcing Kelly out of the game with an injury. The Bills hit on a field goal before Irvin and Aikman connected on two second quarter touchdown passes and the Cowboys took control 28-10 before the half ended.

Dallas began strong again in the third quarter with a 77 yard drive and field goal to extend their lead to 31-10. Soon after, the Bills connected on a 40 yard touchdown pass to Don Beebe and were only down two touchdowns, 31-17, entering the fourth quarter. Troy Aikman's air attack continued, this time to Alvin Harper on a 45-yard touchdown pass, before Buffalo found their hole too deep to dig out of. The final margin of victory for Johnson's talented boys was 52-17.

Troy Aikman was awarded the MVP for his shining play and his 144.2 passer rating demonstrated it. He was 22/30 for 273 yards and 4 touchdowns with no interceptions. Emmitt Smith rushed for 108 yards.

<u>What Actually Happened?</u>

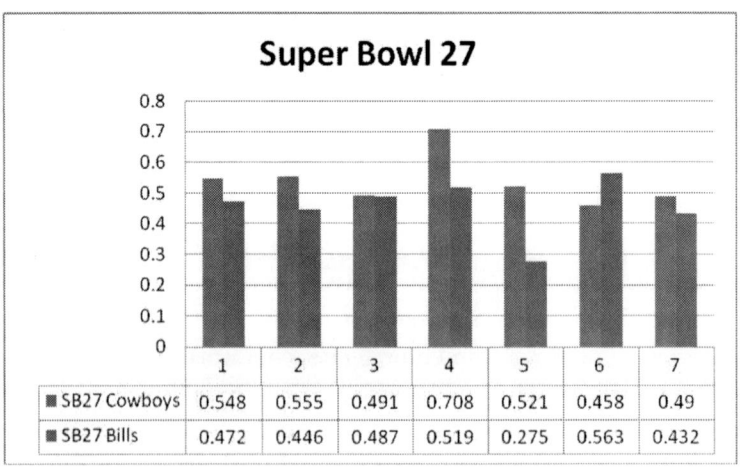

	1	2	3	4	5	6	7
■ SB27 Cowboys	0.548	0.555	0.491	0.708	0.521	0.458	0.49
■ SB27 Bills	0.472	0.446	0.487	0.519	0.275	0.563	0.432

MPI-T MPI-O MPI-D MPI-ST MPI-OP MPI-DP MPI-TP

While the credit usually goes to offense and defense, and Aikman certainly deserved his MVP award, most do not even know that this was the team with the best performing special teams unit in Super Bowl history (MPI-ST=.708)! As such, we categorized it in this section although it could have appeared in several. While this is not to say that special teams won the game, it does say that this unit did their job better than 87 other teams on Super Bowl Sunday.

The Cowboys were also first in takeaways minus giveaways (T-G=7), but the special teams play was even more impressive to such an extreme level that its graph above looks more like a city skyscraper. Dallas also had the second best point production in Super Bowl history with 52.

The Bills were 30th in net passing yards, similar to their performance in the previous Super Bowl but far too one dimensional as a team to win the big game. Unfortunately for the Bills, they did not take care of the ball. They were the worst team in Super Bowl history on both turnovers (9) and takeaways minus giveaways (-7).

Dr. John's Super Bowl 27 Lesson

"Fumble 8 times and you don't win"

The Dallas Cowboys won this game decisively, but they were also aided greatly by the self-destructive Buffalo Bills in their third straight Super Bowl loss. The Bills turned the ball over 9 times with 8 fumbles and 4 interceptions. Some truths do not require extra discussion.

Super Bowl 44 – February 4, 2010 – Sun Life Stadium, Miami, FL

New Orleans Saints 31 (.548) Indianapolis Colts 17 (.480)

Brief Game Review

New Orleans Saints coach Sean Payton and Indianapolis Colts coach Jim Caldwell each brought their #1 seeded teams to the Super

Bowl. This was the first time in sixteen years that # 1 seeds in their Conferences would butt heads on Super Sunday.

The Saints made it to the Super Bowl for the first time in franchise history after finishing the season with an NFC best 13-3 record. The New Orleans offense had led the NFL in scoring during the regular season. Saints quarterback Drew Brees, who finished the season as the NFL's top rated quarterback, threw for 4,338 yards and 34 touchdowns.

The Colts completed the regular season an NFL best 14-2. As in previous years, Indianapolis was led with a high powered offense directed by star quarterback Peyton Manning. Manning won the regular season MVP for the fourth time after throwing for 4,500 yards and 33 touchdowns. The offensive line was also superb in allowing only 13 sacks, fewest in the league.

The Saints were forced to punt on their first possession. The Colts then drove twice down the field to score, the second time on a 96-yard record-tying longest Super Bowl drive to take a 10-0 lead. Early in the second quarter New Orleans got on the board with a 46-yard field goal to cut the lead to 10-3. They moved again and had the ball at the Colts 3 yard line on 1st and goal when they were stopped on downs. The Colts took over and tried to run out the clock but the Saints prevented a first down and following a punt the Saints kicked another field goal as time expired. The Colts led 10-6 at halftime.

Sean Payton's Saints surprised everyone by executing and recovering an onside kick to begin the second half. It was the first onside kick attempted before the fourth quarter in Super Bowl history. The Saints drove 58 yards and finished it off with a Brees to Pierre Thomas 16 yard touchdown pass and a 13-10 lead. The Colts on their next possession drove 76 yards in ten plays, and scored on Joseph Addai's 4 yard touchdown to take the lead back 17-13. Before the end of the 3rd quarter the Saints added a field goal to cut their deficit to one.

Early in the 4th quarter the Colts had a chance to add to their lead, but Matt Stover missed a 51 yard field goal. The Saints then drove 59 yards down the field and scored on a 2 yard touchdown pass to Jeremy Shockey and a successful two point conversation to take a 24-17 lead. On the next drive, Manning was intercepted by Tracey Porter who returned it

74 yards for a touchdown to make the final score 31-17. Saints quarterback Drew Brees was awarded the Super Bowl MVP after throwing for 288 yards and two touchdowns. His 32 completions in the game tied a Super Bowl record.

<u>What Actually Happened?</u>

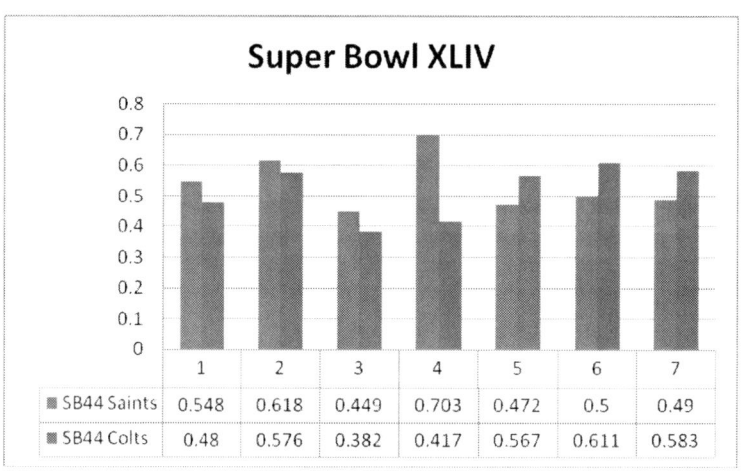

Drew Brees and the Saints offense were brilliant, the 4th best offensive performance in Super Bowl history (MPI-O=.618) just behind the Super Bowl VIII Dolphins and Super Bowl XXIX and XIX 49ers overall. Clearly Brees earned his MVP award for the game. But don't forget the Saints special teams unit. It was even better! The Saints special teams performance (MPI-ST=.703) and dominance ranked 2nd overall in Super Bowl history, only behind the Cowboys of Super Bowl XXVII and above 70% of perfection! Perhaps their most memorable play was the onside kick surprise to start the second half that worked to a charm. Another factor was not turning the ball over.

As for the Colts, the offense played well and ranked 14th overall (MPI-O=.576) and 7th in net passing yards (333), outgaining the Saints through the air who had 281 yards. The special teams play for the Colts was horrible (MPI-ST=.417) and ranked 81st overall in performance and 87th in dominance.

By playing extremely efficient error free football on offense, and with nearly the best special teams performance in Super Bowl history, the Saints were able to outclass the Colts in a fairly well played game.

Dr. John's Super Bowl 44 Lesson

"Take smart risks to change your fate"

Saints coach Sean Peyton should have received the Super Bowl MVP award for ordering an onside kick to start the third quarter to beat another Peyton named Manning. It gave the Saints the ball, took it out of Manning's dangerous hands, led to points, and boosted the confidence of the number two ranked special teams unit in Super Bowl history.

Super Bowl 28 – January 30, 1994 – Georgia Dome, Atlanta, GA

Dallas Cowboys 30 (.540) Buffalo Bills 13 (.466)

Brief Game Review

This was the first time in Super Bowl history that the same two teams with the same two coaches, Jimmy Johnson of Dallas and Marv Levy of the Buffalo Bills, met in two consecutive Super Bowls. Johnson's team crushed the Bills in the previous Super Bowl (XXVII) 52-17. This was also the last time #1 seeds from each conference met in the Super Bowl. Rumors swelled that Johnson would leave the Cowboys.

Both teams had achieved 12-4 regular season records. Cowboys' quarterback Troy Aikman led a strong passing attack supported by NFL MVP running back Emmitt Smith and a strong defense. The Bills were led by now 4 time starting Super Bowl quarterback Jim Kelly, their no-huddle offense, and star running back Thurman Thomas. The Bills defense was a weakness going in, ranked 28th that season in the NFL.

The Cowboys opened the scoring on their first drive of the game by marching to the 24 yard line and kicking a 41 yard field goal for a 3-0 lead. The Bills responded with a record 54 yard field goal by Steve Christie to tie the game 3-3 (still the longest field goal in Super Bowl history). After a Bills turnover, Dallas added a field goal to lead 6-3, but the Bills soon responded with a 17 play, 80 yard drive and 4 yard touchdown run by Thurman Thomas to go up 10-6. Then Christie kicked another field goal as time expired to give the Bills a 13-6 lead at the end of the first half.

The Cowboys dominated the second half. Defensive linemen Leon Lett forced a Thurman Thomas fumble and James Washington grabbed it at the 46 and ran for a touchdown to tie the game. Thurman Thomas would later say, "Dallas didn't wear us down in the second half, I fumbled… I cost us the game." Several Bills agreed it was the key factor. Bills center Kent Hull said "We were high in the first half, and then boom! The turnover took a big chunk out of our confidence." The Cowboys defense was exceptional in the second half and kept the Bills scoreless. The Dallas offense would add two more touchdowns and a field goal largely on the dominant blocking and running of Emmitt Smith who earned the MVP award for his 132 yard performance and Dallas won 30-13. A few weeks after the Super Bowl, Jimmy Johnson left the Cowboys.

What Actually Happened?

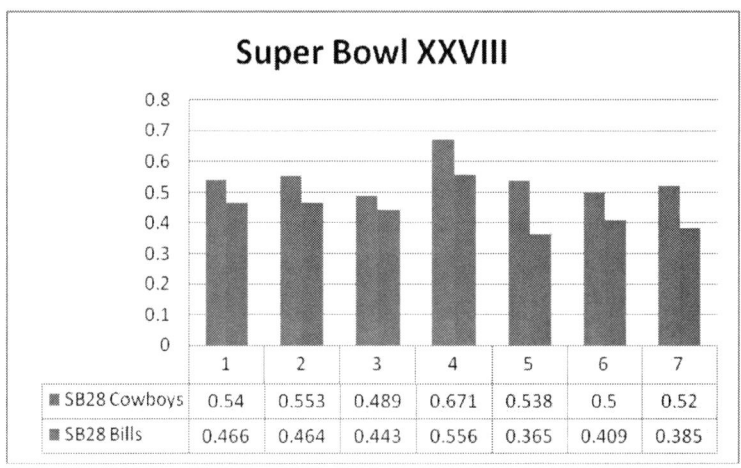

While the Cowboys running game, and MVP Emmitt Smith, certainly deserve praise, a closer analysis shows that their rushing was not spectacular compared with other teams in Super Bowl history. Net yards rushing (137) ranked only 28th and overall offense ranked just 25th (MPI-0=.553). Time of possession was good but not rare or superb (18th ranking, 34:29 to 25:31). Even on defense the Cowboys only ranked 40th overall (MPI-D=.489). What might have looked like another Cowboys blowout win like the year before did not shine by Super Bowl standards.

It is more likely that the Bills inept defense contributed to the Cowboys success. The Bills were ranked 67th in overall defense (MPI-D=.443) and 65th in defensive dominance (MPI-DD=-.114). The Cowboys were a team mired in controversy before the game and might have easily lost if not for the fumble return for a touchdown by James Washington, and superior special teams play.

The overall best performing unit on the field was the Dallas special teams unit (MPI-ST=.671) which ranked 4th in Super Bowl history only behind the same unit for the 1992 Cowboys the year before (.708) (Cowboys special teams coaches Joe Avezzano and Steve Hoffman really deserve credit), the 2009 Saints (.703) and the 1973 Dolphins (.673). A review of every play shows that special teams were an influential positive factor in the Cowboys victory. Even though Steve Christie hit the longest field goal in Super Bowl history for the Bills, it was kicker Eddie Murray for Dallas who starred, connecting on 3 of 3 field goals and a nice touchback kickoff. John Jett added a couple beautiful punts, one that pinned the Bills at the one yard line.

Even though there was a running into the kicker penalty that gave the Bills the ball back, there were enough good assignments executed, solid hits, and good runbacks on special teams to make up for that, and if the running into the kicker penalty were replaced by a better than average play, this would have been the best special teams performance in Super Bowl history! Special teams are an often forgotten element, but this was still the 4th best performance in the history of the Super Bowl and it might have saved the day even though nobody discusses this today.

Dr. John's Super Bowl 28 Lesson

"Appreciate who takes care of you"

The Dallas Cowboys escaped a bullet. Mired in pre-game controversy, they were 7 down in the third quarter to a team with the 28th ranked defense. While their rushing game got the most credit, Cowboy fortunes owe more to special teams and a fumble returned for a touchdown. Dallas' special teams ranks 4th in history and one play would have made them 1st. Dallas ranked 28th in rushing and 37th in total yards. That doesn't come close with how well their special teams played in Super Bowl 28!

Most Dominant Special Teams Unit (MPI-STD)

MPI-STD (Special Teams Dominance) represents relative dominance of a team's special teams over its opponent's special teams. It is calculated as "MPI-ST of team 1" – "MPI-ST of team 2."

#1--1973 Miami Dolphins (.308)--Reviewed in "Best Teams Ever"
#2--2009 New Orleans Saints (.286)--Reviewed in "MPI-ST"
#3--2005 Pittsburgh Steelers (.254)
#8--2008 Pittsburgh Steelers (.181)

Super Bowl 40 – February 5, 2006 – Ford Field, Detroit, MI

Pittsburgh Steelers 21 (.478) Seattle Seahawks 10 (.479)

Brief Game Review

The Pittsburgh Steelers led by jut-jawed Coach Bill Cowher and rookie quarterback "Big Ben" Roethlisberger began the 2005 season by winning seven of its first nine games. Although the team suffered a major setback when both Roethlisberger and his backup, Charlie Batch, went down with injuries, the Steelers still ranked fourth in the NFL with a strong offense and defense. Roethlisberger's return did not mean a guaranteed Super Bowl especially after falling to the then-undefeated Indianapolis Colts. The postseason hopes of the Steelers were in peril, but the team recovered in time to win its final four regular season games and finish 11-5.

The Seattle Seahawks marched into Ford Field in Detroit led by one-time Packer coach Mile Holmgren and quarterback Matt Hasselbeck, having added 11 wins in a row to a 2-2 start, setting a new team record at an NFC best of 13-3. The Seahawks were tops in the NFL with 50 quarterback sacks. It was the Seahawks first Super Bowl appearance in their 30 year history.

Holmgren versus Cowher, Rothlisbeger versus Matt Hasselbeck! The stage was set. Could the Steelers stop the Seahawks? Would the Steelers self-destruct?

After the first four possessions of the game ended with punts, the Seahawks seized field position after a short punt and 12 yard return to midfield. Hasselbeck threw a pair of completions to receivers Darrell Jackson and Joe Jurevicius for 20 and 11 yards, then found Jackson for a 16 yard touchdown pass, but it was nullified by an interference penalty on Jackson for pushing off and Seattle eventually settled for a field goal and 3-0 lead. Defenses held tight and Seattle would intercept Roethlisberger before the Steelers finally scored. On 3rd down and 28 from the Seattle 40, Roethlisberger found Hines Ward for a 37 yard pass. After being stopped twice, the Pittsburgh quarterback ran it in himself and the Steelers led 7-3 at halftime.

On the second play of the third, Willie Parker ran off right tackle for an improbable 75 yard touchdown, beating Marcus Allen's Super Bowl XVIII record by one yard and the Steelers led 14-3. On the next major drive all the way to the Seahawks 7, defensive back Kelly Herndon intercepted a pass from Roethlisberger and returned it for yet another Super Bowl record of 76 yards to the Steelers 20. Two plays later, Hasselbeck connected with tight end Jerramy Stevens and brought the game closer at 14-10.

By the start of the fourth the Seahawks were driving near midfield and made it all the way to the Steelers 19 yard line. After a huge pass to the one was called back for holding on right tackle Sean Locklear,

Hasselbeck was intercepted by Steelers defensive back Ike Taylor, and he returned it 24 yards. A penalty on Hasselbeck for a low block brought the ball even further near midfield. After one first down, Pittsburgh connected on a 43 yard fancy reverse touchdown pass in which Rothlisberger pitched to Parker who handed to Randle El who threw the ball to Hines Ward for a touchdown. This was the first time a wide receiver had thrown a touchdown pass in a Super Bowl. The Steelers' deception defeated the Seahawks massive efforts and multiple mistakes.

<u>What Actually Happened?</u>

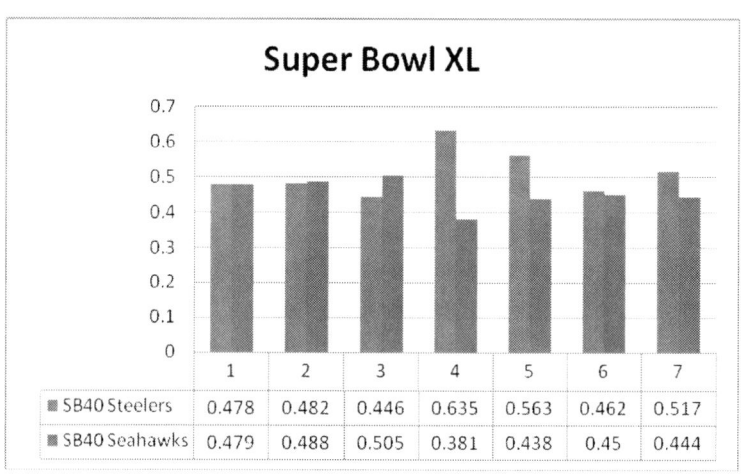

Super Bowl XL

	1	2	3	4	5	6	7
▪ SB40 Steelers	0.478	0.482	0.446	0.635	0.563	0.462	0.517
▪ SB40 Seahawks	0.479	0.488	0.505	0.381	0.438	0.45	0.444

MPI-T MPI-O MPI-D MPI-ST MPI-OP MPI-DP MPI-TP

This was one of the four oddest games in Super Bowl history in that the Seahawks actually performed a touch better the Steelers (MPI-T=.479 to .478 advantage) but still lost the game. Officiating was horrendous and disadvantaged the Seahawks multiple times from almost anyone's account, and there was even an apology issued by the head official after the game. Excuses, however, are unacceptable, and there will always be factors to deal with. Pittsburgh still had to make it happen.

The Steelers won this game most significantly on the dominance of their special teams (MPI-STD=.254) which ranked 3rd overall amongst 88 teams (see bar graph in #4 above). The special teams performance of

Seattle ranked 84th of the 88 teams who have played on Super Sunday (MPI-ST=.381). Stated another way, Seattle's special teams played at an awful 38% of capacity. The combination of ten huge Seattle mistakes on special teams and good special teams play by the Steelers was decisive and represented the most extreme difference between the teams. The other factor that was huge is that Pittsburgh had some big and rare plays that decided the game by putting points on the board or taking them off, but they were not characteristic of Pittsburgh's overall performance (e.g., Parker's 75 yard run, Ward's touchdown on a reverse pass, a touchdown pass called back many say unfairly, and more).

In pressure situations of this game, Pittsburgh prevailed, and they especially ruled in defensive pressure situations where they were 29th overall (MPI-TPD=.073) and the Seahawks were ranked a poor 60th. Doing well in key moments is what wins championships and it is what characterized the New England Patriots in the 2000s even if their overall performance did not look extraordinary. Getting the job done in key moments is a huge advantage for any team.

While not taking away from this great Pittsburgh victory, it is also unrealistic to ignore how rare and odd this outcome was given the relative performance of the teams. Seattle outperformed the Steelers on both sides of the ball and should have won. If not for one or two of those extremely rare plays and/or questionable officiating, the overall performance of the Seahawks might have easily resulted in victory, but that is why you play the game on the field! Congrats Pittsburgh again!

Dr. John's Super Bowl 40 Lesson

"Pay attention to details"

The Seattle Seahawks played well enough to beat the Pittsburgh Steelers in Super Bowl 41 but did not pay attention to details, especially on special teams. They lapsed in focus on three big plays that reversed their fortunes. That is the nature of mental mistakes. Just one bug ruins a meal no matter how good the food might be. The Steelers creatively cooked up success in a few key plays to beat a higher performing team.

Super Bowl 43 – February 1, 2009 – Raymond James Stadium, Tampa, FL

Pittsburgh Steelers 27 (.494) Arizona Cardinals 23 (.488)

Brief Game Review

Coach Mike Tomlin's favored Pittsburgh Steelers led by 28-year old quarterback Ben Roethlisberger completed the 2008 season with the second-best record in the AFC at 12-4 and earned a seventh Super Bowl trip. Coach Ken Whisenhunt's Arizona Cardinals were led by the reemergence of 37 year old quarterback Kurt Warner who, after a period of injuries, would post one of his best seasons in 2008, throwing for 4,583 yards and 30 touchdowns with only 14 interceptions. His top receivers Larry Fitzgerald, Anquan Boldin, and Steve Breaston made the Cardinals the fifth team ever to feature three players with more than 1,000 receiving yards.

During the Recession this Super Bowl offered an exciting distraction to the U.S. audience, making it the second most-watched Super Bowl in history. Dubbed the "The Recession Bowl," its tagline was "Believe in Now."

The Pittsburgh Steelers quickly drove down the field and scored twice (one field goal and a touchdown) becoming the first team to score on its first two drives since the Denver Broncos in Super Bowl XXXII. The Steelers held the Cardinals to just one first down in the first quarter, while gaining 135 yards. The Cardinals eventually responded on a 45 yard completion by Kurt Warner to Antoine Boldin. Next Warner found tight end Ben Patrick on a 1 yard touchdown pass to make the score 10-7. Seven plays later the Cardinals had a first down on the Steelers' 1 yard line and 18 seconds remaining in the half and a chance to take the lead when Warner's pass was intercepted in the end zone by linebacker James Harrison, who then took off down the sideline for a 101 yard touchdown return, bringing the Steelers a lead of 17-7 at halftime. A booth review was called to verify whether Harrison had broken the plane, as he was tackled at the goal line, and the ruling stood.

The Steelers began the third quarter with another long scoring drive leading to a field goal and a 20-7 lead. Warner later made one of the most memorable plays finding Larry Fitzgerald, who made a leaping catch in tight coverage for a touchdown, closing the margin to 20-14. Several plays after getting the ball back, the Cardinals connected again on a touchdown pass to Fitzgerald on a post route, and led 23-20. The Steelers had the ball on their own 22 yard line with 2:37 left when Roethlisberger marched his team down the field completing two passes for 27 yards and another for 11. A few plays later, Roethlisberger hooked up with Santonio Holmes in the corner of the end zone for a touchdown, managing to keep his toes in bounds. The booth review held and the Steelers won 27-23.

<u>What Actually Happened?</u>

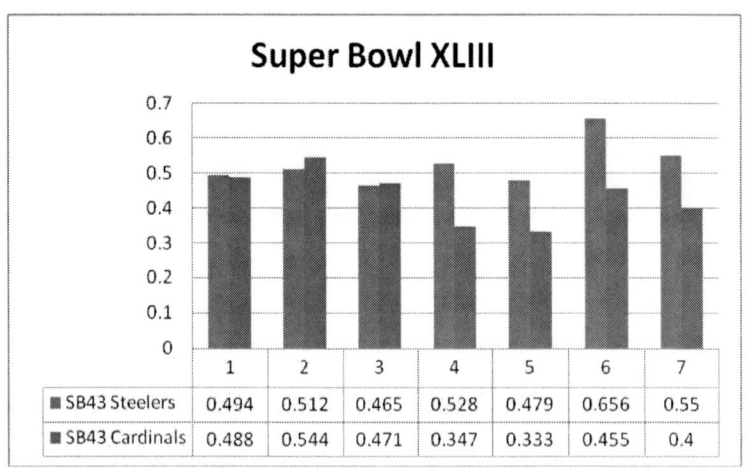

	1	2	3	4	5	6	7
■ SB43 Steelers	0.494	0.512	0.465	0.528	0.479	0.656	0.55
■ SB43 Cardinals	0.488	0.544	0.471	0.347	0.333	0.455	0.4

MPI-T MPI-O MPI-D MPI-ST MPI-OP MPI-DP MPI-TP

While this was a very sloppy game with 18 penalties, it was also one of the most exciting Super Bowls in memory. The final Roethlisberger drive was reminiscent of a Tom Brady or Joe Montana led drive. The game had big plays and the 2nd net yards passing in Super Bowl history as Kurt Warner amassed 374 yards, just below his previous best in Super Bowl XXXIV when he threw for 407 with the Rams. Despite these numbers through the air, the Cardinal's overall performance on offense was only 29th ranked (MPI-O=.544), edging out the Steelers offense in this game (MPI-O=.512) which ranked 41st.

Three extreme factors in this game were big plays in pressure situations, special teams, and penalties. While Pittsburgh trumped the Cardinals in all three areas, the defensive pressure play was by far most influential and the best example was James Harrison's interception and record return for a touchdown which was ironic because Harrison was supposed to have blitzed on the play and instead found himself in perfect position for a pick. Arizona was poised to go up 14-10 and instead went down 17-7, a 14 point swing on one play. The "Big Ben" to Santonio Holmes pass in the corner of the end zone for the win was obviously huge and Holmes won the MVP, but looking more closely at what won this game is interesting.

The Steelers were the 8th most dominant special teams unit overall (MPI-STD=.181) but due mostly to a dismal special teams performance by Arizona which ranked second to last overall (MPI-ST=.347) while the Steelers special teams unit was an adequate unit ranked 39th (MPI-ST=.528). In total pressure situations the Steelers ranked 25th (MPI-TP=.550) whereas Arizona was a poor 76th (MPI-TP=.400). The story is really told on defense where the Steelers defense in pressure situations (.656) dominated the Cardinals offense (.333 and 17th best in Super Bowl history). Finally, the Cardinals committed 11 penalties to Pittsburgh's 7, both poor numbers, but Arizona ranked 86th of 88 teams on penalties and yards penalized, and these included three holding penalties by left tackle Mike Gandy. Only two teams, the Cowboys in Super Bowl XXII and Panthers in Super Bowl XXXVIII had more penalties (12).

In sum, while the Steelers' dominance over the Cardinal's offense in pressure situations was decisive, it only represented a relative strength for Pittsburgh in history as there were 16 better teams in this category. The game was categorized in MPI-STD because there were only 7 more dominant special teams units than Pittsburgh on this day, and it occurred mostly because the Cardinals were so horrible on special teams.

Dr. John's Super Bowl 43 Lesson

"Sometimes being bad pays off"

Mistakes happen and 70% of perfection in any area is rare. Rare instincts at times win. When James Harrison intercepted Kurt Warner's pass and ran it back for a touchdown, some credited Harrison's instincts. He might have had a hunch about where the ball was coming. However, experts claim he blew his assignment and should have blitzed. His mistake of staying back paid off when the ball came to him wrapped in a gift box made of steel with a yellow and black ribbon. Had Harrison not been bad, his Steelers might have lost. It was a 14 point swing.

Most Opportunistic Teams (T – G)
Takeaways minus Giveaways are expressed as highest number.

#1--1992 Dallas Cowboys (7) – Reviewed in "MPI-ST"
#2--1977 Dallas Cowboys (6)
#3--2000 Baltimore Ravens (5) – Reviewed in "MPI-D"
#4-- 1968 New York Jets (4) tie
#4-- 1980 Oakland Raiders (4) tie
#4-- 1991 Washington Redskins (4) tie
#4-- 1969 Kansas City Chiefs (4) tie – Reviewed in "MPI-TPD"
#4--1985 Chicago Bears (4) tie – Reviewed in "Best Teams Ever"
#4--1989 San Francisco 49ers (4) tie – Reviewed in "Best Teams Ever"
#4-- 1996 Green Bay Packers (4) tie – Reviewed in "Most Error Free"
#4-- 2002 Tampa Bay Buccaneers (4) tie – Reviewed in "MPI-D"
#5-- 2004 New England Patriots (3) tie
#5-- 2001 New England Patriots (3) tie

Super Bowl 12 – January 15, 1978 – Louisiana Superdome,
New Orleans, LA

Dallas Cowboys 27 (.487) Denver Broncos 10 (.436)

Brief Game Review

This was the first time in Super Bowl history that the game matched two teams that had met each other in the regular season. On the last week of the regular season the Cowboys beat the Broncos 14-6 at Texas Stadium but the Broncos had rested 6 starters, so many thought they were a stronger team than they revealed.

Coach Tom Landry's Dallas Cowboys were six point favorites after finishing the regular season with a 12-2 record and an NFC East title. Ed "Too Tall" Jones, Thomas "Hollywood" Henderson and Mel Renfro led a very tough Dallas defense. Star quarterback Roger Staubach threw for 2,620 yards and 18 touchdowns during the regular season. Rookie running back Tony Dorsett, despite not becoming the full-time starter until the 10th game, led the Cowboys in rushing with 1,007 yards and 13 total touchdowns.

Coach Red Miller's Denver Broncos got to the Super Bowl on a 12-2 record. They were led by quarterback Craig Morton who won the NFL Comeback Player of the Year Award after finishing the season with 1,929 yards passing and 14 touchdowns. Morton also ran for 125 yards and 4 touchdowns. Denver had a solid defense with the nickname "Orange Crush" and was led by star linebackers Randy Gradishar and Tom Jackson.

"Sloppy" would not be nearly a strong enough adjective to describe the play at Super Bowl XII. On the Cowboys' first two possessions Dallas nearly turned the ball over three times, but they were lucky to keep possession all three times. On Denver's second drive of the game, Morton threw an interception to Dallas Defensive back Randy Hughes and five plays later Dorsett put the Cowboys on the board on a 3-yard touchdown run to give Dallas a 7-0 lead. When Denver got the ball back, Morton would throw yet another interception, this time leading to a Dallas field goal and a 10-0 lead. The second quarter involved more mistakes, but Dallas scored on a 43 yard field goal to go up 13-0. Before the half would be out, Denver turned the ball over four more times and Dallas lost a fumble and missed on three field goals! The score remained 13-0 at halftime.

To open the second half Denver put together their first good drive of the game, marching deep inside Cowboys territory and making a 47 yard field goal to cut the Dallas lead to 10. Dallas, however, responded on a Staubach 45-yard touchdown pass to Butch Johnson and increased their lead to 20-3. Denver answered back on their next drive and scored a touchdown on a 1-yard touchdown run by running back Rob Lytle to cut Dallas lead to 20-10 after 3 quarters.

Midway through the fourth Dallas put the game away on a 29-yard halfback option play to make the final score 27-10. Two players shared Super Bowl MVP honors, defensive end Harvey Martin and defensive tackle Randy White.

What Actually Happened?

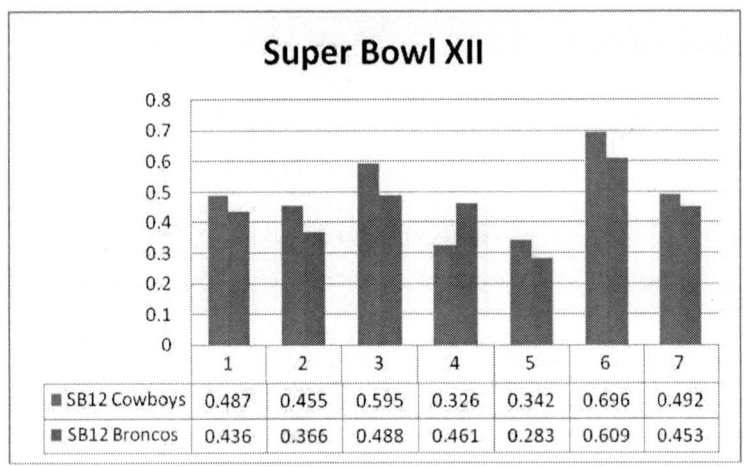

This was a very poorly executed game on both sides of the ball. Winning Dallas' overall performance (MPI-T=.487) ranked 54 in Super Bowl history, which is another way to say that 14 losing Super Bowl teams outperformed the Dallas Cowboys in this game. The game was filled with almost as many mental errors as can be seen in one football game. To start, the game was played at a low level of execution. Adding MPI-T scores together yields a .923 value, and the further below 1.0 this number goes the lower the quality of the game, and vice versa for games in which this number is above 1.0. Contributing to this reduction in performance were an almost unheard of 10 fumbles, 4 interceptions, and 20 penalties!

The two teams were so different in character, but both had strong defenses. The passion of the "orange crush" versus Tom Landry's methodical offensive machine made good copy before the game, and it resulted in mass chaos on the field. The team that suffered most by far was Denver as they turned the ball over 8 times versus Dallas 2. This +6 takeaway minus giveaway statistic (T-G=6) was the single most extreme and influential factor in the Dallas victory and the 2nd ranked T-G in history. Teams like the Broncos with a -6 value on this statistic have probably not won more than 1 in 5000 games in NFL history, and it would be an interesting fact to check for anyone with access to this. What is amazing is that Dallas fumbled 6 times themselves but recovered 4 of their own fumbles, or this game would have been even worse.

At the same time, credit must go to the strong Denver and Dallas defensive units for forcing mistakes, but sharp offenses hold onto the ball. The 4th ranked defensive dominance displayed by Dallas (MPI-DD=.229) and 4th ranked overall defensive performance (MPI-D=.595) were the second most decisive factors, and Denver's offense was absolutely atrocious (MPI-O=.366)! Dallas should also be credited for not throwing an interception versus 4 for the Broncos. Dallas also had the 7th overall ranked time of possession (38:38 to 21:22), giving the offense some credit.

Dr. John's Super Bowl 12 Lesson

"If you want to lose, turn it over 8 times!"

Denver Quarterback Craig Morton's passer rating was 0. Dallas committed 12 penalties and Denver 8, but Denver also turned the ball over 8 times versus Dallas' 2. The team with the least mistakes won.

Super Bowl 3 – January 12, 1969 – Orange Bowl, Miami, FL

New York Jets 16 (.543) Baltimore Colts 7 (.457)

Brief Game Review

This was the third championship between the AFL and the NFL, but first to officially be named the "Super Bowl." Coach Don Shula's Baltimore Colts went into the game as 18-point favorites after finishing the regular season 13-1 and dominating with one of the best offenses and defenses in the NFL. Coach Weeb Ewbank's New York Jets got to the Super Bowl after an 11-3 record, and winning the AFL championship on the arm of their star quarterback Joe Namath. Three days before the game, Joe Namath boldly announced to a crowd at the Miami Touchdown Club "We're gonna win the game, I guarantee it." Because the Jets were such heavy underdogs and the AFL had been destroyed in the first two Super Bowls, his comments seemed ridiculous at the time.

The Jets got the ball first, but were forced to punt after just five plays. Baltimore next drove down to the Jets 19-yard line but missed a 27-yard field goal. Defense prevailed throughout the first quarter and the game was scoreless entering the second. In the beginning of the second quarter Baltimore again failed to convert on an opportunity. With the Jets pinned inside their own 20-yard line, the Colts recovered a fumble. Three plays later Colts quarterback Earl Morrall's pass was deflected and intercepted in the end zone for a touchback. The Jets began running the ball effectively and Namath drove his team 80-yards with Matt Snell scoring on a 4 yard run to put the Jets up 7-0 going into the half.

The Jets dominated the third quarter with ball control and added a couple field goals to pad their lead to 13-0 entering the final quarter. The Colts ran a total of only seven plays and gained only 11 yards in the entire third quarter. In the fourth quarter, New York added a final field goal for a commanding 16-0 lead before Coach Don Shula replaced Morrall with the injured Johnny Unitas. Unitas moved the team but then was intercepted midway through the quarter. When the Colts finally got on the board with a 1 yard run by Jerry Hill there were only 4 minutes remaining and the score was 16-7. The Jets killed the clock and became champions. Joe Namath's famous "guarantee" is still talked about as this was one of the biggest upsets in sports history.

What Actually Happened?

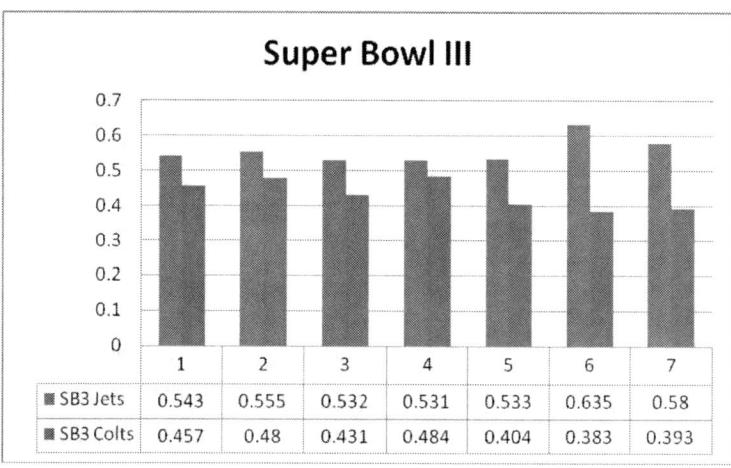

Super Bowl III

	1	2	3	4	5	6	7
■ SB3 Jets	0.543	0.555	0.532	0.531	0.533	0.635	0.58
■ SB3 Colts	0.457	0.48	0.431	0.484	0.404	0.383	0.393

MPI-T MPI-O MPI-D MPI-ST MPI-OP MPI-DP MPI-TP

The clear difference in this game was turnovers. Earl Morrall threw three interceptions and Unitas threw one as opposed to Joe Namath of the Jets who had none. Each team fumbled once and lost it, so the T-G for the Jets (4) was the 4th ranked in Super Bowl history. Give credit to the Jet's defense (MPI-D=.532) which ranks 18th amongst 88 teams in Super Bowl history. The best two other areas for the Jets were in the areas of time of possession (36:10 to 23:50) which ranked 13th overall, and total dominance in pressure situations which ranked 13th (MPI-TPD=.187).

The Colts performance was nowhere near expected, and what happened is likely a case that their team was slightly over-rated and overconfident at the same time, a lethal mix. The Colt's overall performance (MPI-T=.457) ranked 73rd in Super Bowl history. The Colts did have the 23rd most rushing yards (143) but Morrall's passer rating at 9.3 showed how difficult it was to throw against the surprisingly strong Jet's defense.

Ball control, Joe Namath, a strong defense, and most importantly takeaways minus giveaways of +4 helped the Jets become the first AFL team to win the Super Bowl.

Author's Note: This New York Jets victory over the Baltimore Colts is my pick for the most influential game in Super Bowl history because it forced the NFL to take the AFL seriously, and led directly to the merger and thriving NFL and Super Bowl format that we enjoy today. Anyone in my Palm Beach office will see a signed photo of Joe Namath adorning the wall!

Dr. John's Super Bowl 3 Lesson

"Develop a killer instinct or be killed"

The Colts squandered opportunity after opportunity in Super Bowl 3. Had they listened too much to predictions making them an 18 point favorite? They lacked "killer instinct" and repeatedly made careless errors and turnovers. The sharper and hungrier Jets who had nothing to lose forced turnovers and controlled the ball. The brash young quarterback's ridiculous guarantee suddenly made sense.

Super Bowl 15 – January 25, 1981 – Louisiana Superdome, New Orleans, LA

Oakland Raiders 27 (.523) Philadelphia Eagles 10 (.471)

Brief Game Review

After the Raiders started the 1980 season with a 2-3 record, starter Dan Pastorini broke his leg and Jim Plunkett, the 33-year old Heisman Trophy winner with a disappointing NFL career, took the helm. After a slow start, Plunkett led his team to victories in 9 of their last 11 games and Oakland made playoffs as a wild card. Plunkett had thrown for 2,299 yards and 18 touchdowns.

The Raiders' offensive line was led by 2 future Hall of Famers in tackle Art Shell and guard Gene Upshaw. Oakland's defense was anchored by defensive tackle John Matuszak and defensive back Lester

Hayes led the league in interceptions (13) and was the league's Defensive Player of the Year.

Under Head Coach Dick Vermeil, Philadelphia advanced to their first ever Super Bowl led by quarterback Ron Jaworski, who had thrown for 3,529 yards during the regular season, including 27 touchdowns and only 12 interceptions. Halfback Wilbert Montgomery had rushed for over 1,200 rushing yards in the last 2 seasons. The other main deep threats on offense were wide receivers Harold Carmichael and Charlie Smith. The Eagles defense led the league in the fewest points allowed during the regular season (222) and was a major factor in their hard fought 10-7 victory over the Raiders in the regular season in which they sacked Plunkett 8 times.

Oakland linebacker Rod Martin intercepted Eagles quarterback Ron Jaworski's first pass of the game and returned it 17 yards to Philadelphia's 30-yard line, setting up Jim Plunkett's 2-yard touchdown pass to Cliff Branch and a 7-0 lead. The Raiders later scored another touchdown with about a minute left in the period when on third down from the Oakland 20-yard line, Plunkett threw the ball to running back Kenny King at the 39-yard line as he was scrambling. King caught the pass as it carried just over the outstretched arms of defensive back Herman Edwards and took off to the end zone for a Super Bowl record 80-yard touchdown reception and the Raiders led 14-0. The Eagles drove back but were forced to settle for Tony Franklin's 30-yard field goal to cut the score to 14-3. After the Raiders missed a field goal, the Eagles drove to Oakland's 11-yard line but on the Eagle's 28 yard field goal attempt, linebacker Ted Hendricks extended his 6'7" frame at the line and blocked the kick and the score remained 14-3 at halftime.

In the second half, the Raiders drove quickly on Plunkett completions of 13 yards to King and then 32 yards to Bob Chandler. After a short run, Plunkett connected with Cliff Branch on a 29 yard touchdown pass increasing Oakland's lead to 21-3. The Eagles responded by driving 56 yards to the Raiders 34-yard line, but on third down and 3, Jaworski threw his second interception of the game to Rod Martin. Oakland drove 40 yards and scored on Chris Bahr's 46-yard field goal to go up 24–3.

The Eagles finally scored a touchdown early in the fourth after an 88 yard 12-play drive capped by Jaworski's 8-yard touchdown pass to tight end Keith Krepfle. But on their ensuing drive, Oakland marched from their own 11 to the Eagles 17-yard line after which Bahr kicked his second field goal, increasing Oakland's lead to a final score of 27-10. Later, Rod Martin recorded a Super Bowl record third interception. After the game, the NFL Commissioner Pete Rozelle presented the Lombardi Trophy to owner Al Davis and praised Plunkett, head coach Tom Flores, the players, and the entire Raiders organization for being the first wild card team to win the Super Bowl.

What Actually Happened?

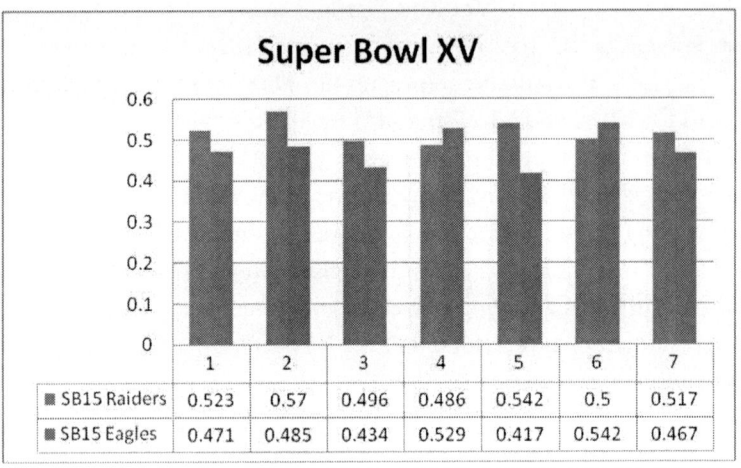

	1	2	3	4	5	6	7
■ SB15 Raiders	0.523	0.57	0.496	0.486	0.542	0.5	0.517
■ SB15 Eagles	0.471	0.485	0.434	0.529	0.417	0.542	0.467

MPI-T   MPI-O   MPI-D   MPI-ST   MPI-OP   MPI-DP   MPI-TP

Jim Plunkett (passer rating = 145.0) and the Raider's offense played great in this game, and Coach Tom Flores cleverly kept his team loose compared with the Eagles who were bussed right to the practice field after arriving into New Orleans. Since this was the first wild card team to win the Super Bowl, Flores' efforts to ease up a little and keep his players fresh were clearly justified.

It could also be argued that this victory was mostly due to ball-hawking and not turning the ball over, and since this area represented the greatest strength overall for the Raiders, the game is categorized here.

Only two other franchises, the Dallas Cowboys (Super Bowls XII & XXVII) and the Baltimore Ravens (Super Bowl XXXV) have done better than the Raiders' +4 on takeaways minus giveaways, so the Raiders are tied for the 3rd ranked franchise in Super Bowl history in this category.

The Raiders offense was very effective and ranked 17th in pure performance (MPI-O=.570) and 16th in dominance (MPI-OD=.136), and the defense was 9th best in points allowed (10). The most awesome effort on defense by far was put in by linebacker Rod Martin who had three interceptions, and many said he should have been the MVP instead of Plunkett. It is a valid argument.

The Eagles' best ranking came in net passing yards (291) at 17th among 88 teams. This game would have been a lot closer if not for the 3 Ron Jaworski interceptions to Martin. The Eagles were better than the Raiders on special teams (MPI-ST=.529 to .486) and defense in pressure situations (MPI-DP=.542 to .500), but worse in the other 5 classic areas as shown on the graph above.

Dr. John's Super Bowl 15 Lesson

"Never give up hope"

Jim Plunkett's career was long considered dead. He had never lived up to his Heisman Trophy hype. He got one final chance when the starting quarterback was injured. He came in and most wrote him off … but not Tom Flores. A former star quarterback himself, he saw hope. A dynamic Hispanic coach/quarterback combo started winning. The backup blossomed. Jim Plunkett would go on to throw 4 touchdowns with no interceptions in winning two Super Bowl titles in four years. Tom Flores re-discovered Jim Plunkett by not giving up on him.

Super Bowl 26 – January 26, 1992 – Metrodome, Minneapolis, MN

Washington Redskins 37 (.551) Buffalo Bills 24 (.469)

<u>Brief Game Review</u>

Washington had performed very well in 1991 but they were not known as an exceptionally talented team in terms of all stars. They just came together and overachieved as a team and ended the season with a league leading 485 points at the hands of quarterback Mark Rypien. Coach Joe Gibbs' talent at bringing out the best in his players was on full display. Rypien had thrown for 3,564 yards and 28 touchdown passes. He was accompanied by wide receivers Gary Clark and Art Monk among others, and running backs Earnest Byner and Ricky Ervins, and the team had gone 14-2 in the regular season.

Media before the game reported that Buffalo was talking brashly and confidently about their chances of winning. They were trying to atone for the difficult loss to the Giants the previous year. Jim Kelly's "no-huddle" offense had done damage to opposing defenses in 1991 with a league leading 6,525 yards and 458 points. They had the familiar cast of receiver Andre Reed and running back Thurman Thomas on offense where they excelled, but they were suspect on defense and only ranked 27th. It was a very unbalanced team with an extraordinary offense and weak defense. Bruce Smith and Jeff Wright had missed most of the season with injuries and the Bills still posted a 13-3 record.

The game started slowly with sloppy play on both sides of the ball and no scoring until the second quarter, but what a quarter it was for the Redskins. After kicking a field goal, Mark Rypien found his targets and got good run support and threw a 10 yard touchdown pass to Byner before Gerald Riggs ran it in twice from short yards, and a blowout seemed imminent in the third quarter with a 24-0 lead. Redskins linebacker Kurt Gouveia had intercepted Kelly on the first play of the third quarter leading to the second short run for Riggs.

Buffalo appear to be making it close after some big pass plays, a nice drive and an interference call, and before long it was 24-10. Hope of any comeback faded, however, when Washington drove 79 yards in 11 plays culminating in a 30 yard touchdown strike to Gary Clark and this game was more or less finished. Buffalo made some noise at the end on two touchdown passes from Kelly, but it was too little too late and the Redskins were champions 37-24.

Mark Rypien was awarded the MVP and achieved a passer rating of 92.0, going 18/33 for 292 yards and 2 touchdowns with 1 interception.

<u>What Actually Happened?</u>

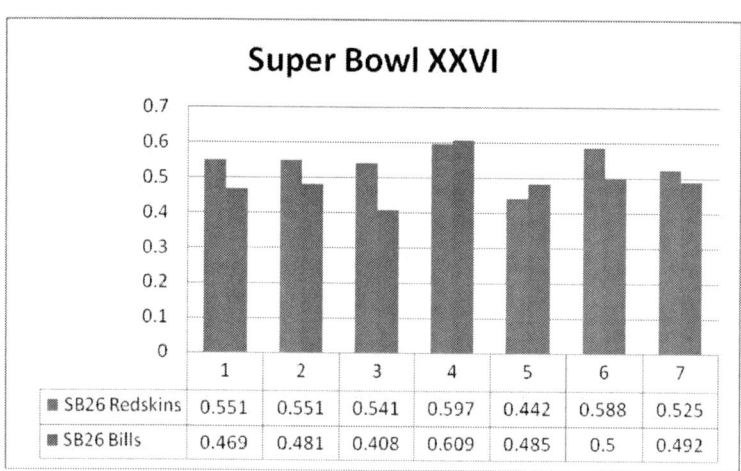

	1	2	3	4	5	6	7
■ SB26 Redskins	0.551	0.551	0.541	0.597	0.442	0.588	0.525
■ SB26 Bills	0.469	0.481	0.408	0.609	0.485	0.5	0.492

MPI-T MPI-O MPI-D MPI-ST MPI-OP MPI-DP MPI-TP

A quick scan of the data in the graph above shows how clearly the Redskins outperformed the Bills (MPI-T=.551 to .469) and that it occurred on both offense and defense, but more so on offense (MPI-0=.551 to MPI-D=.408 for Buffalo) while the Bills were slightly better on special teams. Total pressure performance favored Washington (MPI-TP=.525 to .492).

As a team performance overall, the greatest factor was takeaways minus giveaways (T-G=4) for the Redskins and it ranked 4th best in Super Bowl history. This was due to 4 interceptions, 2 by Brad Edwards. This was also a very solid Redskins team that ranked 9th in Super Bowl history in total performance with the .551 posting.

The Bills were 13th ranked in special teams performance and 34th in net passing yards, but they just did not have the weapons on this day to beat a vastly superior Redskins team.

Dr. John's Super Bowl 26 Lesson

"When you think you are on top of the world, watch out!"

The Bills might have appeared a little overconfident before this game whereas the Redskins kept a lower profile and went about making headlines on the field. Jim Kelly, a wonderful quarterback, perhaps showed some overconfidence in throwing into double coverage on two of his four interceptions in this game. It's better to appear humble and then surprise your opponent with your intense resolve on game day than to project an image of being on top of the world with only one way to go ... and an opponent motivated to lead you there!

Super Bowl 39 – February 6, 2005 – Alltel Stadium, Jacksonville, FL

New England Patriots 24 (.518) Philadelphia Eagles 21 (.498)

Brief Game Review

Coach Bill Belichick's New England Patriots entered the game as 7 point favorites after finishing the regular season with a 14-2 record. Led by their star quarterback Tom Brady, the Patriots offense finished with the fourth most points with 437 and seventh in yards gained with 5,773. Brady's 3,692 passing yards and 28 touchdowns earned him Pro Bowl honors. The running attack was also productive with Corey Dillon signed in the off-season. In his first year with the Patriots Dillon ran for 1,635 yards which was good enough to join Brady with Pro Bowl honors.

Coach Andy Reid's Philadelphia Eagles got to the Super Bowl after finishing the regular season 12-4 led by quarterback Donovan McNabb who threw for 3, 875 yards and 31 touchdowns with just 8 interceptions. McNabb became the first quarterback ever to have more than 30 touchdowns while throwing less than 10 interceptions. The Eagles also had a very strong defensive secondary with three out of the four starters being selected to the Pro Bowl.

The first quarter was scoreless as the Eagles turned the ball over twice, and the Patriots were stopped and forced to punt every time they had the ball. Philadelphia got the first score of the game early in the second quarter after putting together a 9 play, 81 yard drive that ended on a 6-yard touchdown pass to tight end L.J. Smith for a 7-0 lead. Later in the quarter the Patriots got great field position at the Eagles 37-yard line after a horrible punt by Eagles punter Dirk Johnson. The Patriots capitalized by driving 37 yards, and scored on David Givens' 4-yard catch to tie the game at seven heading into halftime. It was only the second time in Super Bowl history that the game was tied at half.

To begin the second half the Patriots marched right down the field and scored on a 2-yard touchdown pass to linebacker Mike Vrabel who had lined up as a tight end. Later in the third quarter the Eagles responded by driving 74 yards in 10 plays and a 10 yard touchdown pass to Brian Westbrook that knotted the game up at 14. It was the first time a Super Bowl went into the fourth quarter in a tie.

Early in the fourth quarter the Patriots drove 66 yards in 9 plays and scored a touchdown on Corey Dillon's 2 yard run to put the Patriots ahead again 21-14. After the Eagles were forced to punt, the Patriots increased their lead on a 22 yard field goal by kicker Adam Vinatieri to give New England a 24-14 lead. Late in the 4th quarter the Eagles came back on a 79 yard drive in 13 plays ending in a 30 yard touchdown pass to receiver Greg Lewis that cut the New England lead to 24-21, but there was only 1:55 left on the clock. The ensuing on-side kick was unsuccessful and the Patriots recovered and ran out the clock. New England wide receiver Deion Branch would be awarded Super Bowl MVP after tying a Super Bowl record for catches with 11 and he had a total of 133 yards receiving. Branch was the 3rd Super Bowl MVP to have won it without throwing or scoring a touchdown.

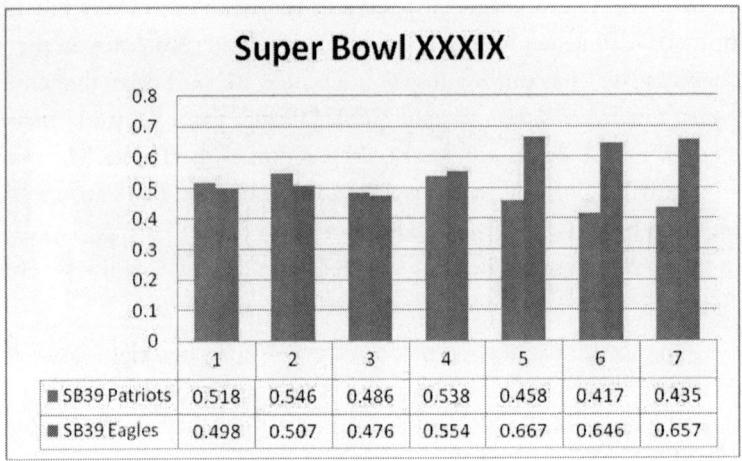

	1	2	3	4	5	6	7
■ SB39 Patriots	0.518	0.546	0.486	0.538	0.458	0.417	0.435
■ SB39 Eagles	0.498	0.507	0.476	0.554	0.667	0.646	0.657

MPI-T MPI-O MPI-D MPI-ST MPI-OP MPI-DP MPI-TP

This was a very close and conservative game overall in which the Patriots performed slightly better and won the game as they should (MPI-T=.518 to .498 for New England). The game really hinged on mistakes and the team with the least mistakes, New England, was left standing after the game. There were no extreme statistics, just good precise play from Tom Brady who had 0 interceptions compared with Donovan McNabb's 3. The T-G of +3 for New England was decisive and it was the 5th best T-G in Super Bowl history.

A close analysis of how well each unit performed shows that both offenses performed better than their respective defensive units, but that the Patriots advantage was greater (MPI-OD=.070) and ranked 30th compared with the Eagle's 45th ranking (MPI-OD=.021).

It was interesting that the Eagles did so much better in key pressure moments of the game (MPI-TP=.657 to .435 for the Patriots) and their offense in pressure moments was the 4th ranked in Super Bowl history (MPI-OP= 667)! It shows why they were able to come back and make it close at the end, but it was not enough to overcome a 3 turnover disadvantage, or the poor punt that led to the Patriots first touchdown.

Had the teams been equal on mistakes, the Eagles would have probably won this game, but making fewer mistakes is what made New England such a great champion.

Dr. John's Super Bowl 39 Lesson

"Before you learn to win, learn not to lose"

Tom Brady, Deion Branch and the Patriots were a well oiled machine of efficiency and smarts who knew not to give it away. The Eagles might have had more talent and performed well in pressure moments, but all that talent and skill was negated by critical mistakes.

Super Bowl 36 – February 3, 2002 – Louisiana Superdome, New Orleans, LA

New England Patriots 20 (.514) St. Louis Rams 17 (.510)

Brief Game Review

Coach Bill Belichick's New England Patriots were a 14 point underdog to Mike Martz and the St. Louis Rams who displayed both one of the most explosive offenses in history and a tough defense ranked third in the NFC. Behind the Rams' quarterback, Kurt Warner, and league MVP running back Marshall Faulk, this St. Louis powerhouse had gone 14-2 and led the league in total offensive yards (6,930) and scoring (503)!

New England, by contrast, had gone 11-5 in the regular season after losing their first two games. Theirs was the story of backup quarterback Tom Brady taking over after Drew Bledsoe was injured and having instant success. However, nobody in the world gave the surprise Patriots much of a chance against this growing Mike Martz dynasty. Little did everyone know that it would be New England coach Bill Belichick's team that would dominate the decade instead. The Rams went up 3-0 on a 50 yard field goal and the score remained like that until Patriots cornerback Ty Law intercepted a Warner pass and ran it back for a touchdown and a 7-3 lead early in the second quarter. Just before the half Brady found David Patten in the end zone for another touchdown and the Patriots led 14-3 at half.

Defense prevailed in the third quarter but the Pats added 3 to go up 17-3 as they began the final period. The Rams kicked it into gear finally when, after a long drive, Kurt Warner ran it in from 2 yards out to make the score 17-10. After both teams held for two series' each, the Rams got the ball with only 1:51 left in the game and down by 7. In just three quick passes from Warner the Rams struck again, tying the game at 17 on a 26-yard pass to Ricky Proehl. With no timeouts left and 1:30 remaining, many argued for New England to run out the clock and play for overtime, but Brady instead fired three complete passes to his 41 and then after an incomplete he hit Troy Brown for 23 yards and Jermaine Wiggins for 6 to put the ball on the Rams 30 yard line with 6 seconds to play. Adam Vinatieri nailed the 48 yarder and the Pats were champs. Tom Brady was named MVP for going 16 of 27 for 145 yards. This game had been moved back one week after the entire Season due to the September 11 attacks. It was the first time a Super Bowl had been played in February and, with the exception of the following year, when the game was played in January, all subsequent Super Bowls from 2004 on have been played in February.

What Actually Happened?

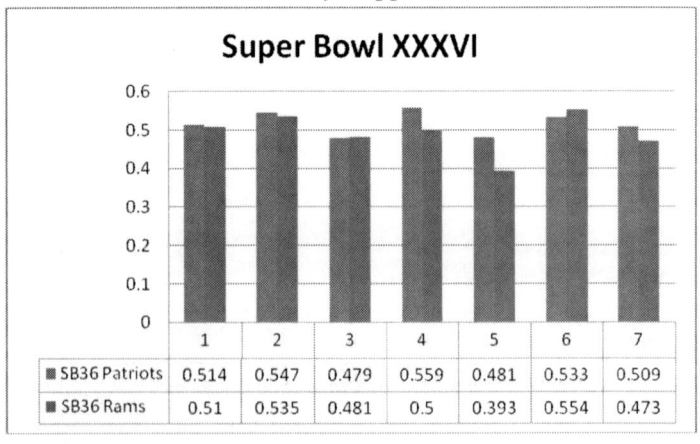

MPI-T   MPI-O   MPI-D   MPI-ST   MPI-OP   MPI-DP   MPI-TP

One thing interesting about the Patriots Super Bowl wins is that they do not usually look great or on the extremes statistically. Coach Bill Belichick just finds ways to win and this usually involves forcing turnovers, operating efficiently on offense with few mistakes, and kicking game winning field goals at the end! In this game the Patriots appeared to be the surprise victors given all the pre-game hype, but football is a team sport and a close analysis (see chart above) of the data shows that they should have won because they performed better on 5 of 7 key categories. These included overall performance (MPI-T=.514), offense (MPI-O=.547), special teams (MPI-ST=.559), pressure offense (MPI-OP=.481), and overall pressure play (MPI-TP=.509). The Rams were better on overall defense (MPI-D=.481), and pressure defense (MPI-DP=.554).

The Patriots greatest accomplishment might have been holding Rams quarterback Kurt Warner to only throw one touchdown pass even though he threw the ball all over the field for 337 yards, the 5th best passing performance in Super Bowl history! But this 5th best performance in passing only translated to a 33rd best overall offensive ranking among the 88 teams. They were 59th best in rushing, so the Patriots did a marvelous job shutting that down. One dimensional usually loses.

However, praise of Kurt Warner is in order too. Of the 5 greatest passing yard performances in Super Bowl history, Kurt Warner owns 3 including best overall (407 yards with the Rams in Super Bowl 34), second best (374 yards with the Cardinals in Super Bowl 43), and fifth best here versus the Patriots! Only Tom Brady (354 yards in Super Bowl 38) and Joe Montana (341 yards in Super Bowl 23) are in the same class as Warner as far as passing yards.

Individual accomplishments look great on paper but do not win titles. Balance and big plays win. Warner is a Super Bowl champion, but he also lost two Super Bowls. The Patriots were the more complete team in Super Bowl 36. They were more balanced and they came up with the big plays when they needed to and this is a great tribute to Tom Brady who was deserving of the MVP award.

Dr. John's Super Bowl 36 Lesson

"Teamwork trumps individual glory every time"

Teamwork requires sharp timing, consistent effort, reduced mistakes, and big plays when it counts. The New England Patriots played smart football and stole the Rams' budding dynasty, replacing it with a New England Patriots dynasty that is still thriving a decade later.

Most Error Free Teams (T + P)

Penalties plus Turnovers are expressed as lowest number, but since turnovers are much more damaging, teams are sequenced as those with 0 turnovers first, then with 1 turnover, and so on.

#1--1975 Pittsburgh Steelers (0 + 0 = 0)
#2--1973 Miami Dolphins (0 + 1 = 1) tie--Reviewed in "Best Teams Ever"
#2--1967 Green Bay Packers (0 + 1 = 1) tie
#3--1996 Green Bay Packers (0 + 3 = 3) tie
#3--1994 San Francisco 49ers (0 + 3 = 3) tie--Reviewed in "MPI-O"
#3--2009 New Orleans Saints (0 + 3 = 3) tie--Reviewed in "MPI-ST"

Super Bowl 10 – January 18, 1976 – Orange Bowl, Miami, FL

Pittsburgh Steelers 21 (.478) Dallas Cowboys 17 (.479)

Brief Game Review

Coach Chuck Noll's Pittsburgh Steelers and Coach Tom Landry's Dallas Cowboys were by far the most popular and two of the most successful teams in the league at the time of this game. The pre-game hype swirled around whether Steelers star receiver Lynn Swan would play after suffering a severe concussion that had hospitalized him and caused him to miss practice. Cowboy players tried to intimidate Swan including safety Cliff Harris who said, "I'm not going to hurt anyone intentionally but getting hit again while he's running a pass route must be in the back of Swann's mind. I know it would be in the back of my mind." Later in the week Swan responded to Harris by saying, "I'm still not 100 percent. I value my health, but I've had no dizzy spells. I read what Harris said. He was trying to intimidate me. He said I'd be afraid out there. He needn't worry. He doesn't know Lynn Swann. He can't scare me or the team. I said to myself, 'The hell with it, I'm gonna play.' Sure, I thought about the possibility of being re-injured. But it's like being thrown by a horse. You have to get up and ride again immediately or you may be scared the rest of your life."

The game started off with excitement on the first play when Cowboys quarterback Roger Staubach was sacked and fumbled. Dallas recovered the ball and was forced to punt. The Steelers were also stopped, but on the punt Steelers punter Bobby Walden fumbled the snap and Dallas recovered the ball at the Steelers 29. On the next play, Staubach threw to an open Drew Pearson for a touchdown and a 7-0 lead. Pittsburgh then drove down the field and scored on quarterback Terry Bradshaw's pass to tight end Randy Grossman to tie the game at seven. Dallas charged back but had to settle for 36 yard field goal to take a 10-7 lead into the half.

The third quarter was scoreless with the only real opportunity coming when the Steelers drove to the 16 -yard line, but Steelers kicker Roy Gerela missed his second field goal and the score stayed 10-7 going into the fourth quarter. Early in the fourth quarter, the Cowboys were forced to punt from their own goal line. Reggie Harrison blocked the punt out of the end zone for a safety and the Dallas lead was cut to 10-9. The Steelers got the ball back and drove to the Dallas 20 and kicked a field goal for a 12-10 lead. On Dallas' next play from scrimmage, Pittsburgh intercepted and returned to the Dallas 7-yard line where they again had to settle for a field goal and a 15-10 lead.

When the Steelers got the ball back, many believed they would run time off the clock, but on 3rd and 6 Terry Bradshaw threw it a mile and hit Swann on a 64 yard touchdown to give the Steelers a 21-10 lead. The extra point was missed and after the play Bradshaw had to leave the game with a concussion. Dallas scored only one more time and the game ended 21-17 in favor of Steelers. The game had only two penalties called, both against the Cowboys for 20 yards. Swan who had four catches for a Super Bowl record 161 yards and one touchdown was named Super Bowl MVP. He became the first wide receiver to win the award.

What Actually Happened?

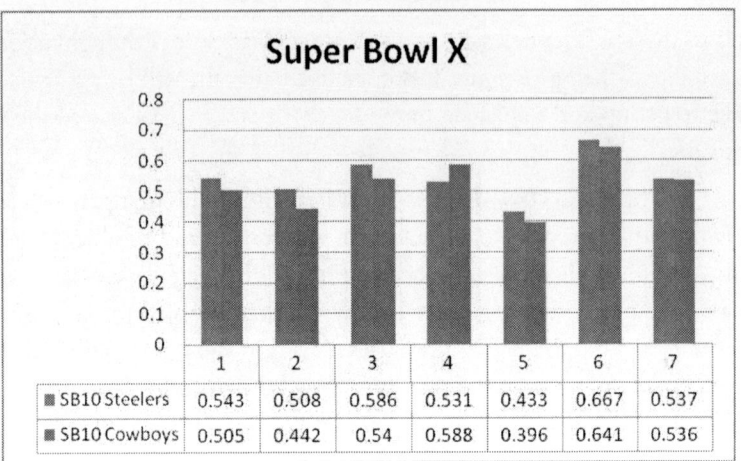

Super Bowl X

	1	2	3	4	5	6	7
■ SB10 Steelers	0.543	0.508	0.586	0.531	0.433	0.667	0.537
■ SB10 Cowboys	0.505	0.442	0.54	0.588	0.396	0.641	0.536

MPI-T MPI-O MPI-D MPI-ST MPI-OP MPI-DP MPI-TP

This game was very rare in that Pittsburgh is the only team in Super Bowl history to have no penalties or turnovers in a game, and the 2 penalties overall were the lowest in Super Bowl history. While Pittsburgh fumbled 4 times, they recovered each ball and never turned it over to Dallas.

It was a very good defensive battle as each unit performed well (MPI-D=.586 and 6th ranked for Pittsburgh; MPI-D=.540 and 15th ranked for Dallas).

Pittsburgh might have easily lost this game to a very solid Cowboys team with just one or two lost fumbles of the 4, or a couple key penalties, but the fact remains that it was the most error free performance by one team in the history of the Super Bowl. Not making mistakes saved the Steelers skin in this game and credit must certainly go to Pittsburgh coach Chuck Noll and his entire coaching staff for preparing the team well.

The MVP, Pittsburgh receiver Lynn Swann, had 4 catches for 161 yards after spending time in the hospital and being taunted by Cowboys before the game. His 64 yard touchdown catch was the biggest play of the game. Terry Bradshaw also deserves credit for no interceptions and a 122.5 passer rating.

Dr. John's Super Bowl 10 Lesson

"Don't beat yourself and you always have a chance!"

The Steelers had no turnovers and no penalties in the most error free performance in Super Bowl history. They still barely won a tough defensive struggle against a very strong Cowboys team. Credit goes to Lynn Swan for his courage and clutch performance, but by not beating themselves with mistakes the entire Steelers team earned a title.

Super Bowl 2 – January 14, 1968 – Orange Bowl, Miami, FL

Green Bay Packers 33 (.547) Oakland Raiders 14 (.466)

Brief Game Review

Coach Vince Lombardi's NFL Green Bay Packers who had won the previous AFL-NFL championship game easily (Super Bowl I) entered as 14 point favorites. Pre-game hype concerned whether head coach Vince Lombardi would retire. Many thought this would be his final game. Because so many Packers players believed this, they were motivated for their coach to go out on top as a winner.

Coach John Rauch's Oakland Raiders had no success moving the ball on their first two series and were forced to punt each time. Green Bay, on the other hand, moved the ball well on their opening drive and kicked a 39-yard field goal for an early 3-0 lead. To open the second quarter, the Packers started from their own 3 and drove 84 yards before settling for a second field goal and a 6-0 lead. Later in the second quarter Green Bay quarterback Bart Starr hit receiver Boyd Dowler for a 62-yard touchdown pass and a 13-0 lead. The Raiders offense finally woke up on their next possession with a 9 play 79-yard drive capped by a 23 yard touchdown pass from quarterback Daryle Lamonica to wide receiver Bill Miller to cut the Packers lead to 13-7, but Green Bay added a field goal before the half and went up 16-7.

The second half was dominated by the Packers. During the third quarter Green Bay had the ball three times and kept it almost 13 minutes with expert blocking and impressive ball control. On their first drive, they scored on a 2 yard run by Donny Anderson, then added another field goal to take a 26-7 lead into the fourth quarter. Just a few minutes into the fourth quarter, Green Bay put the game away when Herb Adderley intercepted a Lamonica pass and returned it 60 yards for a touchdown and a 33-7 lead. Oakland scored a meaningless touchdown on another pass to Miller, but the Green Bay Packers were Super Bowl II champions 33-14. Vince Lombardi was carried off the field and quarterback Bart Starr was named Super Bowl MVP after throwing for 202 yards and a touchdown.

<u>What Actually Happened?</u>

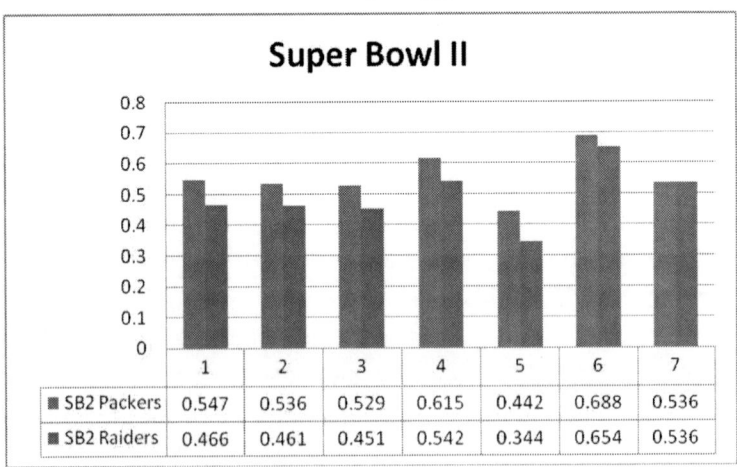

	1	2	3	4	5	6	7
■ SB2 Packers	0.547	0.536	0.529	0.615	0.442	0.688	0.536
■ SB2 Raiders	0.466	0.461	0.451	0.542	0.344	0.654	0.536

MPI-T MPI-O MPI-D MPI-ST MPI-OP MPI-DP MPI-TP

This game was all Green Bay. Credit the team for playing the second most error free game in Super Bowl history for their legendary coach. They had no turnovers and just 1 penalty. Only the 1973 Miami Dolphins matched this performance, and only the 1975 Pittsburgh Steelers exceeded it by committing no turnovers and no penalties. A closer analysis shows that it was also the 13th most dominant defensive pressure performance (MPI-DP=.688) in Super Bowl history. They ran and threw well and Bart Starr got the MVP with a 96.2 passer rating, but the offense, while good, was only ranked 31st overall (MPI-O=.536) by comparison. The Packers special teams unit deserves credit for putting in the 12th best performance overall (MPI-ST=.615).

The Raiders defense did reasonably well in key moments of the game (MPI-DP=.654) and ranked 23rd among the 88 teams and 30th overall in pressure moments (MPI-TP=.536). But they had no chance compared with the determined Packer effort to make their coach proud. With error free play seen only twice in the history of the Super Bowl and four field goals by Don Chandler, the Packers easily dominated.

Dr. John's Super Bowl 2 Lesson

"Play for a higher purpose"

The Green Bay Packers played even better than expected for the higher purpose of honoring their great coach. This provides exceptional motivation. Everything Vince Lombardi preached for years came to a terrific crescendo in 60 minutes, especially on key defensive plays. While Bart Starr got the MVP for the second straight year, it should have gone to a key defensive player such as Willie Davis or Herb Adderley because it was on defense where the Packers were best.

Super Bowl 31 – January 26, 1997 – Louisiana Superdome, New Orleans, LA

Green Bay Packers 35 (.539) New England Patriots 21 (.495)

Brief Game Review

Six days prior to this Super Bowl, an article in the Boston Globe reported that New England Coach Bill Parcells would be leaving the Patriots after the Super Bowl to become the head coach of the New York Jets. These rumors often took center stage more than the game. The Patriots had gone 11-5 and swept their two playoff opponents entering the game. Coach Mike Holmgren's Green Bay Packers came in as obvious favorites to win the game, having posted an NFC best 13-3 record led by their powerful defense which was NFL best in both yards and points allowed. On offense, the Packers were led by quarterback Brett Favre, who won the league MVP award that year.

Green Bay opened the scoring when Favre connected with Andre Rison on a 54 yard touchdown pass on only their second offensive play of the game. Next the Packers kicked a field goal to go up 10-0 but New England kept it close by scoring touchdowns on their next two possessions on short passes by quarterback Drew Bledsoe. Down 14-10 in the second quarter, the Packers scored on an 81 yard pass from Favre to Antonio Freeman, and before halftime the Packers added another field goal and touchdown for a commanding 27-14 lead.

Midway through the third quarter, the Patriots scored on an 18 yard Curtis Martin run to close the gap, but on the ensuing kickoff Desmond Howard returned the ball a record 99 yards for a touchdown and a 35-21 lead. There was no more scoring for the rest of the third and fourth quarters as Green Bay's defense finished strong.

Patriot's quarterback Drew Bledsoe threw four interceptions and Packers defensive lineman, Reggie White, set a new Super Bowl record with three sacks in the game. The MVP of the game belonged to Packers kick and punt returner Desmond Howard who accumulated 154 kickoff return and 90 punt return yards. Howard became the first special teams player to win Super Bowl MVP.

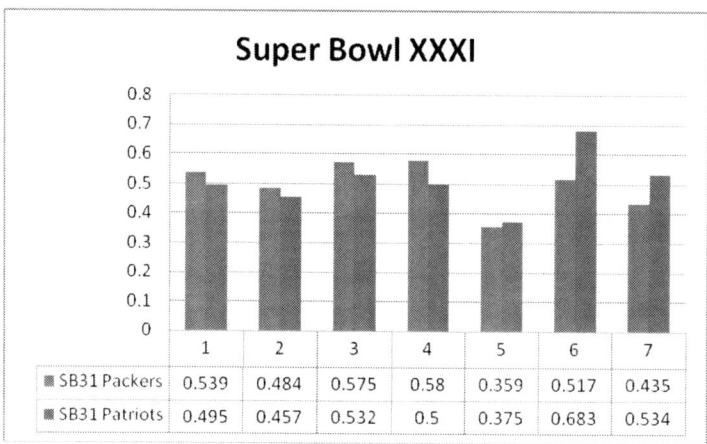

	1	2	3	4	5	6	7
SB31 Packers	0.539	0.484	0.575	0.58	0.359	0.517	0.435
SB31 Patriots	0.495	0.457	0.532	0.5	0.375	0.683	0.534

MPI-T MPI-O MPI-D MPI-ST MPI-OP MPI-DP MPI-TP

Green Bay's Special Teams unit was given a lot of credit and Desmond Howard was a worthy recipient of the MVP for his rare and terrific individual performance. Looking closer, there were more influential factors. The Packers' special teams ranked 19th in Super Bowl history (MPI-ST=.580) and 21st in dominance (MPI-STD=.080). By contrast the Packers defense did relatively better, ranked 8th overall (MPI-D=.575), but an even more extreme factor in Green Bay's favor was their 4th ranked takeaways minus giveaways (T-G=4) and 3rd ranked error free play (T+P=3). The Packers had no turnovers and only 3 penalties.

The Patriots defense beat the Packers offense in key moments of this game (MPI-DPD=.324) with a 16th ranked performance, and were ranked 15th overall in pressure play on defense (MPI-DP=.683). The Patriots put themselves in position to win this game, but costly mistakes on offense hurt while Green Bay played almost error free.

Dr. John's Super Bowl 31 Lesson

"What you don't do may help most"

Desmond Howard was the recognized star in this Packers Super Bowl victory for what he did. What many do not realize is that what the Packers did not do helped them even more. They did not turn the ball over and they did not commit more than 3 penalties and these were huge.

Teams with Best Time of Possession (Min:Sec)

Time of Possession is expressed numerically in minutes and seconds.

#1--1990 New York Giants (40:33 to 19:27)
#2--1989 San Francisco 49ers (39:31 to 20:29)
#3--1985 Chicago Bears (39:15 to 20:45)--Reviewed in "Best Teams Ever"
#5--2003 New England Patriots (38:58 to 21:02)

Super Bowl 25 – January 27, 1991 – Tampa Stadium, Tampa, FL

New York Giants 20 (.514) Buffalo Bills 19 (.493)

Brief Game Review

Dubbed the "Battle of New York," this was the first Super Bowl between two teams representing the same state. Coach Marv Levy's Buffalo Bills and Bill Parcell's New York Giants entered the game with two completely different styles of football. The Giants built their team around playing power football with a strong defense, and with an offense that would sustain long drives that killed the clock. The Giants offensive goal was to wear down the defense and keep the opposing team's offense off the field and prevent them from scoring. During the regular season the Giants defense ranked first in fewest points allowed and second in the league in fewest total yards allowed.

The Bills had a completely different high-powered offense with quick scoring drives led by hall of fame quarterback Jim Kelly and they led the league in total points scored. They ran a no-huddle offense, which prevented opposing teams from making defensive substitutions and reading the Bills' formation. The Bills were favored by seven and a lot of experts believed the Bills' high-powered offense would be too much for the Giants defense. The teams had played each other in week 15 of the regular season and the Bills won 17-13.

After Buffalo was forced to punt on the opening drive, the Giants did what they did best, taking 6:15 off the clock, driving 58 yards, and kicking a 28 yard field goal to go up 3-0. The Bills high-octane offense kicked in as they zipped 66 yards up the field in 1:23 and tied the game with a 23 yard field goal. After a Giants punt, the Bills offense struck again, going 80 yards in 4:27 and scoring on a 1 yard run for a 10-3 lead. Later in the second quarter, all-pro defensive end Bruce Smith sacked Giants' quarterback Jeff Hostetler in the end zone for a safety to give the Bills a 12-3 lead. On the last drive for the Giants before the half, New York marched 87 yards and Hostetler found Stephen Baker for a 14 yard touchdown pass with 25 seconds left in the half to pull within two points 12-10.

The Giants stuck with their methodical game plan on the opening drive of the second half and drove 75 yards in 14 plays to score a touchdown and take their first lead of the game 17-12. The drive took nine minutes and 29 seconds, at the time a Super Bowl Record. After the Bills and Giants traded possessions, Buffalo got the ball back on their own 37 and went 63 yards in four plays, scoring on a 31 yard run from Thurman Thomas to take a 19-17 lead. But before the Bills defense could take a break they were back out on the field trying to stop the Giants plodding and pounding offense. On the next drive the Giants took 7:32 off the clock in 14 plays and drove 74 yards for a Matt Bahr second field goal that gave New York a 20-19 lead. After an exchange of punts, the Bills began at their own 10 with 2:16 remaining and drove all the way to the Giant's 29 yard line setting up a potential game winning field goal with only 8 seconds left. Scott Norwood's kick sailed one foot wide right and the rest is history. Running back Otis Anderson got the MVP for 102 yards rushing and a touchdown.

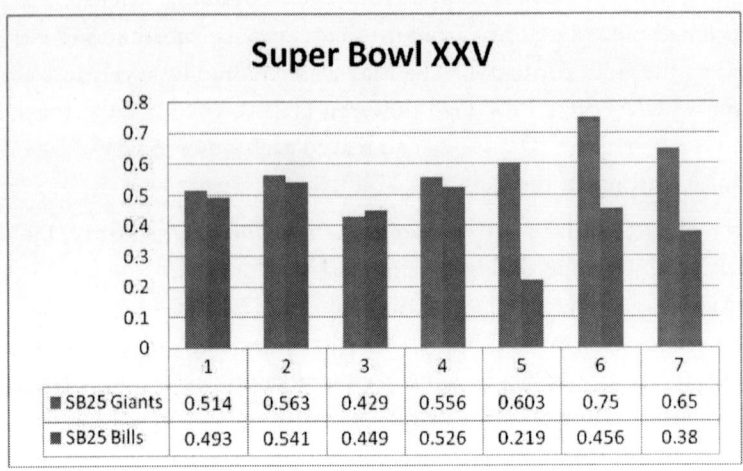

Super Bowl XXV	1	2	3	4	5	6	7
■ SB25 Giants	0.514	0.563	0.429	0.556	0.603	0.75	0.65
■ SB25 Bills	0.493	0.541	0.449	0.526	0.219	0.456	0.38

MPI-T MPI-O MPI-D MPI-ST MPI-OP MPI-DP MPI-TP

To begin, the Giants outperformed the Bills in this game and should have won (MPI-T=.514 to .493). Both offenses were dominant with the Giants holding a slight advantage and the Giants were also slightly better on special teams. But it was in pressure moments of the game where the Giants destroyed the Bills most in this game, as can be vividly seen on the above graph above numbers 5, 6 and 7.

The Giants had the 3rd best overall defensive performance in pressure (MPI-DP=.750) and 3rd best defensive dominance in pressure (MPI-DPD=.531). But the Giants biggest asset by far was time of possession (40:33 to 19:27) and it ranks number 1 amongst all 88 teams in Super Bowl history!

The Bills, like the Giants, played a clean game with no turnovers and had the 15th best net rushing yards in Super Bowl history (166) but the Giants matched it with the 13th best performance (172). Still, the Bills could have won this game if the ball had been one more foot left on the field goal, but they did not play well in pressure, and the missed field goal at the end was just one example. The Bills offense in pressure moments was second worst in history and ranked 87th (MPI-OP=.219).

Since the Bills did very poorly in critical moments throughout this game, there was anything but confidence when Scott Norwood was asked to reverse those fortunes with a 47-yard kick. That distance is not a sure bet, and he did not lose this game, the entire Bills team lost, and the effective ball control and strong pressure defensive team of the Giants team won it.

Dr. John's Super Bowl 25 Lesson

"Stop Blaming Scott Norwood!"

He almost won it for the Bills, but Scott Norwood did not by himself lose this game. Since when is a 47 yard field goal a sure bet? The Bills had been horrible in pressure situations before he missed, so Norwood would have only helped save his team that had one of the worse pressure performances overall. The better team won this game, so it would have been more of a surprise if Norwood had made the kick. Scott Norwood should not be blamed even if he could have been praised as the hero.

Super Bowl 24 – January 28, 1990 – Louisiana Superdome, New Orleans, LA

San Francisco 49ers 55 (.574) Denver Broncos 10 (.416)

Brief Game Review

Coach George Seifert's San Francisco 49ers were attempting to win back to back titles as they had beaten the Bengals the previous year in Super Bowl XXIII. They completed a successful 14-2 regular season campaign led by star quarterback Joe Montana throwing to Jerry Rice in amassing 3,512 yards passing and 26 touchdowns against 8 interceptions. Roger Craig ran for over a thousand yards as this powerful offense was almost unstoppable. On defense, the 49ers were 3rd best in points allowed in the NFL as Pierce Holt had 10.5 sacks along with Charles Haley.

Over in Denver, Coach Dan Reeves had top quarterback John Elway direct an 11-5 season with his cast of receivers including Vance Johnson with his best ever season of 76 catches for 1,095 yards, and a running crew including Bobby Humphrey who ran for 1,151 yards. The defensive line was strong led by Ron Holmes, who had 9 sacks, and the always tough Karl Mecklenburg.

In the first half, the 49ers moved the ball almost at will as Montana threw three touchdown passes, two to Jerry Rice and one to Brent Jones, and Tom Rathman ran it in from one yard away as the 49ers were in total control 27-3 at the half.

The same pattern of domination continued in the second half as the 49ers ran and threw at will and went up 41-3 on two sharp touchdown passes to Rice and Taylor. Denver got on the board to make it 41-10 before San Francisco slammed the door shut with more ball control and running touchdowns and the final score was 55-10.

Joe Montana was the Super Bowl MVP for his 5 touchdown passes and no interceptions. Many say this was the best team in history.

What Actually Happened?

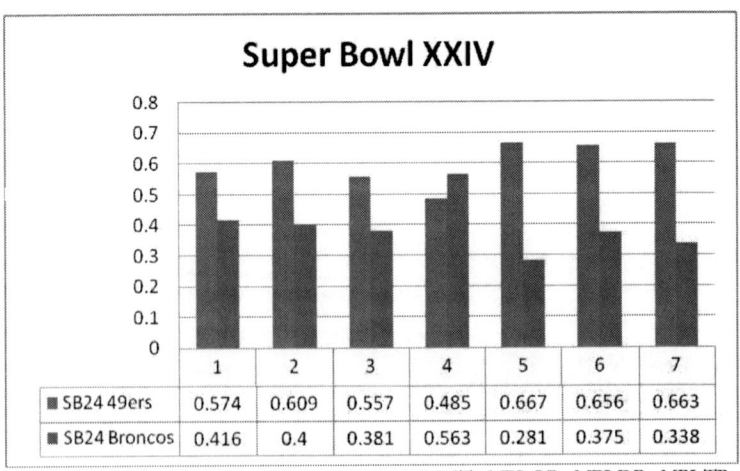

	1	2	3	4	5	6	7
■ SB24 49ers	0.574	0.609	0.557	0.485	0.667	0.656	0.663
■ SB24 Broncos	0.416	0.4	0.381	0.563	0.281	0.375	0.338

MPI-T MPI-O MPI-D MPI-ST MPI-OP MPI-DP MPI-TP

The magnitude of 49ers domination in this game cannot be overemphasized. Here are just a few of the most impressive stats. The 49ers were 1st in points scored (55), point differential (45), net yards gained differential (294), and turnovers (0). They also had the ball control mindset and came out 2nd in time of possession (39:31 to 20:29), 3rd in total dominance (MPI-TD=.158), just below the Super Bowl VIII Dolphins and Super Bowl XX Bears, and 4th in overall performance (MPI-T=.574).

The Broncos were the 21st best team in special teams (MPI-ST=.563) and 23rd in special teams dominance (MPI-STD=.078), but much worse in everything else against this powerhouse.

<u>Dr. John's Super Bowl 24 Lesson</u>

"Wear out the defense and freeze the offense by stealing time"

This 49ers had everything, especially on offense, and their demonstration of steady ball control and punishing possession offense was exemplary. Add the fast strike ability of Joe Montana and this offense was almost unstoppable. Possession offense is very effective against a team with a top quarterback like John Elway. The offense only gets better as the game wears on and the defense wears out. It puts a chill in the opposing offense which can't do anything from the bench.

Super Bowl 38 – February 1, 2004 – Reliant Stadium, Houston, TX

New England Patriots 32 (.516) Carolina Panthers 29 (.424)

Brief Game Review

New England Patriots' coach Bill Belichick faced the Carolina Panthers' John Fox. The Patriots had gone 14-2 in the regular season, winning their last 12 games after some player controversy and a terrible shutout loss to the Bills. When they righted the ship, Tom Brady had another stellar year, throwing for 3,620 yards and 23 touchdowns. Deion Branch was his primary receiver with 57 catches. The Panthers, on the other hand, were a story of major recovery, having been 1-15 only two years prior, but with the arrival of Fox as head coach and the infusion of talent brought in by Bill Polian things changed rapidly. They completed an 11-5 record on the strong running of Stephen Davis who amassed 1,444 yards on the ground with 8 touchdowns. The passing did not disappoint either as Jake Delhomme replaced Rodney Peete early in the season and finished with 3,219 yards passing and 19 touchdowns. Both teams also had strong defenses and the Panther's strength was on the line which featured Julius Peppers, Kris Jenkins, and Mike Rucker.

Early on it was a defensive battle with neither team scoring until late in the second quarter despite several early opportunities for the Patriots. The Patriots finally scored on a pass from Brady to Branch and it opened up a ton of offense on both sides. This first score came at 26 minutes and 55 seconds into the game, setting a record for the longest amount of time a Super Bowl remained scoreless.

Tom Brady set a Super Bowl record with 32 completions in 48 attempts for 354 yards, 3 touchdowns and 1 interception. The Panthers quarterback Jake Delhomme countered with 16 completions of 33 pass attempts for 323 yards and 3 touchdowns, with no interceptions.

With 4 seconds left in the game, Patriot place kicker Adam Vinatieri kicked a 41 yard field goal to win the game for New England, 32-29. New England's Tom Brady was named Super Bowl MVP for the second time in three years.

What Actually Happened?

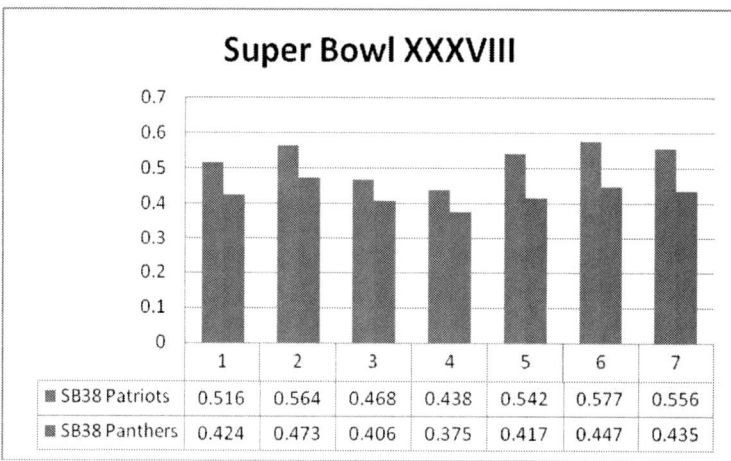

Super Bowl XXXVIII

	1	2	3	4	5	6	7
■ SB38 Patriots	0.516	0.564	0.468	0.438	0.542	0.577	0.556
■ SB38 Panthers	0.424	0.473	0.406	0.375	0.417	0.447	0.435

MPI-T   MPI-O   MPI-D   MPI-ST   MPI-OP   MPI-DP   MPI-TP

Media after the game said this was one of the best games ever and it was indeed exciting, but many wrongly asserted said that this game had been well played. How could it from a performance standpoint when it was filled with 20 penalties (12 for Carolina, 8 for New England) and many other mistakes resulting from carelessness. The Patriots played very well in the last minute when they needed to move the ball into position to kick the game winner. This pattern has been seen often with New England in Super Bowl history where it seems like they are just barely able to win at the end, but a closer view shows that they have usually played much better than the scoreboard indicates.

Data shows that despite a close game on the scoreboard, the Patriots outplayed the Panthers (MPI-T=.516 to.424, ranked 14th overall on MPI-TD=.092), and totally dominated the Panther's defense with their offense at a 12th ranked level (MPI-OD=.158). The Patriots did it with the 5th best time of possession in Super Bowl history (38:58 to 21:02), 3rd ranked net passing yards (354), and 3rd ranked net yards gained (481).

What kept this game so close is that the Panthers offense was up to the task against the Patriots defense and even performed slightly better (MPI-O=.473 to .468). The Panthers also had the 15th best net passing yards (295) and 21st overall net yards gained (387) in Super Bowl history.

Both teams showed poor special teams play but the Patriots were better (MPI-ST=.438 to .375) and the Patriots were much better in pressure situations on offense, defense, and overall (see above graph).

<u>Dr. John's Super Bowl 38 Lesson</u>

"Act rather than react to be resilient"

Tom Brady bounces back! After he threw a critical interception in the 4th quarter to Reggie Howard, and the Panthers came back to score a touchdown and take the lead, Brady could get upset and "react". Or he could "act" by directing his offense. He chose to act and after an 11 play drive, short touchdown pass, and run for two, the Patriots led by 7. When Carolina tied the game, Brady led his team into the winning field goal position. That is resilience and that is Tom Brady.

<u>Outperformed Teams that Won</u>

Better team performance almost always leads to victory, but exceptions occur. Just a couple broken assignments or rare big plays can lead to a 14 or 21 point swing as it did for Pittsburgh in winning Super Bowl XL despite being outperformed by Seattle on MPI-T (see below). Of the 44 Super Bowl games, only 4 times did the outperformed team on the MPI-T win. When this happens it is still helpful to analyze why it happened and learn from it. Teams are listed below in order from biggest surprise down based on relative MPI-T scores.

#1--1999 St. Louis Rams (.487) defeated Tennessee Titans (.495)
#2--1970 Baltimore Colts (.469 defeated Dallas Cowboys (.471)
#3--1995 Dallas Cowboys (.497) defeated Pittsburgh Steelers (.498)
#3--2005 Pittsburgh Steelers (.478) defeated Seattle Seahawks (479)--
Reviewed in "MPI-ST"

Super Bowl 34 – January 30, 2000 – Georgia Dome, Atlanta, GA

St. Louis Rams 23 (.487) Tennessee Titans 16 (.495)

Brief Game Review

St. Louis Rams coach Dick Vermeil and quarterback Kurt Warner were up against the Tennessee Titans' coach Jeff Fisher and quarterback Steve McNair, a matchup to be remembered for years. Both teams had finished the regular season 13-3, but the Titans had to get in as a wild card as they finished second in their division to the 14-2 Jacksonville Jaguars.

The Rams had experienced a major turnaround from 4-12 the previous year and it was mirrored in their star quarterback Warner who had the year before been working in a grocery store and now found himself throwing for 4,353 yards and 41 touchdowns to earn the NFL MVP award! He was supported by star running back Marshall Faulk, the NFL Offensive Player of the year with 1,381 rushing yards, 87 receptions and 12 scores. This was truly a phenomenal offense and the defense was astounding as well, leading the league in fewest rushing yards allowed and 4th in total yards permitted!

Over in Tennessee, Steve McNair took the reins as quarterback and despite being out for 5 games due to injuries still put up impressive passing and running statistics (2,179 yards passing and 337 yards rushing). His star running back was Eddie George who ran for 1,304 yards and caught 47 passes. It should be noted that the playoffs were not easy for the Titans and their first win over Buffalo came on what is now known as the "Music City Miracle," the famous trick kickoff return play that won in the end! They also had a surprise comeback win over Minnesota in which they scored 35 points in the second half to win 49-37 and a nail-biting defensive victory over Tampa Bay 11-6 in the NFC Championship game.

Consider what happened. McNair completed 22 of 26 passes for 214 yards. Warner completed 24 of 45 passes for 414 yards and two touchdowns. The Rams appeared to be in full control of this game in the third quarter up 16-0. Then the Titans came all the way back and tied the game at 16 apiece with 2:12 left in the game. Kurt Warner then completed a 73 yard touchdown pass to wide receiver Isaac Bruce. The score now favored the Rams 23-16.

But it wasn't over. The Titans worked themselves to the Ram's 10 yard line with only six seconds remaining. This game was on its way into overtime. Tennessee's wide receiver Kevin Dyson took a Steve McNair pass and raced for the score, only to be pinned by Rams linebacker Mike Jones one yard short of the goal line -- as time expired! The photograph is burned forever into the memories of anyone who watched this game as Dyson desperately reaches for goal line and comes up just inches short as Jones applied pressure!

The final: A nervous St. Louis 23, a woeful Tennessee 16. Believe it or not! Kurt Warner was named the MVP. He was not intercepted once.

What Actually Happened?

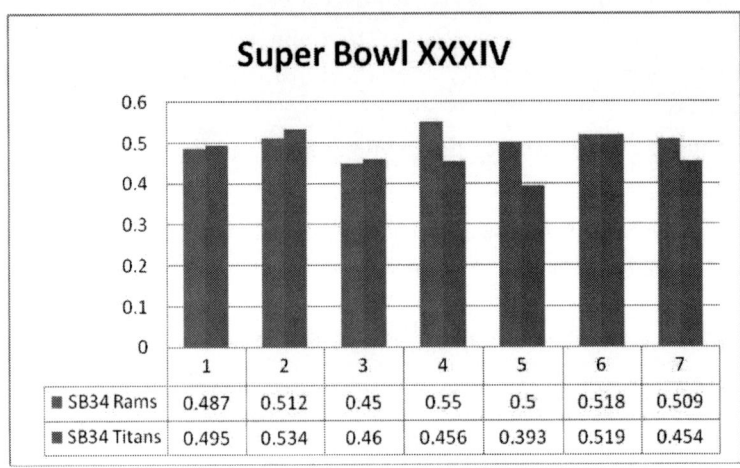

Super Bowl XXXIV

	1	2	3	4	5	6	7
▪ SB34 Rams	0.487	0.512	0.45	0.55	0.5	0.518	0.509
▪ SB34 Titans	0.495	0.534	0.46	0.456	0.393	0.519	0.454

MPI-T MPI-O MPI-D MPI-ST MPI-OP MPI-DP MPI-TP

This was an extremely exciting game that went down to the one last iconic play. Kevin Dyson will probably be stretching to reach the end zone in his dreams for the rest of his life. Maybe he gets a little closer to the goal line each night as Mike Jones' grasp lessens until finally he'll break the plane of the goal line like a golf ball dropping into the cup at the last possible second, and we'll all get the updated game account on ESPN!

What really happened? For one, the Titans should have won the game because they outperformed the Rams (MPI-T=.495 to .487), an anomaly that has only happened 4 times in 44 games and is deserving of this special category. The Titans offense outperformed the Rams defense

(MPI-OD=.084) and the Rams offense did the same with the Titans defense to a slightly less extent (MPI-OD=.052). Special teams favored the Rams decisively (MPI-STD=.093, 18th best) and so did defensive dominance in pressure situations (MPI-DPD=.125) and overall pressure situations (MPI-TP=.509 to .454), and while these pressure differences were not huge, combined with special teams dominance the Rams had slightly more weapons.

The Rams had the most net passing yards in Super Bowl history (407) with Kurt Warner firing away, yet they still almost lost the game with only 23 points on the board! What does that tell us about individual accolades in football? The Rams also had the 8th best net yards gained (436). What does that say about yards gained? The logic of an MPI system makes sense when one realizes how faulty traditional statistics can be for failing to include mental factors and also for giving only a partial snapshot of one portion of reality rather than a comprehensive view of every key moment in the game as MPI-T does.

Here is another one: The Rams were the 41st best performing offense in Super Bowl history (MPI-O=.487) despite have the most passing yards among 88 teams. Being great on offense is much more than throwing a ball. Compare that with how easily the Baltimore Ravens with a poorer than average offense destroyed the Giants in Super Bowl XXXV.

The Titans had no turnovers, to their credit, but they did commit 7 penalties. The Titans also controlled the clock in an 11th ranked fashion (36:26 to 23:34) and should have barely won this game and might have done so had Dyson made it across the goal line. But their overall MPI-T score of .495 hardly qualifies for a Super Bowl champion. It is the 46th ranked performance among 88 teams.

The bottom line is that if you play with fire by performing under .500 on the MPI-T, you are never guaranteed a win, and this game really could have gone either way. Congrats to Mike Jones for making "The Tackle" of Kevin Dyson near the goal line!

Dr. John's Super Bowl 34 Lesson

"Out of the muck appears a blue lotus"

Mike Jones is the hero of this chaotic Super Bowl for making his game winning tackle and preserving victory for the Rams. In chaos, individual heroes arise. Examples include Jim O'Brien for his game winning kick in Super Bowl V, Joe Montana for his calm during the final touchdown drive in Super Bowl XXIII, or David Tyree's clutch helmet catch in Super Bowl XLII. The legend of the blue lotus in eastern cultures signifies wisdom and the victory of the spirit over the senses. It is said that "out of muck will appear a lotus," a beautiful flower of goodness. Mike Jones played the role of blue lotus for the St. Louis Rams in Super Bowl XXXIV.

Super Bowl 5 – January 17, 1971 – Orange Bowl, Miami, FL

Baltimore Colts 16 (.469) Dallas Cowboys 13 (.471)

Brief Game Review

Coach Don McCafferty of the Baltimore Colts came to Miami to face Tom Landry's Dallas Cowboys in the first Super Bowl played after the AFL-NFL merger. The Colts had finished the regular season 11-2-1 with veteran quarterback in Johnny Unitas throwing for 2,213 yards but he also threw for more interceptions than touchdowns. Backup quarterback Earl Morrall was solid but Unitas won in the playoffs and McCafferty went with him. The Colts were very tough on defense led by all pro Bubba Smith at defensive tackle, and star linebackers Mike Curtis and Ted Hendricks.

The Cowboys' quarterback Roger Staubach switched off with Craig Morton and Landry chose to go with Morton in the Super Bowl. He had thrown for 1,819 yards and 15 touchdowns and had a higher passer rating than Staubach. The Cowboys were mostly a running team, however, with Duane Thomas who had galloped for 803 yards in the season. Defense was also strong led by Bob Lilly, Chuck Howley, and Charlie Waters who had 5 interceptions. The Cowboys were 10-4 in the regular season.

The game was far from eye pleasing unless your taste in art happens to be abstract expressionism. Penalties, turnovers, miscues, and footwork problems made this game look more like a junior varsity high school matchup than the NFL title game. It did have a most memorable ending when the Colts' Jim O'Brien, with five seconds left, kicked a 32-yard field goal to hand Baltimore a 16-13 victory.

This was the first Super Bowl played on artificial turf. The two teams committed 11 turnovers combined and it was the only Super Bowl in which a member of the losing team, Linebacker Chuck Howley, was named the Most Valuable Player. After the game, he refused to accept the reward because his team lost. That's a team player!

Bubba Smith of Dallas said he was so embarrassed by the game that he refused to wear his Super Bowl ring, and Bill Curry claimed that his ring "symbolized the most mixed sense of achievement that I've ever experienced in my career."

<u>What Actually Happened?</u>

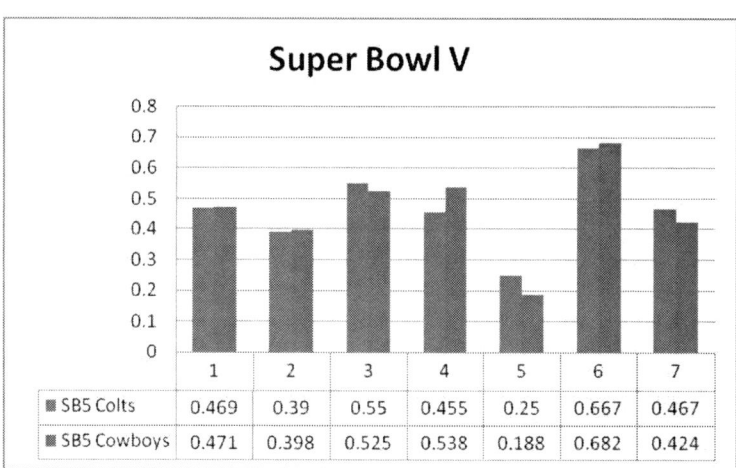

	1	2	3	4	5	6	7
■ SB5 Colts	0.469	0.39	0.55	0.455	0.25	0.667	0.467
■ SB5 Cowboys	0.471	0.398	0.525	0.538	0.188	0.682	0.424

MPI-T MPI-O MPI-D MPI-ST MPI-OP MPI-DP MPI-TP

While this game is appropriately categorized as one of the games where the outperformed team won, neither team "performed" in this game and the winner, the Colts, had the fortune of getting 2 of their 3 interceptions at the end that led to 10 points. Dallas would have outperformed Baltimore by much more and probably won without those interceptions, but it still would have been a sloppy win. The Colts made more mistakes and still won. Both teams' offensive units were beaten soundly by their defensive counterparts, and the Cowboys played better on special teams (MPI-ST=.538 to .455). The key problem for the Cowboys, however, came in critical pressure situations where they registered a mere .188 on MPI-OP which ranked worst with an 88th ranking! The Colts were not much better on MPI-OP and ranked 83rd with a .250 score. Both defenses did very well in dominating the game in pressure, and the Colts in this area were the 4th best in Super Bowl history (MPI-DPD=.479) only behind the Super Bowl XI Raiders, Super Bowl XXXV Ravens and Super Bowl XXV Giants!

In sum, the Colts won a tough and sloppy defensive struggle even though they were slightly outperformed. The Cowboys made mistakes at inopportune times at the end of the game on ill advised passes to lose it.

Dr. John's Super Bowl 5 Lesson

"Dance with who brung you!"

The Dallas Cowboys had an awesome defense. Coach Tom Landry was a master. In a rare loss of character, Landry abandoned his conservative running and defensive game plan and directed quarterback Craig Morton to pass. Morton was intercepted twice at the end of the game and both led to Colts scores. When it happened the second time with the score tied, Jim O'Brien was in winning field goal range. Rather than "dancing with who brung him" by running, punting, and letting his defense work, Landry ordered a pass on 2nd and 35 from his own 27! After an interception and game winning field goal, the Colts, rather than Cowboys, became world champions. Landry would correct his error in the next Super Bowl by allowing Duane Thomas to dance Mardi Gras Mambo all over Dolphin's defenders in New Orleans.

Super Bowl 30 – January 28, 1996 – Sun Devil Stadium, Tempe, AZ

Dallas Cowboys 27 (.497) Pittsburgh Steelers 17 (.498)

Brief Game Review

Coach Barry Switzer's Dallas Cowboys and quarterback Troy Aikman met with Coach Bill Cowher's Pittsburg Steelers and quarterback Neil O'Donnell for Super Bowl XXX. The 13 ½ point underdog Steelers were matched up with the Cowboys for the third time in a Super Bowl.

The Cowboys were trying to win their 3rd Super Bowl in 4 years and had completed a successful 1995 season with a 12-4 record. Aikman at quarterback (3,304 yards passing with 16 touchdowns) and Smith running the ball (1,773) was still a terrific combination that many thought would be hard to beat.

The Steelers were back in the Super Bowl for the first time in over 15 years. They finished the regular season 11-5 led by quarterback Neil O'Donnell who threw for 2,970 yards with 17 touchdowns and the leading receiver was Yancey Thigpen with 85 catches for 1,307 yards. Runners for Pittsburgh were Bam Morris and Erric Pegram. The defense was rock solid, as Pittsburgh defenses have been so many times in Super Bowl history, and they ranked second in the NFL.

Neil O'Donnell completed 28 of 49 passes for 239 yards including a touchdown pass to Thigpen in the second quarter that cut Dallas' 13-0 lead to 13-7, but it was his 3 interceptions, and 2 to Dallas cornerback Larry Brown that would lead to 14 Cowboys points and make the difference in this game. In fact Pittsburgh was in a position to win this game only down 20-17 when the second O'Donnell interception sealed the deal for Dallas.

Troy Aikman was excellent for Dallas at 15 of 23 for 209 yards and 1 touchdown with no interceptions (passer rating was 108.8).   Larry

Brown was the big difference maker for the Cowboys and it earned him the MVP. Brown became the first cornerback to be a Super Bowl MVP.

What Actually Happened?

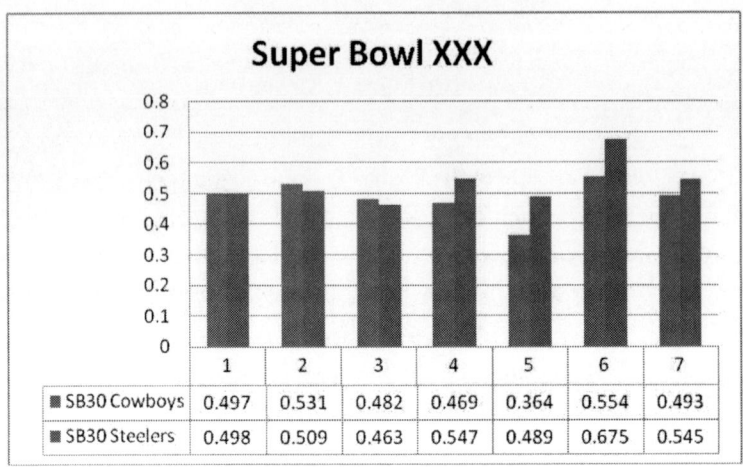

	1	2	3	4	5	6	7
■ SB30 Cowboys	0.497	0.531	0.482	0.469	0.364	0.554	0.493
■ SB30 Steelers	0.498	0.509	0.463	0.547	0.489	0.675	0.545

MPI-T MPI-O MPI-D MPI-ST MPI-OP MPI-DP MPI-TP

This was one of the rarest games in Super Bowl history as the team that performed better, Pittsburgh (MPI-T=.498 to .497) lost the game. History has a way of evening things out, because 10 years later Pittsburgh would win a Super Bowl after they were outperformed by Seattle. Both the Cowboys and Steelers offenses beat their respective defensive rivals in this game but special teams play (MPI-ST=.547 to .469) and total pressure performance favored the Steelers (MPI-TP=.545 to .493).

The winning Cowboys have a great knack in Super Bowl history for ball hawking and not turning the ball over! They were 12th ranked on (T-G=3) and 7th on error free play (T+P=4) whereas the Steelers ranked 67th on (T-G) with a -3 value.

The clean play of the Cowboys with no turnovers versus the 3 interceptions by Pittsburgh changed fate and history because the Steelers would have probably won this game without the picks, and it would have been a great upset in Super Bowl history. Larry Brown was very deserving of his MVP.

Dr. John's Super Bowl 30 Lesson

"Are you starting to see a trend here?!"

Your author is dumbfounded. The Dallas Cowboys hold the top two takeaway minus giveaway (T-G) performances in Super Bowl history and here they do it again with a +3 that wins a game that they should have lost! In this Super Bowl 30 lesson I give up and ask you the reader to tell me why the Cowboys are so good at taking the ball away and not giving it up. I am sure every football team in the country would like to improve on this one and if you know and can tell me I will share it with others. Email your ideas to me for this rare trend to info@johnfmurray.com because I have no idea why they have mastered this so well!

A Note about Other Rare Wins: Some Super Bowl performances were also rare and not well represented by team performance categories and statistics. Brief Game Reviews are still found in the category that most closely fits the team's performance. The comments below clarify briefly what made this game rare.

1968 New York Jets – The heavily favored Baltimore Colts of the NFL lost to Joe Namath, the brash young gunslinger of the New York Jets who boldly guaranteed a Jet's victory and then went out and made good. The Jets came to play and the Colts looked lost when they were supposed to win by three touchdowns.

1988 San Francisco 49ers – The offense led by quarterback Joe Montana saved their best for last with rare poise and superior offensive pressure performance on the last drive of the game only. Trailing the Cincinnati Bengals 16-13 with 3:10 remaining and the ball on their own 8, the 49ers drove 92 yards and won 20 – 16 on a 10 yard touchdown pass to John Taylor. The 49ers' +218 yards passing advantage is the largest passing yards differential in Super Bowl history but the game was still extremely close. Offensive pressure dominance won it on the last drive.

1997 Denver Broncos – This was a huge upset for the Broncos when the NFC had won 13 straight Super Bowls, the Packers were being called a dynasty as 12 point favorites, and Brett Favre was the NFL MVP three years in a row. Team performance statistics do not capture the heart and guts of the 37-year-old John Elway in the third quarter going for his first Super Bowl title with a courageous dive and spin into the air for a first down while being hit. The play led to a touchdown, 24-17 point lead, and ultimate victory from an inspired team.

2001 New England Patriots – It was one of the biggest upsets in Super Bowl history and an odd game as the Rams were favored by 14. A resourceful team led by Tom Brady, error free play, Brady's final drive, +3 take away ratio, and strong special teams play helped negate Kurt Warner's third best passing dominance in Super Bowl history. Both offenses played extremely well in a low scoring game.

2007 New York Giants – It was arguably the biggest upset in NFL history. The Giants stopped a Patriots team that could have been undefeated. Eli Manning was clutch in pressure situations. The David Tyree helmet catch is iconic as best the catch ever in a Super Bowl.

BEST PERFORMING TEAMS EVER

These are the best teams in Super Bowl history, as shown by performance and measured by the MPI-T or overall team performance. As you can see below, the 1985 Chicago Bears are champions of MPI Bowl I, and the best performing team of all time. They were also the most dominant team of all time as you can tell by the first category reviewed! See Chapter 4 for the ranking tables on all MPI and traditional measures.

MPI Bowl I (January 1, 2011) West Palm Beach, FL
#1 - 1985 Chicago Bears
Super Bowl XX (01-26-1986) Louisiana Superdome - New Orleans, LA
Chicago Bears 46, New England Patriots 10

#2 - 1984 San Francisco 49ers
(Reviewed in MPI-OD)
Super Bowl XIX (01-20-1985) Louisiana Superdome - New Orleans, LA
San Francisco 49ers 38, Miami Dolphins 16

#3 - 1973 Miami Dolphins
Super Bowl VIII (01-13-1974) Rice Stadium – Houston, TX
Miami Dolphins 24, Minnesota Vikings 7

Others reviewed in this section that best fit here

#5--1982 Washington Redskins (.572)
#8--1983 Los Angeles Raiders (.553)

Super Bowl 20 – January 26, 1986 – Louisiana Superdome, New Orleans, LA

Chicago Bears 46 (.591) New England Patriots 10 (.411)

Brief Game Review

The roaring 1985 Chicago Bears, rated by some as the most powerful football team ever assembled, had finished the regular season 15-1 only losing to Dan Marino and the Miami Dolphins in a night game. They were coached by Mike Ditka who won the NFL Coach of the Year award and the defense had allowed the fewest points (198) and total yards (4,135) of any team that season. Quarterback Jim McMahon had thrown for 2,392 yards and 15 touchdowns while Walter Payton rushed for 1,551 yards and was at the time the NFL's leader in rushing yards gained with 14,860. Defensive Player of the Year went to Bears' linebacker Mike Singletary.

Raymond Berry was the New England Patriots coach and the team had gone 11-5 in 1985 and 6 of the games with Steve Grogan filling in for Tony Eason at quarterback, but Eason was back for the Super Bowl. The team entered the playoffs as a wild card. Young Stanley Morgan provided firepower at wide receiver and Craig James was a successful halfback who rushed for 1,227 yards. The defense was a solid

5th in the league led by linebacker Andre Tippett who recorded 16.5 sacks.

The Patriots took the second quickest lead in Super Bowl history after recovering a fumble on the second play of the game and then kicking a field goal to go up 3-0. Chicago took no time in retaliating with a quick drive and field goal to tie the game at 3 and they would add another 3 points to go up 6-3 before Craig James fumbled and set up a touchdown run by Matt Suhey and the Bears led 13-3. The Bears extended the lead, after stopping New England, on a 59 yard drive in 10 plays to make it 20-3. At this point Berry replaced quarterback Tony Eason with Steve Grogan, but it ended in a punt followed by another long drive and field goal, and Chicago led 23-3 at the half.

In the second half, the Bears scored on a one yard run after a Super Bowl longest 96 yard drive, and then scored on the Patriots' series when cornerback Reggie Phillips intercepted a Grogan pass and ran it back for a touchdown and lead of 37-3. Following yet another turnover, and McMahan pass, William "the Refrigerator" Perry scored to make it 44-3. Each team would score again and the final score was 46-10.

Bears defensive end Richard Dent had 1.5 sacks, forced two fumbles, blocked a pass, and was Most Valuable Player. Mike Ditka became the second player to win a Super Bowl ring as player and coach.

What Actually Happened?

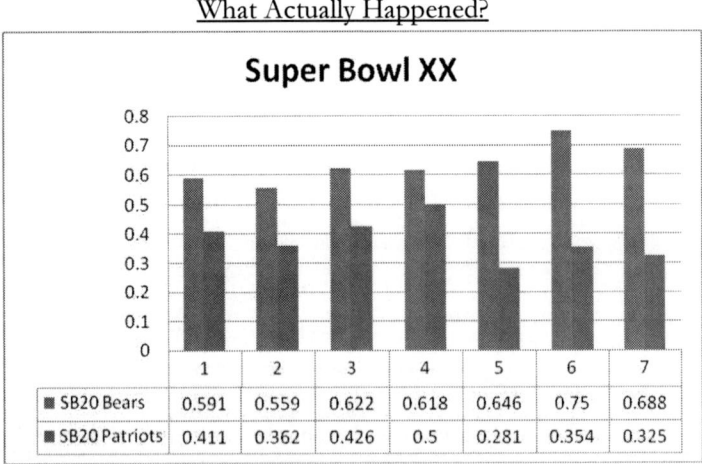

	1	2	3	4	5	6	7
■ SB20 Bears	0.591	0.559	0.622	0.618	0.646	0.75	0.688
■ SB20 Patriots	0.411	0.362	0.426	0.5	0.281	0.354	0.325

MPI-T MPI-O MPI-D MPI-ST MPI-OP MPI-DP MPI-TP

Not enough can ever be said about this 1985 Super Bowl 20 Chicago Bears team and first MPI Bowl winner and how they so completely destroyed the New England Patriots. Let's look at the data. The Bears rank 1st on total performance (MPI-T=.591), 1st on total dominance (MPI-TD=.180), 2nd on total dominance in pressure (MPI-TPD=.363), 2nd on net yards gained (537), 2nd on net yards allowed (123), 2nd on point differential (36), 3rd in total performance in pressure (MPI-TP=.688), 3rd in overall defense (MPI-D=.622), 3rd in defensive dominance (MPI-DD=.260), 3rd in defensive performance in pressure (MPI-DP=.750), 4th in takeaways minus giveaways (T-G=4), and 3rd in time of possession (39:15 to 20:45)! Were the Bears bad at anything? They did commit 7 penalties, but it made no difference, they were on top of the world for one night and for an entire season except for one magical night for Dan Marino and the Dolphins.

The Patriots were better in just two areas, penalties (5) and yards penalized (35 versus 40 for the Bears). This small advantage made no difference at all. New England had no chance.

Many assert that this 1985 Bears team is the best team ever while others will argue that the 1972 undefeated Dolphins team was best and better than the Bears because they did not lose all year. Both are valid arguments, but deciding on a best team for an entire season is entirely different than looking statistically at how each team played in the Super Bowl, just one game in the season, but the most important one.

As far as the best playing team in a Super Bowl, the 1972 Dolphins were not even close to the 1985 Bears in their performance against Washington in Super Bowl VII, but the 1973 Dolphins team in Super Bowl VIII was. The Super Bowl XIX and XXIV 49ers teams would have also possibly challenged Chicago.

The best ever team on Super Bowl Sunday is the 1985 Super Bowl XX Chicago Bears. Congrats to the Super Bowl 20 Bears for becoming the first champion of MPI Bowl I.

Dr. John's Super Bowl 20 Lesson

"There is no such thing as the greatest football team of all time"
- Chicago Bears Head Coach Mike Ditka

Coach Ditka is entitled to his view, but there is such a thing as the "Best Team Ever" on Super Bowl Sunday and his Super Bowl 20 Chicago Bears were best. Congratulations to the Super Bowl XX Champion Chicago Bears! You are Champions of MPI Bowl I and will hold that title until a better performing Super Bowl team comes along.

The MPI Bowl is the Super Bowl of Super Bowls

Super Bowl 8 – January 13, 1974 – Rice Stadium, Houston, TX

Miami Dolphins 24 (.580) Minnesota Vikings 7 (.421)

Brief Game Review

In Super Bowl VIII, Don Shula's Miami Dolphins became the first team to appear in three consecutive Super Bowls. Miami went into the game as 6 1/2 point favorites having finished the regular season with a 12-2 record. They were powered by an impressive offensive line that fueled a dominant rushing game led by bruising fullback, Larry Csonka, who ran for 1,003 yards, and speedy running back Mercury Morris who added 954 yards rushing and 10 touchdowns. The Vikings also finished 12-2 with their veteran quarterback Fran Tankenton. During the regular season Tankenton threw for 2,113 yards and 15 touchdowns. The Vikings were more known for having one of the best defenses in the NFL.

The Dolphins dominated the Vikings from the opening kickoff. On the first drive of the game, Miami drove down the field and scored on Larry Csonka's 5-yard touchdown run to take an early 7-0 lead. After Minnesota was forced to punt after 3 plays, the Dolphins again marched methodically 56 yards in 10 plays ending the drive on a Jim Kiick one yard touchdown run and a 14-0 lead. After the first quarter the score remained 14-0, with the dolphins gaining 118 yards of offense and 8 first downs, while the Vikings had just 25 yards of offense and one first down. In the second quarter Miami would add a field goal to go up 17-0. Midway through the second quarter the Vikings had an opportunity to score, but on 4th and 1 from the goal line the Dolphins defense held and the score remained 17-0 going into the half.

The game remained the same as Minnesota was forced to punt on their first possession. Miami got the ball back and drove 43 yards in eight plays, scoring on another Larry Csonka run to make the score 24-0. The running attack of Miami kept the clock ticking and it wasn't until the fourth quarter that Minnesota got going and put together a 57 yard 9 play drive ending on 4-yard touchdown run by Tarkenton to make it 24-7 and that was the end of the scoring. Dolphin's running back Larry Csonka was named Super Bowl MVP. He ran for two touchdowns and 145 yards, which at time was a Super Bowl record. Miami only threw the ball seven times the entire game, a Super Bowl record for fewest pass attempts.

What Actually Happened?

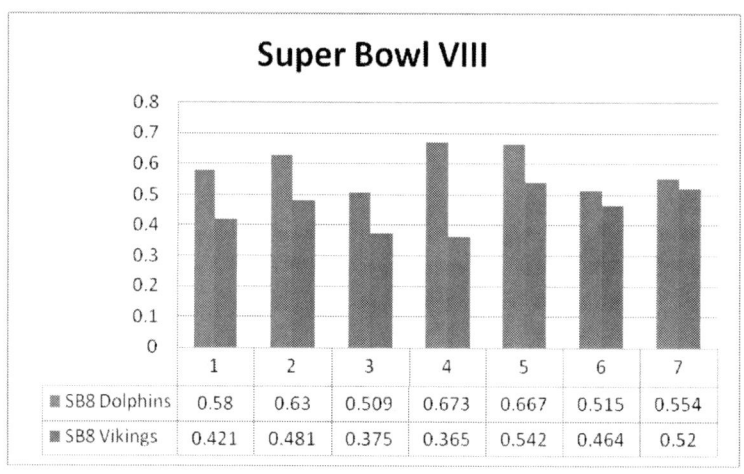

	MPI-T	MPI-O	MPI-D	MPI-ST	MPI-OP	MPI-DP	MPI-TP
SB8 Dolphins	0.58	0.63	0.509	0.673	0.667	0.515	0.554
SB8 Vikings	0.421	0.481	0.375	0.365	0.542	0.464	0.52

Any way you look at this game, the Miami Dolphins completely annihilated the Minnesota Vikings and it happened mostly on offense, and more specifically running the ball. Consider these impressive rankings. The Dolphins were the 3rd overall best performing team in Super Bowl history (MPI-T=.580) only behind the Bears of Super Bowl 20 and the 49ers of Super Bowl 19. Even better, Miami was the 2nd most dominant team (MPI-TD=.159) only behind the Bears. They were the 2nd in error free play (T+P=1) with only 1 penalty and no turnovers, 3rd in points allowed (7), 1st in special teams dominance (MPI-STD=.308), 3rd in special teams performance (MPI-ST=.673), 3rd in offensive performance (MPI-O=.630), and 3rd in offensive dominance (MPI-OD=.255). It quickly becomes clear that this team was easily one of the top 5 teams of all time and an argument could be made for them being the best of all time.

To the Vikings credit, they did reasonably well on offense in pressure moments (MPI-OP=.542) but it was only enough to generate 7 points on the scoreboard and Miami was never threatened. They also had the 18th ranking on yards allowed (259) but that was primarily because quarterback Bob Griese did not have to throw more than 7 passes, completing 6 for a passer rating of 110.1.

In sum, Miami moved the ball at will with MVP fullback Larry Csonka who gained 145 yards on 33 carries. They scored after long and methodical drives and let the clock do the rest. When you can win this way there is no reason to pass. Credit must also go to an offensive line led by Wayne Moore, Bob Kuechenberg, Jim Langer, Larry Little, and Norm Evans, and to Don Shula and his coaching staff for using an innovative cross block scheme to frustrate the Viking's defensive line all day.

Dr. John's Super Bowl 8 Lesson

"Why use nuclear weapons if stone-age battering rams work?"

Passing wasn't even necessary as the Miami Dolphins offensive line so completely dominated the Minnesota Vikings' defensive line. Shula's innovative cross-block and other blocking schemes made it even more difficult for the hapless Vikings defenders to do anything productive. This was an awesome display of power running. The degree of domination was so total that this is one of the best teams ever, if not the very best. Some will be surprised to learn that this team totally outperformed the Dolphins "perfect season" 1972 team of the year before. There is no comparison. The 1973 team played much better. If not for the World Football League stealing Csonka, Kiick and Warfield the next season, Miami might have easily won three more Super Bowl titles.

Super Bowl 17 – January 30, 1983 – Rose Bowl, Pasadena, CA

Washington Redskins 27 (.572) Miami Dolphins 17 (.472)

Brief Game Review

Super Bowl XVII between Coach Don Shula's Miami Dolphins and Coach Joe Gibbs' Washington Redskins came at the end of a strike shortened season. The 1982 season began with a 57-day long NFL players strike forcing the league to reduce the season to a 9 game schedule. The playoff format was altered to a 16-team format with 8 teams making the playoffs from each conference. This was the only season where division standings didn't matter.

The Redskins finished first in the NFC with an 8-1 record. They were led by their great quarterback Joe Theismann, a group of burly offensive linemen known as the "hogs" and a deadly accurate kicker, Mark Moseley, who became the first placekicker ever to win the NFL most valuable player. The Dolphins finished the season second in the

AFC with a 7-2 record. They were led by their very tough and league leading defense nicknamed the "Killer Bees" because six out of their eleven starters' last names started with a B.

Miami opened up the scoring on their second possession when quarterback David Woodley hit wide receiver Jimmy Cefalo for a 76 yard touchdown pass. On the Dolphins next possession the Redskins recovered Woodley's fumble and kicked a field goal. On the ensuing kickoff, Miami returned almost to midfield and then drove to the 3, but the Redskins defense held and forced a 20-yard field goal giving Miami only a 10-3 lead. The Redskins next drive would be a preview for how they ultimately won this game, pounding away at an 80 yard ball control drive in 11 plays and scoring on Alvin Garret's 4 yard TD reception to tie the game at 10-10 with less then two minutes in the half. On the ensuing kickoff, Miami's Fulton Walker returned the kick for a 98 yard touchdown to take a 17-10 lead into half. Walker's kickoff return for a touchdown was the first in Super Bowl history.

The Redskins fought back admirably and consistently in the second half, but it still seemed like the Dolphins had a chance when AJ Duhe intercepted quarterback Joe Theismann late in the third quarter. The Redskins' Mark Murphy soon intercepted Woodley, however, and the much better team ultimately won this game. Perhaps one of the most iconic plays came late in the third quarter when Dolphins lineman Kim Bokamper tipped a Theismann pass into the air deep in the Redskins zone and appeared about to catch it and run for a game changing touchdown. Instead, Joe Theismann dove at the ball at precisely the last fraction of a second and knocked it away to save the day for Washington.

The Redskins hogs had been pounding the Miami line all day and their momentum was about to pay off. With Miami hanging on for dear life and a 17-13 lead with just a little more than 10 minutes left, the Redskins faced a fourth and one from the Dolphin's 43 yard line. Riggins had been running well and Coach Gibbs decided to go for it. In the most memorable play of the game, a run to the left called "70-Chip," John Riggins followed perfect blocking by the hogs to his left and cornerback Don McNeal, the only player with a chance to make the play, slipped a little and then tried to tackle Riggins too high. Riggins ran through the defense and onto a 43 yard sprint for the touchdown that won the game.

The game was won by an old fashioned slugfest. Washington would hold Miami to a mere 34 yards in the second half, allowing only two first downs and no pass completions. The Redskins won the way the Dolphins were familiar to winning in the past with great blocking and punishing running not unlike Super Bowl VIII. After the game Dolphins left tackle, Bob Kuechenberg, would say, "Their way is what we called Dolphin football. They controlled the second half and they're fitting world champions."

Washington Redskins running back John Riggins won the Super Bowl MVP award with his 166 yards rushing yards and a touchdown. Riggins also set two Super Bowl records in the game. He had the most rushing yards in a Super Bowl with 166 and the most rushing attempts by one player in a Super Bowl with 38.

What Actually Happened?

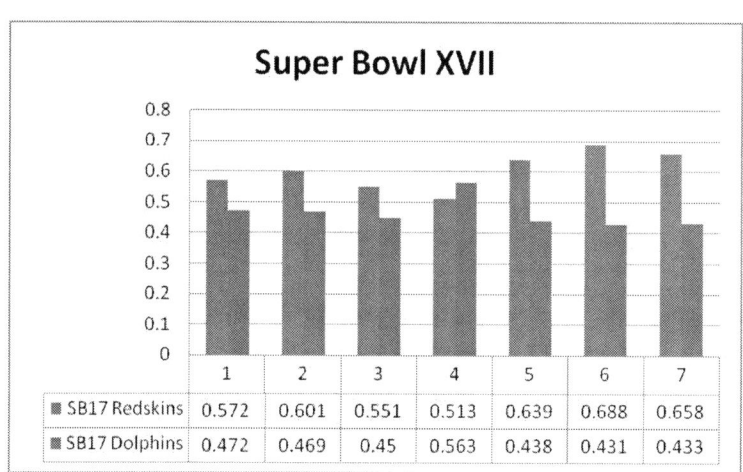

MPI-T MPI-O MPI-D MPI-ST MPI-OP MPI-DP MPI-TP

This performance by the Redskins was the fifth best pure performance in Super Bowl history as shown on MPI-T (.572). A closer analysis reveals why. Washington was 2nd in net rushing yards (276), 4th overall in net yards differential, 6th in pressure moments of the game as seen on MPI-TP (.658), 6th in net yards allowed (176), 9th in total dominance on MPI-TD (.100), and 11th on defense (.551).

Considering the domination by the Redskins in this game, it is amazing that the Dolphins were even in the game. The Redskins should have put the Dolphins away much earlier in the game but the Dolphins were very successful on two huge plays resulting in 14 points, a 76 yard touchdown pass to Jimmy Cefalo and a 98 yard kickoff return by Fulton Walker. This forced Washington to bear down, focus and execute and they did just that in a most overwhelming fashion to avert a rare upset when they clearly had the upper hand in terms of performance.

This game shows just how fragile victory can be. While the best team usually wears down a much weaker opponent, as the Redskins clearly did, a few big plays can also change history dramatically. If not for Joe Theismann's head's up "smart play" in knocking the ball away the Dolphins might have won their third Super Bowl title and a better performing team would have lost as has happened only 4 times in 44 Super Bowl games. As it stood, the Redskins displayed tremendous balance and power, especially in running the ball, and they should be extremely proud of being the 5th best of all time. The Dolphins almost pulled a rabbit out of their hat and were just one big play from doing so!

Dr. John's Super Bowl 17 Lesson

"When you are better like the Redskins you are still vulnerable."

You need to scrap, claw and fight even harder like the Hogs, John Riggins and Joe Theismann because your opponent will be even more aggressive, creative and resourceful.

Super Bowl 18 – January 22, 1984 – Tampa Stadium, Tampa, FL

Los Angeles Raiders 38 (.553) Washington Redskins 9 (.453)

Brief Game Review

Coach Joe Gibbs' Washington Redskins came into this game as three point favorites over Coach Tom Flores' Los Angeles Raiders. The Redskins had beaten the Raiders in the regular season and some say they were a little overconfident going into this game. Washington had finished the regular season an NFL best 14-2. Gibbs' offense, led by quarterback Joe Theismann, NFL MVP in 2003, had scored 541 points in 1983, a new NFL record. He had passed for 3,714 yards and 29 touchdowns. Washington also had a very strong defensive line which limited opposing teams to 1,289 yards rushing, tops in the NFL.

The Los Angeles Raiders reached the Super Bowl on a 12-4 record featuring running back Marcus Allen who had rushed for more than 1,000 yards and scored 11 touchdowns in only his second NFL season. Raiders' quarterback Jim Plunkett had thrown for 2,935 yards and 20 touchdowns. Pro Bowlers Matt Millen, Rod Martin, Lyle Alzado and Howie Long marshaled a very strong Raider defense.

The Raiders got on the scoreboard in the 1st quarter when Derrick Jensen blocked a punt into the end zone and recovered for a touchdown and a quick 7-0 lead. Then early in the 2nd quarter Plunkett connected with wide receiver Cliff Branch for a 12-yard touchdown pass and a 14-0 lead. The Redskins came back with an impressive 73 yard drive to the Raiders 7, but were stopped and settled for a 24-yard field goal. After the Raiders were forced to punt, quarterback Joe Theismann made perhaps the biggest mistake of the game. Throwing a pass with only 12 seconds left in the half and backed up to his 12 yard line, his pass was intercepted by Raider linebacker Jack Squirek for an easy touchdown and a 21-3 Raider halftime lead.

The Redskins charged out in the second half, drove down the field, and scored on a 1-yard John Riggins run on a drive reminiscent of Super Bowl XVII. The extra point was blocked, but the Redskins had 9 points on the board. The Raiders wasted no time in replying with their own drive, scoring on Marcus Allen's 5 yard touchdown run for a 28-9 Raiders' lead. The Redskins never threatened again but the Raiders added another touchdown and field goal before the final whistle and a 38-9 victory. Marcus Allen was named Super Bowl MVP for his 191 yards rushing and 2 touchdowns. The Raiders became the first team in Super Bowl history to score a touchdown on offense, defense, and special teams.

<u>What Actually Happened?</u>

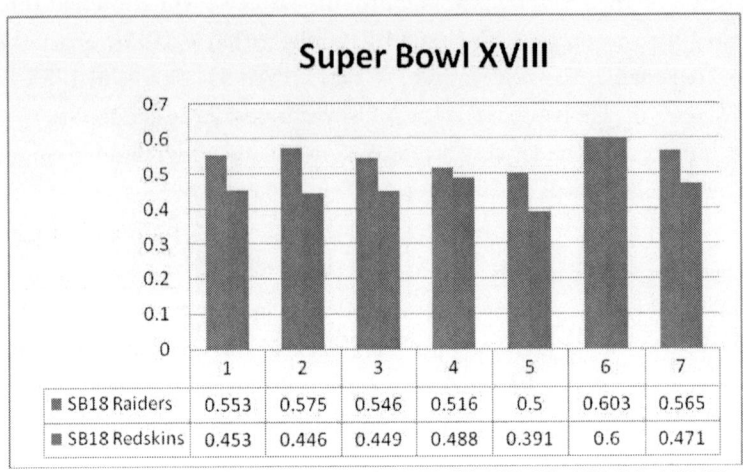

Super Bowl XVIII

	1	2	3	4	5	6	7
■ SB18 Raiders	0.553	0.575	0.546	0.516	0.5	0.603	0.565
■ SB18 Redskins	0.453	0.446	0.449	0.488	0.391	0.6	0.471

MPI-T MPI-O MPI-D MPI-ST MPI-OP MPI-DP MPI-TP

The Los Angeles Raiders were the 8th best pure performing team of all time in this game (MPI-T=.553) and the graph above shows that they were better in each of the 7 MPI categories. It was a classic whipping by a team that was a 3 point underdog. They were also the 9th most dominant team (MPI-TD=.100).

The Raiders achieved their success primarily with a fabulous running game, led by MVP Marcus Allen (191 yards on just 20 carries), and it was 6th best in Super Bowl history in net yards rushing (231). They showed balance on both sides of the ball as the 15th best overall offense (MPI-O=.575) and 13th best defense (.546) too. Corners Mike Haynes and Lester Hayes were outstanding and it changed Washington's game plan by taking away their air threat. It was the 8th most points scored (38) and 5th greatest point differential (29).

The Redskins were overmatched in this game. Congrats to Coach Tom Flores and his staff for getting the team ready with his "total commitment" message, congrats to Jim Plunkett for his second Super Bowl title, and congrats to the entire Raiders organization for a day that became known to the Redskins as "Black Sunday."

Dr. John's Super Bowl 18 Lesson

"Put the past behind you and make a total commitment"

The Redskins were the favorite, they had beaten the Raiders in the regular season and most thought they would do so again. Rather than be intimidated, the Silver and Black bought into Tom Flores' "total commitment" message and just went out and gave the Redskins a good old fashioned whipping.

Chapter Four: Where Does Your Team Rank?

"Whatever you are, be a good one."
—Abraham Lincoln

Top Teams in Every Category
(Note: Teams with the same rank have the same score)
Results of MPI BOWL I

Best Teams Ever: Top 32 Teams

    Below are the Top 32 performing teams that have played in the first 44 Super Bowl Games from 1967 to 2010. The list will be updated each year based on the new Super Bowl game played. The top team on the list is the current MPI Bowl I Champion. This list is based on performance in one game in a comprehensive manner as reflected on the MPI Total score. It is about performance and not outcome. This list represents the teams that were overall best based on their play on Super Bowl Sunday, not during the season. Feel free to disagree. It is based on how the team actually performed, and it includes mental factors too!

MPI BOWL I RESULTS

RANK	32 BEST TEAMS	MPI-T
1	Bears-Super Bowl-20	0.591
2	49ers-Super Bowl-19	0.586
3	Dolphins-Super Bowl-8	0.580
4	49ers-Super Bowl-24	0.574
5	Redskins-Super Bowl-17	0.572
6	49ers-Super Bowl-29	0.563
7	Steelers-Super Bowl-14	0.557

8	Raiders-Super Bowl-18	0.553
9	Raiders-Super Bowl-11	0.551
9	Redskins-Super Bowl-26	0.551
11	Buccaneers-Super Bowl-37	0.550
12	Chiefs-Super Bowl-4	0.549
12	Ravens-Super Bowl-35	0.549
14	Packers-Super Bowl-1	0.548
14	Redskins-Super Bowl-22	0.548
14	Cowboys-Super Bowl-27	0.548
14	Saints-Super Bowl-44	0.548
18	Packers-Super Bowl-2	0.547
19	Giants-Super Bowl-21	0.545
20	Jets-Super Bowl-3	0.543
20	Steelers-Super Bowl-10	0.543
22	Cowboys-Super Bowl-28	0.540
23	Steelers-Super Bowl-9	0.539
23	Packers-Super Bowl-31	0.539
25	Cowboys-Super Bowl-6	0.538
25	49ers-Super Bowl-16	0.538
27	Broncos-Super Bowl-33	0.531
28	Colts-Super Bowl-41	0.525
29	Raiders-Super Bowl-15	0.523
30	49ers-Super Bowl-23	0.521
31	Patriots-Super Bowl-39	0.518
32	Patriots-Super Bowl-38	0.516

25 Best Teams in Other Categories

RANK	TEAM	MPI-TD	RANK	TEAM	MPI-TP
1	BearsSB20	0.180	1	PackersSB1	0.716
2	DolphinsSB8	0.159	2	RaidersSB11	0.700
3	49ersSB24	0.158	3	BearsSB20	0.688
4	ChiefsSB4	0.140	4	SteelersSB14	0.675
4	49ersSB19	0.140	5	49ersSB24	0.663
6	RedskinsSB22	0.129	6	RedskinsSB17	0.658
7	RavensSB35	0.128	7	EaglesSB39	0.657
8	49ersSB29	0.115	8	CowboysSB6	0.655
9	RedskinsSB17	0.100	9	GiantsSB25	0.650
9	RaidersSB18	0.100	10	VikingsSB9	0.641
11	RaidersSB11	0.098	11	49ersSB29	0.630
12	BuccaneersSB37	0.097	12	49ersSB16	0.620
13	CowboysSB6	0.093	13	DolphinsSB7	0.619
14	PatriotsSB38	0.092	14	49ersSB19	0.618
15	JetsSB3	0.086	15	GiantsSB42	0.615
15	SteelersSB9	0.086	16	ColtsSB41	0.611
17	PackersSB1	0.084	17	ChiefsSB4	0.596
18	RedskinsSB26	0.082	18	BroncosSB33	0.594
19	PackersSB2	0.081	19	ColtsSB44	0.583
20	GiantsSB21	0.078	20	JetsSB3	0.580
21	CowboysSB27	0.076	21	BroncosSB32	0.567
22	CowboysSB28	0.074	22	RaidersSB18	0.565
23	SaintsSB44	0.068	23	PatriotsSB38	0.556
24	49ersSB23	0.061	24	DolphinsSB8	0.554
25	SteelersSB14	0.055	25	SteelersSB43	0.550

RANK	TEAM	MPI-TPD	RANK	TEAM	MPI-O
1	PackersSB1	0.368	1	49ersSB19	0.646
2	ChiefsSB4	0.363	2	49ersSB29	0.641
2	BearsSB20	0.363	3	DolphinsSB8	0.630
4	CowboysSB6	0.345	4	SaintsSB44	0.618

RANK	TEAM		RANK	TEAM	
5	RaidersSB11	0.325	5	BroncosSB33	0.615
5	49ersSB24	0.325	6	49ersSB24	0.609
7	49ersSB29	0.315	7	GiantsSB21	0.608
8	GiantsSB25	0.270	8	RaidersSB11	0.604
9	RedskinsSB17	0.225	9	RedskinsSB17	0.601
10	49ersSB19	0.223	10	PackersSB1	0.597
11	EaglesSB39	0.222	11	CowboysSB6	0.592
12	RedskinsSB22	0.198	12	49ersSB16	0.582
13	JetsSB3	0.187	13	RedskinsSB22	0.580
14	VikingsSB9	0.183	14	ColtsSB44	0.576
15	ColtsSB41	0.169	15	RaidersSB18	0.575
16	49ersSB16	0.165	16	FalconsSB33	0.574
17	GiantsSB42	0.164	17	RaidersSB15	0.570
18	DolphinsSB7	0.153	18	BroncosSB32	0.566
19	SteelersSB43	0.150	19	BengalsSB16	0.565
20	SteelersSB14	0.149	20	PatriotsSB38	0.564
21	BroncosSB33	0.139	21	GiantsSB25	0.563
22	BroncosSB32	0.136	22	BearsSB20	0.559
23	CowboysSB28	0.135	23	JetsSB3	0.555
24	RavensSB35	0.134	23	CowboysSB27	0.555
25	PatriotsSB38	0.121	25	CowboysSB28	0.553

RANK	TEAM	MPI-OD	RANK	TEAM	MPI-OP
1	49ersSB19	0.297	1	PackersSB1	0.775
2	49ersSB29	0.258	2	49ersSB16	0.731
3	DolphinsSB8	0.255	3	49ersSB29	0.682
4	SaintsSB44	0.236	4	DolphinsSB8	0.667
5	49ersSB24	0.228	4	49ersSB24	0.667
6	CowboysSB6	0.208	4	EaglesSB39	0.667
7	GiantsSB21	0.203	7	SteelersSB13	0.654
8	BroncosSB33	0.200	8	SteelersSB14	0.650
9	RedskinsSB22	0.197	9	BearsSB20	0.646
10	PackersSB1	0.183	10	RedskinsSB17	0.639
11	RaidersSB11	0.166	11	GiantsSB42	0.625
12	PatriotsSB38	0.158	12	BroncosSB33	0.615

RANK	Team		RANK	Team	
13	RedskinsSB17	0.151	13	GiantsSB21	0.614
14	RedskinsSB26	0.143	14	GiantsSB25	0.603
15	49ersSB16	0.142	15	CowboysSB6	0.596
16	RaidersSB15	0.136	16	BroncosSB21	0.583
17	BearsSB20	0.133	17	VikingsSB9	0.575
18	BroncosSB32	0.132	17	RaidersSB11	0.575
19	ColtsSB44	0.127	19	ColtsSB44	0.567
20	RaidersSB18	0.126	20	ChiefsSB4	0.563
21	JetsSB3	0.124	20	SteelersSB40	0.563
22	GiantsSB25	0.114	22	ColtsSB41	0.559
23	BillsSB25	0.112	23	CowboysSB13	0.558
24	CowboysSB28	0.110	24	BengalsSB16	0.554
25	49ersSB23	0.108	25	VikingsSB8	0.542
			25	RaidersSB15	0.542
			25	PatriotsSB38	0.542

RANK	Team	MPI-OPD	RANK	TEAM	MPI-D
1	PackersSB1	0.480	1	SteelersSB9	0.653
2	49ersSB29	0.432	2	RavensSB35	0.637
3	49ersSB16	0.374	3	BearsSB20	0.622
4	ChiefsSB4	0.341	4	CowboysSB12	0.595
5	BearsSB20	0.292	5	ChiefsSB4	0.587
5	49ersSB24	0.292	6	SteelersSB10	0.586
7	SteelersSB13	0.289	7	BuccaneersSB37	0.585
8	CowboysSB6	0.269	8	PackersSB31	0.575
9	EaglesSB39	0.250	9	SteelersSB14	0.568
10	RedskinsSB17	0.208	10	49ersSB24	0.557
11	DolphinsSB8	0.203	11	RedskinsSB17	0.551
12	RedskinsSB22	0.198	12	ColtsSB5	0.550
13	GiantsSB21	0.182	13	RaidersSB18	0.546
14	GiantsSB42	0.181	14	RedskinsSB26	0.541
15	CowboysSB13	0.173	15	CowboysSB10	0.540
16	JetsSB3	0.150	15	ColtsSB41	0.540
17	GiantsSB25	0.147	17	49ersSB19	0.536
18	BroncosSB33	0.136	18	JetsSB3	0.532

RANK	TEAM	
19	CowboysSB28	0.129
20	SteelersSB14	0.122
21	SteelersSB40	0.113
22	BroncosSB21	0.104
23	PatriotsSB38	0.095
24	49ersSB23	0.073
25	ColtsSB44	0.067

RANK	TEAM	MPI-DD
1	RavensSB35	0.312
2	SteelersSB9	0.286
3	BearsSB20	0.260
4	CowboysSB12	0.229
5	ChiefsSB4	0.217
6	49ersSB24	0.157
7	BuccaneersSB37	0.157
8	ColtsSB5	0.152
9	SteelersSB10	0.144
10	CowboysSB5	0.135
11	RedskinsSB22	0.129
12	PackersSB31	0.118
13	RaidersSB18	0.100
14	RedskinsSB17	0.082
15	ColtsSB41	0.078
16	SteelersSB14	0.077
17	PackersSB2	0.068
18	49ersSB23	0.061
19	RedskinsSB26	0.060
20	RaidersSB11	0.060
21	GiantsSB42	0.057
22	JetsSB3	0.052
23	PatriotsSB31	0.048
24	CowboysSB27	0.045
25	VikingsSB9	0.038

RANK	TEAM	
18	PatriotsSB31	0.532
20	RedskinsSB22	0.531
21	PackersSB2	0.529
22	GiantsSB42	0.526
23	CowboysSB5	0.525
24	49ersSB23	0.523
25	PatriotsSB42	0.520

RANK	TEAM	MPI-DP
1	RaidersSB11	0.825
2	RavensSB35	0.771
3	CowboysSB6	0.750
3	DolphinsSB7	0.750
3	49ersSB19	0.750
3	BearsSB20	0.750
3	GiantsSB25	0.750
8	SteelersSB14	0.700
8	ColtsSB41	0.700
10	CowboysSB12	0.696
11	RedskinsSB7	0.694
12	VikingsSB9	0.692
13	PackersSB2	0.688
13	RedskinsSB17	0.688
15	PatriotsSB31	0.683
16	CowboysSB5	0.682
17	SteelersSB30	0.675
18	PackersSB1	0.667
18	ColtsSB5	0.667
18	SteelersSB10	0.667
21	49ersSB24	0.656
21	SteelersSB43	0.656
23	RaidersSB2	0.654
24	ChiefsSB4	0.650
25	EaglesSB39	0.646

RANK	TEAM	MPI-DPD	RANK	TEAM	MPI-ST
1	RaidersSB11	0.600	1	CowboysSB27	0.708
2	RavensSB35	0.544	2	SaintsSB44	0.703
3	GiantsSB25	0.531	3	DolphinsSB8	0.673
4	ColtsSB5	0.479	4	CowboysSB28	0.671
5	49ersSB19	0.475	5	DolphinsSB19	0.636
6	CowboysSB6	0.469	6	ChiefsSB4	0.635
6	BearsSB20	0.469	6	SteelersSB40	0.635
8	DolphinsSB7	0.442	8	FalconsSB33	0.633
9	CowboysSB5	0.432	9	49ersSB16	0.631
10	ColtsSB41	0.425	10	SteelersSB14	0.618
11	CowboysSB12	0.413	10	BearsSB20	0.618
12	ChiefsSB4	0.400	12	PackersSB2	0.615
13	49ersSB24	0.375	13	BillsSB26	0.609
14	VikingsSB9	0.353	14	BroncosSB22	0.605
15	PackersSB2	0.344	15	RedskinsSB26	0.597
16	PatriotsSB31	0.324	16	CowboysSB10	0.588
17	SteelersSB43	0.323	16	BengalsSB23	0.588
18	SteelersSB30	0.311	18	BuccaneersSB37	0.587
19	RedskinsSB7	0.288	19	PackersSB31	0.580
20	PackersSB1	0.271	20	DolphinsSB6	0.567
20	SteelersSB10	0.271	21	DolphinsSB17	0.563
22	BroncosSB12	0.267	21	BroncosSB24	0.563
23	RedskinsSB17	0.250	23	PatriotsSB36	0.559
24	49ersSB29	0.235	24	GiantsSB25	0.556
25	JetsSB3	0.231	24	BillsSB28	0.556

RANK	TEAM	MPI-STD	RANK	TEAM	T-G
1	DolphinsSB8	0.308	1	CowboysSB27	7
2	SaintsSB44	0.286	2	CowboysSB12	6
3	SteelersSB40	0.254	3	RavensSB35	5
4	49ersSB16	0.249	4	JetsSB3	4
5	ChiefsSB4	0.229	4	ChiefsSB4	4

RANK	TEAM		RANK	TEAM	
6	FalconsSB33	0.211	4	RaidersSB15	4
7	CowboysSB27	0.189	4	BearsSB20	4
8	SteelersSB43	0.181	4	49ersSB24	4
9	DolphinsSB19	0.162	4	RedskinsSB26	4
10	BroncosSB12	0.135	4	PackersSB31	4
11	DolphinsSB6	0.134	4	BuccaneersSB37	4
12	SteelersSB14	0.131	12	PackersSB2	3
13	BroncosSB22	0.121	12	CowboysSB5	3
14	BroncosSB32	0.120	12	SteelersSB9	3
15	BearsSB20	0.118	12	SteelersSB10	3
16	CowboysSB28	0.115	12	RaidersSB11	3
17	BengalsSB23	0.114	12	49ersSB16	3
18	RamsSB34	0.094	12	49ersSB29	3
19	ChargersSB29	0.091	12	CowboysSB30	3
20	CowboysSB5	0.083	12	BroncosSB33	3
21	PackersSB31	0.080	12	PatriotsSB36	3
22	DolphinsSB7	0.079	12	PatriotsSB39	3
23	BroncosSB24	0.078	23	CowboysSB6	2
23	SteelersSB30	0.078	23	DolphinsSB8	2
25	PAckersSB2	0.073	23	RamsSB14	2
			23	RedskinsSB22	2
			23	CowboysSB28	2
			23	ColtsSB41	2

RANK	TEAM	T+P	RANK	TEAM	TIME
1	SteelersSB10	0	1	GiantsSB25	2433
2	DolphinsSB8	1	2	49ersSB24	2371
2	PackersSB2	1	3	BearsSB20	2355
4	PackersSB31	3	4	CowboysSB6	2352
4	49ersSB29	3	5	PatriotsSB38	2338
4	SaintsSB44	3	6	SteelersSB9	2327
7	49ersSB24	4	7	CowboysSB12	2318
7	RaidersSB11	4	8	ColtsSB41	2284
7	CowboysSB30	4	9	BuccaneersSB37	2234
10	RaidersSB15	5	10	49ersSB19	2231

10	GiantsSB25	5	11	TitansSB34	2186
10	PatriotsSB36	5	12	RedskinsSB17	2175
13	GiantsSB21	6	13	JetsSB3	2170
13	BillsSB25	6	14	PackersSB2	2154
15	TitansSB34	7	15	RedskinsSB22	2115
16	RamsSB34	8	16	GiantsSB21	2079
17	RavensSB35	9	17	ChiefsSB4	2073
18	RamsSB14	3	18	CowboysSB28	2069
19	CowboysSB6	4	19	PackersSB31	2055
20	PackersSB1	5	20	RavensSB35	2046
20	ChiefsSB1	5	21	SteelersSB30	2029
20	ChiefsSB4	5	22	DolphinsSB8	2025
20	BroncosSB33	5	23	RedskinsSB26	2023
20	GiantsSB42	5	24	CowboysSB13	2022
20	BroncosSB21	5	25	RamsSB36	2010
20	49ersSB23	5			

RANK	TEAM	POINTS SCORED	RANK	TEAM	PTS GIVEN
1	49ersSB24	55	1	CowboysSB6	3
2	CowboysSB27	52	2	SteelersSB9	6
3	49ersSB29	49	3	JetsSB3	7
4	BuccaneersSB37	48	3	ChiefsSB4	7
5	BearsSB20	46	3	DolphinsSB7	7
6	RedskinsSB22	42	3	DolphinsSB8	7
7	GiantsSB21	39	3	RavensSB35	7
8	RaidersSB18	38	8	RaidersSB18	9
8	49ersSB19	38	9	PackersSB1	10
10	RedskinsSB26	37	9	CowboysSB12	10
11	PackersSB1	35	9	RaidersSB15	10
11	SteelersSB13	35	9	BearsSB20	10
11	PackersSB31	35	9	RedskinsSB22	10
14	BroncosSB33	34	9	49ersSB24	10

14	RavensSB35	34
16	PackersSB2	33
17	RaidersSB11	32
17	PatriotsSB38	32
19	CowboysSB13	31
19	SteelersSB14	31
19	BroncosSB32	31
19	SaintsSB44	31
23	CowboysSB28	30
24	PanthersSB38	29
24	ColtsSB41	29

9	SteelersSB40	10
16	ColtsSB5	13
16	CowboysSB28	13
18	PackersSB2	14
18	RedskinsSB7	14
18	RaidersSB11	14
18	GiantsSB42	14
22	ColtsSB3	16
22	CowboysSB5	16
22	VikingsSB9	16
22	49ersSB19	16
22	49ersSB23	16
22	RamsSB34	16

RANK	TEAM	POINT DIFF.	RANK	TEAM	YARDS GAINED
1	49ersSB24	45	1	RedskinsSB22	602
2	BearsSB20	36	2	49ersSB19	537
3	CowboysSB27	35	3	PatriotsSB38	481
4	RedskinsSB22	32	4	49ersSB24	461
5	RaidersSB18	29	5	BroncosSB33	457
6	RavensSB35	27	6	49ersSB29	455
6	BuccaneersSB37	27	7	49ersSB23	453
8	PackersSB1	25	8	RamsSB34	436
9	49ersSB29	23	9	ColtsSB44	432
10	49ersSB19	22	10	ColtsSB41	430
11	CowboysSB6	21	11	RaidersSB11	429
12	PAckersSB2	19	12	RamsSB36	427
12	GiantsSB21	19	13	RedskinsSB26	417
14	RaidersSB11	18	14	BearsSB20	408
15	DolphinsSB8	17	14	CowboysSB27	408
15	CowboysSB12	17	16	CardinalsSB43	407
15	RaidersSB15	17	17	RedskinsSB17	400

RANK	TEAM		RANK	TEAM	
15	CowboysSB28	17	18	GiantsSB21	399
19	ChiefsSB4	16	19	SeahawksSB40	396
20	BroncosSB33	15	20	SteelersSB14	393
21	PackersSB31	14	21	PanthersSB38	387
21	SaintsSB44	14	22	GiantsSB25	386
23	RedskinsSB26	13	23	RaidersSB18	385
24	SteelersSB14	12	24	RaidersSB15	377
24	ColtsSB41	12	25	BroncosSB21	372

RANK	TEAM	YARDS GIVEN	RANK	TEAM	YARDS DIFF.
1	SteelersSB9	119	1	49ersSB24	294
2	BearsSB20	123	2	BearsSB20	285
3	RavensSB35	152	3	RedskinsSB22	275
4	CowboysSB12	156	4	RedskinsSB17	224
5	49ersSB24	167	4	49ersSB23	224
6	RedskinsSB17	176	6	49ersSB19	223
7	CowboysSB6	185	7	SteelersSB9	214
8	ColtsSB5	215	8	CowboysSB12	169
9	DolphinsSB7	228	9	CowboysSB6	167
10	49ersSB23	229	10	ColtsSB41	165
11	DolphinsSB8	238	11	RamsSB36	160
12	PackersSB1	239	12	RedskinsSB26	134
12	ChiefsSB4	239	13	PackersSB1	122
14	GiantsSB35	244	14	BroncosSB33	120
15	RedskinsSB7	253	15	CardinalsSB43	115
16	SteelersSB30	254	16	ColtsSB5	114
17	PackersSB31	257	17	RaidersSB18	102
18	VikingsSB8	259	18	49ersSB29	101
19	ColtsSB41	265	19	ColtsSB44	100
20	RamsSB36	267	20	BuccaneersSB37	96
21	BuccaneersSB37	269	21	PatriotsSB38	94
22	SteelersSB10	270	22	SteelersSB14	92

RANK	TEAM		RANK	TEAM	
23	VikingsSB4	273	22	RavensSB35	92
24	GiantsSB42	274	24	BengalsSB16	81
25	BengalsSB16	275	25	RaidersSB11	76

RANK	TEAM	RUSH YARDS	RANK	TEAM	PASSING YARDS
1	RedskinsSB22	280	1	RamsSB34	407
2	RedskinsSB17	276	2	CardinalsSB43	374
3	RaidersSB11	266	3	PatriotsSB38	354
4	CowboysSB6	252	4	49ersSB23	341
5	SteelersSB9	249	5	RamsSB36	337
6	RaidersSB18	231	6	BroncosSB33	336
7	49ersSB19	211	7	ColtsSB44	333
8	DolphinsSB8	196	8	49ersSB19	326
9	ColtsSB41	191	9	EaglesSB39	324
10	DolphinsSB7	184	10	RedskinsSB22	322
11	SteelersSB40	181	11	BroncosSB21	320
12	BroncosSB32	179	12	49ersSB24	317
13	GiantsSB25	172	13	49ersSB29	316
14	BearsSB20	167	14	SteelersSB14	309
15	BillsSB25	166	15	PanthersSB38	295
16	PackersSB2	160	16	RedskinsSB26	292
17	TitansSB34	159	17	SteelersSB13	291
18	CowboysSB13	154	17	EaglesSB15	291
19	ChiefsSB4	151	19	DolphinsSB19	289
20	BuccaneersSB37	150	20	ChargersSB29	287
21	SteelersSB10	149	21	BengalsSB16	284
22	49ersSB24	144	22	VikingsSB11	282
23	ColtsSB3	143	23	SaintsSB44	281
23	CowboysSB12	143	24	CowboysSB27	271
25	JetsSB3	142	25	GiantsSB21	263

RANK	TEAM	TOTAL PENAL-TIES	RANK	TEAM	YARDS PENAL-IZED
1	DolphinsSB6	0	1	DolphinsSB6	0
1	SteelersSB10	0	1	SteelersSB10	0
1	BroncosSB24	0	1	BroncosSB24	0
1	FalconsSB33	0	1	FalconsSB33	0
5	PackersSB2	1	5	DolphinsSB8	4
5	DolphinsSB8	1	6	49ersSB19	10
5	DolphinsSB19	1	6	DolphinsSB19	10
5	BillsSB28	1	6	BillsSB28	10
9	CowboysSB10	2	9	PackersSB2	12
9	VikingsSB11	2	10	CowboysSB6	15
9	RamsSB14	2	10	SteelersSB30	15
9	49ersSB19	2	12	VikingsSB9	18
9	SteelersSB30	2	12	49ersSB29	18
9	PatriotsSB31	2	14	SaintsSB44	19
15	ColtsSB3	3	15	CowboysSB10	20
15	CowboysSB6	3	15	SteelersSB40	20
15	DolphinsSB7	3	17	PatriotsSB31	22
15	RedskinsSB7	3	18	ColtsSB3	23
15	49ersSB29	3	19	RedskinsSB7	25
15	PackersSB31	3	19	VikingsSB11	25
15	EaglesSB39	3	19	CowboysSB30	25
15	SteelersSB40	3	22	ChiefsSB1	26
15	SaintsSB44	3	22	RamsSB14	26
24	PackersSB1	4	22	BroncosSB22	26
24	ChiefsSB1	4	25	GiantsSB35	27

THE 17 TEAMS WITH
NO TURNOVERS

PackersSB2

DolphinsSB8

SteelersSB10

RaidersSB11

RaidersSB15

GiantsSB21

49ersSB24

GiantsSB25

BillsSB25

49ersSB29

CowboysSB30

PackersSB31

RamsSB34

TitansSB34

RavensSB35

PatriotsSB36

SaintsSB44

Chapter Five: Win a Championship with the MPI and Sports Psychology

"You don't win once in a while, you don't do things right once in a while ... you do them right all the time."
-- Vince Lombardi

Introducing the MPI to a Football Team

Is Winning Important?

Anyone seriously interested in football wants to win. This applies to the head coach of an NFL team just as much as it does to the high school player trying to make his varsity team for the first time and to fans in every major city. It applies also to what I do, and it is the main reason why I developed the Mental Performance Index. I want to help teams win.

If football and other sports did not have this innate competitiveness, I would find a more worthwhile way to spend my time. Human beings reach their highest states when striving for great achievements. I honestly developed the MPI so that I could one day stand on the sidelines with an NFL team as the head coach was receiving the Lombardi Trophy and know that my contribution played some small role in that team's achievement. My fascination with the ultimate accomplishment applies to other sports too. I'd also love to someday do my part to help teams win Stanley Cups, World Series titles, NBA championships and why stop there? But football holds a special place in my heart and mind, so I developed the MPI for football first. There will be future extensions of the MPI to other sports, but let's do football first.

Relationship with Head Coach

The first thing any head football coach who hires me needs to realize is that I provide him a professional service that he uses as he sees fit. What each coach decides to do with the MPI data and other strategies I provide are for him to decide. I later offer suggestions on the best way to utilize MPI data to help the team, but the coach must approve that before I begin. Like an assistant coach, or athletic trainer, I can be a leader on a team and offer my input as requested, but I am not the main team leader; the head coach is, and I respect that boundary.

Some coaches who are reading this right now might fear the unknown or have concerns about what his players are saying and being told. This is totally understandable. The coach is responsible for the success of the team. At an early meeting with the coach, I think it is crucial to work out logistics in terms of who I will be working with, who will be receiving my reports and suggestions for team improvement, and how I will fit into the organizational structure. My involvement can range anywhere from only having direct contact with the head coach, and giving him advice when necessary, to being granted full access to the coaching and training staff in order to develop programs throughout the organization. The sky is the limit to what we can do, but the scope of my responsibilities needs to be worked out in advance with the coach or in some cases with the owner or a senior executive within the organization who would like my input about his team.

Teams, staff, and executives need to know that I have a duty to preserve confidentiality in my work. However, it is often the case that the athletes encourage discussion with the head coach or any other coach. We are hammered about that for years in graduate school and in state licensing exams. I think our profession actually does a better job of ensuring client welfare than most other professions and that is because it is so important that our clients feel comfortable to give us information and know that we are protecting it. It allows them to open up more. We gain trust when our profession has strict guidelines that go even beyond what you may often see in medicine and law.

How MPI Data Helps

If you enjoyed chapter 3 where I provided a brief analysis and MPI report on every Super Bowl game played, you already have a good idea about how this ongoing information is useful to a team or coaching staff. You saw how the MPI was able to dig deeper than traditional statistics could because of what happened in the game mentally as well as physically on the field. So the first thing anyone considering using the MPI needs to do is sit back, relax and realize that by using this you are gaining a huge advantage over your opponent who is not using it. And your opponent, by definition, will not be using it because I will not allow a conflict of interest by working with two teams at the same time. So the MPI will never backfire on a team getting the service because the information can never be used this way by another team. It is confidential.

The first way the MPI data and reports help are by providing useful feedback to the coach immediately after a game is over or perhaps while a game is going on if I rate a game live. In this case I am able to give MPI scores at any point in the game because the computer program I use updates all the scores after each play rating is entered. More typical is to have a report to the coach or executive within 24 hours by email after receiving the tapes of the game or having seen the game live in person or on television. In consulting with teams, they usually overnight the offense, defense, and special teams' DVDs for my weekly analysis, or direct me on how to watch the game live or shortly after it is played.

Once the coach or executive receives the MPI report, he can then use that information, and especially my final section of recommendations, to formulate his plan for the week of training. Each report also contains an update summary and graph of how the team is performing week to week in key areas in order to alert him to any major changes so that he will be able to address the team as needed.

Knowledge is Power

I have expertise in statistics and even taught it at the graduate school level. But in writing this book, I took great pains to consult with a variety of other statisticians to be sure that I had established reliability and validity for the MPI. Sometimes I did the same analysis twice with a different firm just to make sure it was accurate. The point I am trying to make is that you can never have enough knowledge. If you are misinformed about something relating to your football team, all your great efforts leading up to the big game will be wasted or not used as efficiently as possible.

When I was coaching tennis at the Australian Open and other major tennis tournaments as a sports psychologist/fill-in coach, one of the first things my players wanted me to do after the match was to go to the ATP Tour office and get a printout of the statistics from that match. That would offer new insights into first-serve percentage, or success going to the net, for instance. That is exactly the same kind of information that you gain when you receive an MPI report on your team. You probably already have a good quality control program in place and this just supplements those efforts in a major way for the team or each unit. You have your fingers on knowledge that most will not have. Let's face it, I can't work for every team and there are a lot of teams, so it is likely especially now when the MPI is relatively new, to gain a huge advantage over your rivals. It begins with advanced intelligence about your team.

The other way it can be used is to scout an upcoming opponent. By also reviewing DVDs of the entire performance of an upcoming opponent, MPI reports can be generated so the coach is more prepared for the upcoming battle. He will know what he will face. Just as knowing oneself is key, knowing the competition is equally important. MPI reports like this are encouraged, keeping in mind that there will be no conflicts of interest allowed.

<u>Feedback Provides Confidence</u>

Whether the MPI report stops with the head coach or executive, or is shared with the entire team, there is no question that the feedback alone will enhance coach and team confidence. Just as KR (knowledge of results that we discussed in a previous chapter) helps an athlete greatly in his or her development and training, the MPI is a KR tool which leads to greater and faster skill acquisition and increased performance. It makes sense. How would you feel if when you took your car out for a drive the windshield in front of you was suddenly blocked and you had no idea if there was a car coming straight at you or if you were about to enter a major intersection. We use KR constantly in whatever we are doing. That is what our 5 senses provide us in our daily activities. In a similar way, think of the MPI report as a tool to enhance understanding and perception the same way a hearing aid increases sounds or a microscope helps a biologist to look over a culture. Coaches need this tool to know what they have first, so they can plan an appropriate course of action for the team. The result is a more effective and confident coach who places his energies more efficiently on the proper aspect of team development. Let's face it, we are all busy, and there are only so many hours in a day. Possessing the combined impact of knowledge and confidence is huge.

Goal Setting with the MPI

MPI reports provide a big picture view of team performance. Closer analyses by series, quarter or half are also possible. This information is provided in the report which then allows the football coach to set goals to help his team develop and also prepare for immediate challenges. We know from goal setting research that all kinds of goals are helpful. Short-term or daily goals, weekly goals, monthly goals and seasonal goals all make sense, and MPI data can be used to set such goals. For instance, let's say a team is struggling consistently in defensive pressure situations as shown on the MPI and their scores are averaging in the .460-.480 range. With this specific information, team or unit meetings can be arranged to discuss the problem, talk about what pressure situations are, how they are not being handled well, and setting a team goal to raise that .470 average above .500 within the next two weeks. Players are then held responsible for doing this and provided feedback about whether they accomplished that or not, and if not, what they can do better.

The beauty of the MPI is that it gives a specific and sensitive number that can be easily translated into goals. It is also user friendly because it can be explained in terms of how close the team or unit came to being "perfect" in a particular area. Keeping in mind that 1.000 is perfect, players gain a deep respect for how diligent they really do have to be, play by play, moment by moment. If one player decides to goof off for a play, it causes a significant drop in team rating in that area. He can be shown specifically how his behavior hurt the team on the rating rather then being given a more vague scolding that he might not buy into. In essence, by having a number that constantly changes play by play and that holds players accountable, teams enhance focus and confidence at the same time! People are sometimes funny. Unless you show them the mess they made or, on the other hand, the wonderful benefit they have provided to the team, they often don't get it. Numbers like the MPI are hard to argue with. How can you argue with degree of perfection? If you fall short, it is as clear as can be in both numerical and graphical form. If you succeed, you are rewarded and then set higher standards and higher goals to maintain that standard. The 1974 Pittsburgh Steelers and 2000 Baltimore Ravens established standards of defensive performance that went above .630 or 63% of perfection and these were the two best defenses in Super Bowl history. That is both humbling and inspiring. It is humbling in realizing that even the best teams in history left some 37% of performance on the field. It is inspiring, however, if your current average on defense is .510 and you set a goal to reach .560 by December -- and you reach that goal. A better word perhaps is "realistic," and realistic feedback in order to set smarter goals is one of the big winners in using the MPI. What's nice about the realistic rating system is that it punches you right in the face and you see where you can always get better. You can never be good enough! That keeps teams on their toes!

<u>Suggestions for Getting Started</u>

Let's say you are the head coach or major executive of an NFL, NCAA or high school football program and you would like to hire me to implement an MPI program and possibly a sports psychology/mental coaching program for your team, but you just don't know where to start. Here are some suggestions to help you out.

(1) Decide whether you would like this service to be kept between the sports psychologist and yourself, or extended to your coaching staff or entire team.

(2) Whatever you decide, get copies of this book for all interested parties. If you would like to make a dramatic change throughout your team, buy each player and coach a copy of this book and make it required reading. If it is just going to be for you, make sure to read the book before going forward.

(3) Keep it fun and serious too. If your coaching staff will be involved, assign each coach to read about a Super Bowl and report on what the MPI data showed for that game. Then discuss in group how that relates to your current team. Comparing and contrasting with great performances in history is now possible since the MPI stats are standardized, so your team can be compared with, say, the 1966 Packers. That alone inspires! By opening up these thoughts and discussions, and even putting a coach or player on the spot like this, you are also getting them to buy into your philosophy. In short time, you have them all on the same page pursuing the greatest team performance possible.

(4) During the season, publicly reward a coach representing the highest unit performance on the MPI by allowing him to discuss the MPI data and how they used it with their unit. The same applies to players. Let them talk about how they are having success and use the numbers as a way to introduce their discussion as they speak to represent a successful aspect of team performance.

(5) If you are really bold and would like to get everyone on board fast, post the MPI results in the locker room or training room, or give each player or coach a copy of the relevant information so that he is constantly appraised of how well he has performed. They already know if they won or lost the game, and this just provides added information to encourage discussion, and to discipline players as well when they are not living up to expectations. How the numbers are used is up to the coach, but my inclination would be to encourage openness. Get everyone on the same page striving for high ideals and pushing to get a higher MPI score. In essence, do everything possible to encourage players to stay completely in the moment, to play with passion and consistency, and to execute well while playing smart. In many

ways, the MPI does what coaches have already done for years, but it does it by just putting a mirror up to any unit of the team to show them what they actually did week to week.

Train Based on MPI Data

Whether conducted by a coach or an outside expert, it only makes sense to look at the MPI report early in the week and then by middle of week have a session devoted to the greatest needs revealed on the report. If a team is doing very well in one area you might want to reinforce that and praise them for their efforts. In a deficient area, the specific nature of the MPI decline can be explained with rational and productive solutions to improve. Then in the follow-up meetings the new data can be looked at to assess progress. The news will not always be good, and that is ok. We learn more when we struggle. Knowing where we are is the key to getting better.

Summary

You've already read about the underpinnings of the MPI, why it was needed, and how it corrects a major historical omission in team performance measurement. The section you just read introduced to you how it can be practically applied to help teams, coaches, players and executives. Here are the main points again:

(1) The MPI is for winning. That is why it was developed and only coaches and teams interested in performing better and winning will find it helpful.

(2) The coach or executive who hires me controls the use of the MPI reports and data, and it is always 100% confidential and cannot be used to help a team's competitor.

(3) Useful MPI feedback is provided quickly and painlessly in reports that summarize what happened. These can be turned around within 24 hours of receiving the DVD or sooner if the game is seen live.

(4) The knowledge gained is power to the coach and the team.

(5) The feedback adds a natural confidence boost to the coach and team.

(6) Smarter and more effective goal setting is possible with more specific numerical targets provided in the MPI data and reports.

(7) Using the MPI is fun and allows historical comparisons between current teams and the teams of Super Bowl history, for instance. This itself is inspiring and educational.

(8) The MPI is extremely realistic. There is no getting around a good or poor performance. This encourages accountability.

(9) Discussion, when desired by the coach, is facilitated by using this book and the MPI.

(10) More effective training that targets the greatest needs is made possible with the MPI data and reports. As a result teams win more.

Sports Psychology and Mental Coaching in Football

Just as in the last section, the key to remember is that sports psychology and mental coaching are designed to help teams and players perform better and win more football games. It is my philosophy that without this goal, a football game becomes a much less interesting and productive endeavor. The MPI and the mental coaching that I discuss in this book is not for the faint of heart or for those who just wish to have an enjoyable experience on the golf course. There is certainly a place for that and I have worked with many athletes who use sport for reasons other than fierce competition, but this is not the book for that. This book and this philosophy of mental coaching and the use of the MPI are all about performing better in order to win.

I have previously outlined what I believe are many of the fears that some coaches have about mental coaching and sports psychology. While I cannot speak for other sports psychologists, I always start with the assumption that the coach is the captain of the ship and I am there to provide a needed service just the same way any professional would, all the way from the team physician to the dentist, trainer, assistant coach, and massage therapist. I am not and have not a desire to be the head coach. He brings me in to help with his own philosophy of football. I am there to adapt to his needs to help him and help the team achieve worthy goals.

A Need for Access

One of the first benefits of having a general team psychologist or team sports psychologist (and in my case I provide both as I am both a licensed psychologist and expert in mental skills training or mental coaching for athletes) is that players can more easily access professional help. I believe that many players, out of fear or lack of knowledge, never tap into the help needed. But our society is changing and players are starting to reach out more and more to me in my private practice. I work with some of the best professional athletes in the world as well as juniors looking to get a great start. Many find it hard to get the help they need. Having it readily available in either a team staff position or regular consultancy is a huge benefit. Getting the players what they need and, as a coach, having control over the selection of the professional these players are likely to see, is paramount.

The truth is that while all benefit from mental coaching, there are also general needs that arise that present a need for more general counseling. It is long established that sweeping problems under the rug is not the solution. So a licensed professional available to talk with them in a confidential manner gives the players a way to resolve issues when they come up so that they do not become distractions during the game or practice. It doesn't matter how great a player is as an athlete, the raw facts are that a certain percentage of people each year are going to get depressed, have panic attacks, develop eating disorders, lose total confidence and self-esteem, break-up with spouses, engage in conflicts with another player or coach, lose a relative due to a tragedy, become seriously injured and need to rehab quicker, and so on. The list is really endless. This is not to say that athletes are a disturbed group. Far from it. They are very healthy mentally, but there will still be problems on a team because of nothing more than the fact that there are people on a team.

Having a qualified team psychologist or sports psychologist to address these issues before they get out of hand is often a huge key to winning. We tend to think of winning and performance on the field only, and in fact that is what the MPI measures, but the reality is that a football game is only 3-4 hours a week and then you have the rest of the week for people to have problems. While my approach is to try to help athletes to minimize problems, sometimes just having the right professional there to talk can make a world of difference. Having someone who can relate to the athlete is key.

A Need for Prevention of Problems

We get a dental check-up twice a year without thinking about it, and a haircut at least 6 times a year, but people tend to go for mental help only when things get beyond repair or quite out of control. Are your hair and teeth far more important than your success on the field or your entire well-being?

There should never be shame in going to talk with someone who can help, if nothing more than to get better. It is not a sign of weakness, as I emphasized earlier in this book in the "Tough Guys Talk" initiative. It is actually the opposite as an indication of health and strength to face a problem down and defeat it directly rather than let it fester and affect a person worse -- and hurt the whole team too.

Having a professional qualified in mental health care as well as mental training is one of the smartest moves a professional or collegiate football team can invest in. When you think of all the problems that young athletes get into these days and some of the problems at home, it just makes sense to have a smart professional in place who knows the athletes, wants to do everything possible to help them, and wants to help them win as well.

I believe that winning and mental health go hand in hand and I am always impressed by some of the star athletes I work with in all sports and how really insightful and intelligent they are. This is not to say there are not exceptions. As in any sector of society, there are going to be people you like, people you respect, and those you might not care for as much or respect, but on the whole I would say that I am very impressed with the pro athletes I have worked with. It also makes sense. It is a population that survived against incredible odds to do something that everyone else would love to do but maybe did not have the dedication or talent to achieve. At the same time, athletes at all levels are just people and people need to be watched and cared for. I think sometimes we take care of our plants, cars and dogs better than we do our people. That has to change. If an athlete has a problem, he or she needs to be able to get help and quickly, and not run into the trap of thinking that talking is a sign of weakness.

If there is one thing I have learned from 12 years in private practice as a clinical and sports psychologist it is that holding things in almost never works. It usually backfires. I have also learned that the more I talk with someone, the more they reveal. It is the ongoing and consistent relationship that provides the greatest opportunity for growth and success. Knowing the athlete and having the athlete feel safe to discuss problems is a tremendous relief that validates the person. Then they can go out Friday, Saturday or Sunday and knock the daylights out of somebody on the field, throw great touchdown passes, or sack the quarterback. It allows the player to do his job better unfettered by the worries of the day or week.

The additional expertise in sports psychology/mental coaching provides an easy way to talk with an athlete who is raised in a sports culture that may not easily encourage verbal openness. By keeping it initially to discussions about performance or the upcoming game, it really helps ease the transition to other more serious issues when they come up. But I don't want to give the impression either that this is just for off-field issues. I work with a variety of athletes in all sports and also a variety of business situations in which the focus has nothing to do with general well-being and we spend the session strategizing for improved performance. Again it depends on the individual and what the person needs, and doing this all within a team environment helps to keep the focus also on what is needed to help that athlete do his job better on the field.

So whether problems are anticipated and prevented in advance so that a stale player does not develop burnout and possibly later depression, or whether it involves helping a field goal kicker with a pre-snap routine to better do his thing by not slipping over into negative thinking or to allow outside distractions to intrude, the same principle of prevention applies. By addressing problems proactively you gain a healthier and hungrier team that can spend its energies on defeating the upcoming opponent. I told you it was about winning … and I mean it!

A Great Respect for Coaches

Everything I have said so far in this book has probably already been envisioned and/or realized by a coach or coaches somewhere. I am a professional now in my late 40s who grew up in an era where it was possible to become a sports psychologist and there are very few legitimate ones out there, but there are thousands of good coaches. The coaching professions have been around a lot longer than sports psychology. Football coaching has an entire evolution of its own and I respect that very much. I was a coach myself for 7 years before I went back to graduate school to focus more specifically on the coaching of the mind. I have no inherent insight or powers that go beyond what any other coach might have, but I have taken the time to receive the best education possible in my field and I also have years of experience working with some of the best athletes on the planet.

Still, I provide a professional service, like a football coach does, and I do not pretend to involve myself in technical training. I might ask an athlete to tell me what he knows so that we can perform a better session in imagery or for goal setting. The profession that I am proud to be a part of is both a science and an art. It offers a lot as the "science and profession devoted to success." I love what I do, and the addition of a team psychologist to a team roster represents an evolution in advanced coaching whose time has come. It might take a while still, but I expect that within 15 years every professional sports franchise will have a team psychologist on staff and there will no longer be any stigma or suggestions of weakness associated with it.

It is good that I don't try to be a football technician in terms of teaching on-field blocking or throwing techniques and strategies. I leave that to the experts and they allow me to practice in my area of expertise.

There needs to be a mutual respect between similar professions that overlap. The coaching profession certainly overlaps with sports psychology, but the two are still distinct enough or there would not be the profession of Psychology in the first place.

Summary

This was just a brief introduction to sports psychology and mental coaching and each team and coach has different needs. The great thing about this evolution is that everyone benefits. Teams grow stronger, players develop better mental skills and coaches win more. Nobody is compelled to use mental training services, but if players can see and feel its benefits, I am there for them.

Epilogue: "Triumph of a Beautiful and Tough Mind"

by Lesley Visser
Pro Football Hall of Fame Broadcaster

The Thinker

His imagination was always engaged. I remember the first conversation I had with Bill Walsh in about 1983. I was asking about his innovative offense; he was talking about Muhammad Ali. Walsh wanted to know everything about Ali. Where had his skill come from, his motivation? How did Ali sustain it? And how could Walsh apply the answers? A former amateur boxer, Walsh had studied Ali, watched tapes and read books about the champ. He admired Ali's ferociousness and his grace, the elements Walsh sought in his own 49er team.

In the savage sport of football, Walsh had created and radiated an image of "finesse", the appearance of intellect over muscle. Walsh's white hair and professorial approach only added to the persona. But the image belied the reality. His 49er defense was led by the passionate Ronnie Lott, who once famously cut off the tip of his finger to stay in a game. Walsh himself was tough and no-nonsense, just as he was cerebral and calm.

In 1953, Walsh was a 190-pound boxer who won the all-college tournament at San Jose State. He could often be seen shadow-boxing on the sideline at 49er practices. "He liked the artistic side *and* the violent side of boxing," said former 49er center Randy Cross. "I think he secretly liked the language, too." Walsh enjoyed his reputation as a complex man – well-read, thoughtful, a conceptualist who even looked like Rodin's Thinker. But ultimately, he was a coach, a teacher who loved the art of combat. In the Niner locker room throughout the 1980s, there was a sign on the wall: "I Will Not Be Out Hit ANY Time This Season."

Walsh didn't motivate through intimidation. He did so through attention to detail and an expectation of self-awareness. "He was relentless with us," said Jerry Rice, the Hall of Famer who is widely

250

considered the greatest receiver who ever played. "I remember one game when I had 12 receptions, three touchdowns and more than 200 yards. He called me to his office. I was sure it was for a pat on the back. He told me he needed more." Tight end Brent Jones once said, "Bill wasn't happy with good or very good, it had to be excellent." Former 49er assistant Mike Holmgren said that Walsh "was just different. He understood that football was physical, but while the rest of us were pounding an anvil, he was painting a picture."

With Joe Montana at quarterback, Walsh wanted an offense that flowed, one that moved down the field on little cat's feet. It was football as artistry, and no one could stop it. It's fitting that Walsh coached "Joe Cool", because Montana was perfect for Walsh's formula of short, surgical passes that controlled a game. In 10 years, Walsh led the 49ers to three Super Bowl titles and six division crowns , and put together an organization that won two more Super Bowls under successor George Seifert.

Walsh was born in 1931 in Los Angeles, the son of an auto repair shop worker who moved his family north in the 1940s. A wide receiver at San Jose State, Walsh graduated with a degree in business and earned a master's degree in 1953 with his thesis "Defensing the Spread-T Offense". His college coaching career began in 1960 when Hall of Famer Marv Levy hired him as an assistant at Cal Berkeley. Walsh became a fixture in the Bay Area, coaching as an assistant at both Cal and Stanford, with the Oakland Raiders and even, in 1967, the San Jose Apaches, a semi-pro team that played at San Jose City College. Walsh and his wife, Geri, lived for years in an apartment on North First Street in San Jose. A few months after the Apaches went bankrupt and folded, Walsh was out of a job. The Cincinnati Bengals, an AFL expansion team, were looking for an offensive assistant, and Walsh was hired as the receivers coach for the legendary Paul Brown. From Walsh's modest beginnings, the pro career that would put him at the top of the coaching profession with iconic names like Lombardi and Halas and Paul Brown himself, began with the newly formed Bengals.

Paul Brown was a football and cultural warrior. In the mid-1940s, he modernized the game and brought players from all walks of life to his Cleveland Browns --sons of Italy and Ireland, Poland and Hungary. Many of his players were just home from World War II, so when Brown stressed discipline, they already understood. Brown expected his players to pay attention, to be presentable (white shirts at dinner) and to be self-motivated. In his trench coat and fedora, Brown was a pioneer, inventing the two-guard system in which he shuttled in offensive linemen (most famously Chuck Noll) with his plays. He didn't quick-kick on third and long, like so many others; instead, he used the down for a pass play. He stressed scouting, and his Browns, with Otto Graham and Marion Motley, completely dominated the All-American Football Conference, then moved to the NFL and won three titles.

Walsh took full advantage of the Bengals opportunity. Under Brown, Walsh learned the intricacies of what he called a "full dimensional" passing game. Brown and Walsh worked on the precision offense, in which the quarterback and the receiver connected on a defined pattern, one in which the receiver cut before the ball had arrived, leaving the defender out of the play. For an expansion team with a poor running game, Walsh knew he needed something to ignite the struggling offense. What would become the "West Coast" offense--based on short, quick-timed passes by the quarterback, who went through his progression of possibilities while receivers ran to a certain spot--was Walsh's answer to an injury. Paul Brown had drafted a gifted quarterback out of the University of Cincinnati named Greg Cook, but when Cook tore his rotator cuff and had trouble throwing the deep ball, Walsh went to Plan B, the short passing game. He called it his "nickel and dime" approach. Eventually, Ken Anderson became his Joe Montana prototype and Isaac Curtis was his original Jerry Rice.

This was also the time when Walsh began "scripting" his plays. In the mornings before the games, Brown would ask Walsh what his "openers" were. Brown wanted to know what Walsh had in mind for the first offensive series. Walsh began writing down the plays, in order to be prepared for Brown's intense questioning. Soon the list expanded to 10 or 12 plays, which Walsh said gave the team an advantage. "We were making decisions on Thursday or Friday when we had time to concentrate," he said, "and it also limited our chances of becoming predictable. Coaches might not even realize it, but sometimes they use the same formation every time on third and long. We tried to make the job of the defense harder." His players liked it too. Being able to think about and digest the plays 24 hours ahead of time gave them, according to Walsh, "a better night's rest."

After the 1975 season, Paul Brown, the founder and owner of the Bengals, retired, and almost everyone thought the head coaching job would go to Walsh. But Brown gave the job to another assistant, Bill Johnson, and Walsh was crushed. His hurt turned into a quiet fury when Walsh went back to the West Coast as an offensive coordinator for the San Diego Chargers. Walsh never forgot the snub and went on to beat the Bengals in two Super Bowls, along the way barely mentioning Brown's name. "Many people thought I had a large ego," Walsh said years later, "but it was more a reflection of my insecurity. I'd spent so many years as an assistant coach, never knowing if I'd get an opportunity to be an NFL head coach. I was driven inside."

Walsh might have been insecure on the inside, but on the outside he was charming and confident. Roger Craig, a running back for the 49er dynasty, said that when Walsh came into the locker room, everyone perked up. "He had a glow, a charisma," said Craig, "the glow of a champion."

In 1977, Walsh brought some of what he'd learned from both Paul Brown and Charger legend Sid Gillman with him to Stanford, where he'd been hired as the head coach. Walsh constantly tinkered with his concept of using the pass to set up the run. Sometimes, he'd employ the passing game in place of the run. His newly installed aerial attack led the Cardinal back to national prominence, and 49er owner Eddie DeBartolo took notice. In 1978, at the Doral Hotel in Miami, the 49ers were coming off a 2-14 season and DeBartolo decided to offer the head job to Walsh. Walsh was ready. He had forged steel out of an agile and fragile mind.

Passed over for a professional head-coaching job until he was 47, Walsh put everything on the line for DeBartolo, meticulously crafting the 49er organization from top to bottom. As both the head coach and general manager, Walsh made daring decisions, like drafting a skinny kid named Joe Montana in the third round out of Notre Dame in 1979, and trading for Steve Young in 1987. His drafts included Montana, Lott and Rice, perhaps the three best ever to play their position.

Walsh was hungry, and determined to do it his way. "You know why it took me so long to become a head coach?" he once told me with his teeth clenched. "Because owners wanted people to scream and whip their players into submission. I thought you could treat players intelligently."

Walsh had a plan. He was both an innovator and a motivator. In one of his many boxing metaphors, Walsh told his players that the secret of their success would be "beating the opponent to the punch." In "Building a Champion", the book Walsh wrote with Glenn Dickey, Walsh declared that "our team-wide mentality was to move more quickly than our opponent, whether is was the first step a center would take in blocking a nose guard or a receiver exploding off the line." That quickness would become the 49er trademark. Walsh cited the influence of many coaches in refining his offensive attack. He took from Clark Shaughnessy, who utilized the man in motion; Davey Nelson, who developed the Winged-T,; Gillman, who, according to Walsh, brought "refinement to the game"; Brown and his virtual coach on the field, Graham, whose sprint right option would be seen in "The Catch", Dwight Clark's famous game-winning reception in the 1981 NFC Championship game.

Walsh implemented his new offense in 1979. It took another six years before the system had a name. In 2008, I was sitting in Bill Parcells' box before a Dolphin-Jet game, and we started talking about Walsh, his contributions and his legacy. Parcells told me that he, in fact, had given the name "West Coast" offense to Walsh after his Giants beat the 49ers, 17-3, in the opening round of the 1985 playoffs. I was slightly-- OK, overwhelmingly--skeptical. But there it was. In David Harris' definitive book on Walsh, "Genius", Parcells' trademark defense held the 49ers without a touchdown for the first time in three years. In the locker room after the game, Parcells, beaming, declared for all to hear, "What do you think of the West Coast offense now?"

Walsh's innovative offense required a certain kind of player. He needed a quarterback who could think quickly, and one who had an accurate arm. Walsh found that gem in Montana. Phil Simms had been the big catch in the first round, going at No. 7 to the Giants. Montana was the 82nd selection of the draft. Even though Walsh loved Montana's footwork and perfect mechanics, he didn't rush the future Hall of Famer.

In 1979, Montana played sparingly behind Steve DeBerg, but late in the 1980 season, the 49ers trailed the New Orleans Saints, 35-7. Walsh, who often used military analogies from the Civil War or the Battle of the Midway, told his team they would learn about themselves in the second half. They would show the world if they were battle-ready. Walsh gave the reins to Montana, who directed a stunning comeback --409 yards of offense in the second half ---that tied the score, 35-35, with a minute left. San Francisco kicked a field goal to win in overtime, and Walsh later would declare that "the modern history of the San Francisco 49ers began that day."

Montana proved that he could lead, that he could throw a catchable ball under pressure, and that his ball had enough velocity to eliminate a defender. On the other end of the play, Walsh had exacting standards for his pass-catchers. He wanted tall receivers who couldn't be jammed at the line of scrimmage. Walsh didn't require lightning speed, but he wanted receivers with great quickness and soft hands. And most importantly, he wanted receivers who wouldn't drop the ball. In a pass-first offense, the receiver had to secure the ball, even if it meant gaining only a few yards. The offense couldn't withstand too many 2nd-and-10 situations. Walsh became intrigued with a little-known, Division I-AA receiver from Mississippi Valley State who had grown up in tiny Crawford, Mississippi hauling bricks in the hot sun with his father, a laborer. Before the 1985 draft, Walsh maneuvered to get that receiver, Jerry Rice. Even though Rice was projected to be at best the fifth receiver taken, Walsh worried that he would be snatched earlier, so he traded up for the New England Patriots' 16th pick overall.

Rice was raw and precious, a diamond in the rough. I remember doing an interview with him before his first NFL game. I asked him what he did with his signing bonus. He said he bought two cars. I asked him why he needed two cars, and he looked at me as if I were a fool. "I need one for heah," he said in his soft Delta accent, "and one for theyah." We both laughed. Rice turned out to be everything Walsh wanted and more. As a weapon for the 49ers, Rice had enough speed to stretch the field and near-perfect skill to catch the ball. In his rookie season, Rice combined with Montana to catch 49 passes for an astonishing 18.9 yard average. He became the most feared receiver in the game. What I remember about most about Jerry Rice was that, in every aspect of his life, he had to be close to perfection – the way he ran his routes, the way he dressed after the game. He never looked rushed, just completely organized

Bill Walsh always knew that success wasn't a matter of desire, but preparation. He was the embodiment of John Wooden's legendary saying, "Failure to prepare is preparing to fail." His attention to detail extended to the draft. In 10 years with the 49ers, Walsh made more than 40 trades, moving up, moving down, always selecting only those who interested him. In 1986, the 49ers had one of the most astute drafts in NFL history – wide receiver John Taylor and fullback Tom Rathman (each third round) and defensive end Kevin Fagen (fourth round), offensive tackle Steve Wallace and linebacker Charles Haley (all fourth round), and cornerback Don Griffin (sixth round). It was everything San Francisco needed to replace an aging defense and gain a big blocking back.

Walsh had learned his draft strategy from Paul Brown in Cincinnati, and from Al Davis, where Walsh had been an assistant for the Raiders in 1966. Walsh had learned that one person had to be the unquestioned leader of the team, one man needed to take ultimate responsibility. I covered one of the 49er drafts for ESPN and it was a study in organization. The offices, 30 minutes south of Candlestick Park, are in a sprawling complex where the gleaming Super Bowl trophies are displayed in glass cases for any visitor in the lobby to see. On draft day, Walsh sat in a meeting room with 11 of his coaches and six of his scouts in front of a 10-foot blackboard. There were offensive charts, defensive charts and position charts on either side of him. In the age before cell phones, DeBartolo was on a phone hookup from Youngstown, Ohio, and another line was on hold to the draft headquarters in New York. Before each pick, Walsh would ask one of the area scouts to go to the blackboard and write down which three players should be considered. General Manager John McVay said Walsh was always decisive and in charge. "He'd listened to everyone's input," said McVay, "then he made either the pick or the trade. He was never paralyzed or uncertain." Walsh's approach was historically confirmed. His drafts produced 17 Pro Bowl players.

The degree of readiness extended to the practice field. According to Brian Billick, one of 11 NFL head coaches who could trace their careers to Bill Walsh, the West Coast offense was more than X's and O's. It wasn't just two backs and short passes, it was about preparation. "If you look at Mike Holmgren's Seattle Seahawks or Mike Shanahan's Denver Broncos or my former Ravens, you'd see we all have the same level of preparation," said Billick. "We learned from Bill that offensive innovation starts with attention to detail." The coaching personalities of Walsh's students were variable – from excitable Denny Green to placid George Seifert to stoic Mike Holmgren to voluble Sam Wyche--but all were skillful leaders who made the commitment to be prepared. Many people know that Walsh scripted the first 15 or 20 plays of every game, but he mapped out his practices exactly the same way.

The Walsh style also was to diminish the physicality of the practices as the season wore on, to allow the players to embrace opportunity and to take responsibility. Billick wrote a book with Walsh, called "Finding the Winning Edge", and Walsh shared his secret of excellence. "A system should never reduce the game to a point where it simply blames the players for failure because they didn't physically overwhelm the opposition," Walsh wrote. The player had to know what was his fault, what was the coaching responsibility, and what both could do to improve. Walsh had an interesting way of criticizing his players. Instead of addressing them directly, he would criticize their coaches. If a running back failed to take on a pass rusher, Walsh would ask why the coach couldn't get better pass protection from his player. The player would double his effort to please both his position coach and the head coach.

Walsh's offense had many important facets that were often overlooked. Like the primacy of the left tackle. After the 49ers won their first Super Bowl in 1981, Walsh drafted Bubba Paris to protect Montana's blind side. Paris was quick and active, and also chubby. Walsh wanted Paris to play at 300 pounds, not the 20 or 30 extra that Paris often carried. In 1987, the 49ers had romped through the season 13-2 and were favored to win the Super Bowl by 14 points, no matter who the opponent. But the Minnesota Vikings stopped the 49ers before they ever got to the Super Bowl. Paris, slower and heavier, was repeatedly beaten by 6-5, 270-pound Chris Doleman, who wore No. 56 in honor of his idol, Lawrence Taylor, and who repeatedly came flying from his position at right defensive end.

The pass rush was so heavy that Walsh benched Montana and put Steve Young in the game. Young was a lefty who at least could see Doleman coming and hopefully avoid the pressure.

The next year, Steve Wallace, from that great draft in 1986, was now protecting Montana's blind side. The position of left tackle had been re-imagined in Walsh's pass-happy offense. In the playoffs in 1988, again against Minnesota and the brilliant Doleman (who was now headed to his second straight Pro Bowl), Walsh told Wallace that he would be a key to the game. Walsh knew that the battle between his left tackle and the Vikings rusher would be no less than a heavyweight boxing match. Wallace had spent many hours preparing for Doleman, and he was ready for what Doleman offered. Instead of meeting Doleman at the line of scrimmage, as Paris had done, Wallace backed up on the slick Candlestick Park surface and encountered Doleman as the charging Viking wanted to turn left and take down Montana. In the first half, Montana threw six completions without an interception for a 21-3 lead. It was a performance that CBS analyst John Madden said was "as close to perfect as possible." Montana had thrown three touchdown passes and Wallace hadn't given up one sack. But no one mentioned Wallace's name—which is a tribute. The 49ers won, 34-9, and left tackle became a glamour position. Wallace had signed his first contract for $90,000. Before the 2000 season, the Baltimore Ravens would re-sign their left tackle, Jonathon Ogden to a six-year deal worth $44 million. (In 2008 the Miami Dolphins would make Michigan tackle Jake Long the number one pick of the draft.)

Walsh was always teaching, always thinking. I remember someone in the 49er organization telling me that when Walsh was coaching in 1957 at Washington High School in Fremont, California, he required the cheerleaders to attend a Football 101 class that he taught. He didn't want them cheering at the wrong time, or when his quarterback was calling an audible. It was no surprise. Walsh was able to master the biggest concept and smallest detail. He said that he would often wake up in the middle of the night after a game to design a new play, even if the 49ers had won by 35 points. "We were ready for any situation," said tackle Harris Barton. "At the start of every game, we thought we already had an edge." And Walsh would stand unruffled on the sideline, secure in the knowledge that his 49ers were completely prepared.

In all his years of dedication and success, Walsh said his proudest moment came when watching the 49ers drive 92 yards to the winning touchdown in Super Bowl XXIII. Walsh said it was as if all his years of coaching and practicing came together in those 3 minutes and 20 seconds, what Walsh called "11 plays that made a symphony."

Super Bowl XXIII, like so much of the NFL, had its roots in Paul Brown. The 49ers were playing the Cincinnati Bengals, coached by Sam Wyche. Brown had hired Walsh in the 1960s as an assistant with the Bengals and Walsh had hired Wyche, an original Cincinnati Bengal, in 1979, as the quarterback coach for the 49ers. Together, they had molded the young Joe Montana, who, of course, became the hero of Super Bowl XXXIII.

San Francisco fans lived for a moment like this, for Montana to lead the team down the field in a signature drive to win a championship. It happened in January 1989, in Miami's Joe Robbie Stadium. I remember thinking that the ticket prices were reasonable, $100, and that Miami was a great place for a Super Bowl, although during the week, celebrations were marred when riots broke out in the rough Overtown section. San Francisco was favored, and this greatly annoyed Bengal quarterback Boomer Esiason, who didn't want to echo the famous victory guarantee Joe Namath had made before Super Bowl III, but told me he spent the week biting his lip. When Esiason was tired of answering questions about the Bengals' chances, he took out a camera and snapped pictures of the reporters trying to interview him. On game day, Billy Joel sang the national anthem, and Bob Griese and Nick Buoniconti, former Dolphins who played on the only undefeated team in NFL history, were trotted out for the coin toss. The Air Force flyover was spectacular.

Then the game began, and it wasn't that impressive. The first half ended 3-3. It was a defensive struggle, and Bengals nose tackle Tim Krumrie was taken off the field on a stretcher after breaking his leg just minutes into the first quarter. The game picked up steam in the second half, and with 3:20 left in the fourth quarter, Esiason maneuvered the Bengals into position for a field goal that would give Cincinnati the lead.

Jim Breech's 40-yard kick put the Bengals up, 16-13. On the sideline, backup Steve Young turned to Montana, and said, "OK, it's set up perfectly for us."

It was unexpected for the favored 49ers to be in a comeback situation. Randy Cross said after the game, "I was surprised. I thought we should have been ahead by three touchdowns." After the kickoff and a holding penalty against the 49ers, the final drive started on the 8-yard line. Montana famously said to his team in the huddle, "We only have 92 yards to go." Walsh said the plan was to get the team at least into field-goal position and hope to go for the touchdown. The clock showed 3:10. Walsh told his team that the success of the drive rested on the entire unit, not just Joe. He said no player could afford a breakdown. The offense huddled on the goal line. Montana, not one for loud speeches or declarations, said simply, "Let's go, be tough." On the first play, Montana passed over the middle to Roger Craig for 8 yards, then quickly to tight end John Frank for another 7 and a first down.

Montana, calling his own signals, was in total control, mixing his receivers and moving confidently down the field. "We were functioning like a machine," said Bubba Paris. "It was happening." Montana called his first timeout with 1:54 to play. Esiason was watching from the Bengal sideline. "I was with the guys from Disney, practicing my, 'I'm going to Disneyland,'" Boomer told me. "But out of the corner of my eye, I saw it slipping away. I was filled with dread." Montana hit Rice for 17 yards and Craig for another 13. With their fifth first down of the drive, the 49ers had the ball on the Bengal 18-yard line. An 8-yard pass over the middle to Craig moved the ball to the Bengals 10 with 39 seconds left. Montana called his second timeout.

Walsh wanted a play called "20 Halfback Curl, X Up", designed to go to Craig, who was to run another pattern over the middle. But Craig lined up in the wrong spot in the backfield. With no time to argue, Montana took the snap, looked at Craig as he was supposed to do and went to his second option. Rice was the decoy on the play, lined up wide right and sent in motion to the left to move the defense. Taylor was split wide left and ran straight to the endzone, a skinny post, beating defensive back Ray Horton, who was late coming over to cover him. Montana rifled the 10-yard the winning touchdown to Taylor with 34 seconds left and pumped his arms in the air. The Disney people dropped Esiason and went sprinting across the field. In the final 30 seconds, the Bengals failed to move the ball out of their own territory. Rice, who had played on a tender ankle but amassed a Super Bowl record 215 receiving yards, was named the MVP. The game cemented the legacy of a few of the players and their "Professor" coach.

Appendix I

Dr. John's Super Bowl Lessons I to XLIV - 1967-2010

Dr. John's Super Bowl 1 Lesson

"Get away, relax and come back … then have fun and attack!"

When Max McGee didn't think he would play he could not over-think or get tight. He took his mind off football the night before and inadvertently prepared for a career performance. When facing pressure, get away for a few minutes or hours, then come back to compete like never before.

Dr. John's Super Bowl 2 Lesson

"Play for a higher purpose"

The Green Bay Packers played even better than expected for the higher purpose of honoring their great coach. This provides exceptional motivation. Everything Vince Lombardi preached for years came to a terrific crescendo in 60 minutes, especially on key defensive plays. While Bart Starr got the MVP for the second straight year, it should have gone to a key defensive player such as Willie Davis or Herb Adderley because it was on defense where the Packers were best.

Dr. John's Super Bowl 3 Lesson

"Develop a killer instinct or be killed"

The Colts squandered opportunity after opportunity in Super Bowl 3. Had they listened too much to predictions making them an 18 point favorite? They lacked "killer instinct" and repeatedly made careless errors and turnovers. The sharper and hungrier Jets who had nothing to lose forced turnovers and controlled the ball. The brash young quarterback's ridiculous guarantee suddenly made sense.

Dr. John's Super Bowl 4 Lesson

"The reputation of your opponent is meaningless. History is filled with inferior teams that dominate and great teams that wither"

The Kansas City Chiefs proved once again that winning is achieved in the trenches, and when it counts most, not on paper or in the media.

Dr. John's Super Bowl 5 Lesson

"Dance with who brung you!"

The Dallas Cowboys had an awesome defense. Their coach, Tom Landry, was a master. In a rare loss of character, Landry abandoned his conservative running and defensive game plan and directed quarterback Craig Morton to pass. Morton was intercepted twice at the end of the game and both led to Colts scores. When it happened the second time with the score tied, Jim O'Brien was in winning field goal range. Rather than "dancing with who brung him" by running, punting, and letting his defense work, Landry dumped his date to impress the homecoming queen with a pass on 2nd and 35 from his own 27! After an interception and game winning field goal, Landry was left standing alone as the Colts rather than Cowboys became world champions. Landry would correct his error in the next Super Bowl by allowing Duane Thomas to dance Mardi Gras Mambo all over Dolphin's defenders in New Orleans.

Dr. John's Super Bowl 6 Lesson

"Remove your opponent's top weapon and everything falls into place"

The Dolphins were a powerful running team. The Cowboys neutralized it with a flex defense that gave Dallas another man on the defensive line. With no big running game to rely upon, the Dolphins were forced out of their comfort zone and the more experienced Cowboys prevailed.

Dr. John's Super Bowl 7 Lesson

"A perfect team is far from perfect"

Even though the 1972 Miami Dolphins achieved a perfect season record, they did not even come close to a perfect performance against the Redskins. They dominated this game, but 34 teams performed better on Super Sunday. To show how fragile perfection is, one fluke play by the Redskins could have tied this game, and two could have won it. Still … the Dolphins achieved what no other team has ever achieved, and they deserve the accolades!

Dr. John's Super Bowl 8 Lesson

"Why use nuclear weapons if stone-age battering rams work?"

Passing wasn't even necessary as the Miami Dolphins offensive line so completely dominated the Minnesota Vikings' defensive line. Shula's innovative cross-block and other blocking schemes made it even more difficult for the hapless Vikings defenders to do anything productive. This was an awesome display of power running. The degree of domination was so total that this is one of the best teams ever, if not the very best. Some will be surprised to learn that this team totally outperformed the Dolphins "perfect season" 1972 team of the year before. There is no comparison. The 1973 team played much better. If not for the World Football League stealing Csonka, Kiick and Warfield the next season, Miami might have easily won three more Super Bowl titles.

Dr. John's Super Bowl 9 Lesson

Super Bowl Jeopardy

Answer: *"NICKNAME FOR A DEFENSE THAT*
ALLOWED ONLY 17 YARDS ON
21 CARRIES IN A SUPER BOWL

Question: "WHAT IS THE *STEEL CURTAIN?"*

In this coming out party for the Pittsburgh Steelers, the future most
successful franchise in Super Bowl history set the standard for how tough,
mean and hard hitting defense should be played." The Vikings averaged .8
yards per rush.

Dr. John's Super Bowl 10 Lesson

"Don't beat yourself and you always have a chance!"

The Steelers had no turnovers and no penalties in the most error free
performance in Super Bowl history. They still barely won a tough
defensive struggle against a very strong Cowboys team. Credit goes to
Lynn Swan for his courage and clutch performance, but by not beating
themselves with mistakes the entire Steelers team earned a title.

Dr. John's Super Bowl 11 Lesson

"Be offensive on defense! Instill fear with toughness and aggression and make hits
hurt."

The 1976 Oakland Raiders had a habit of playing nasty, aggressive and
violent defense. It paid off against the Vikings and to this day still
remains the toughest, best, and most dominant defense in key moments
of a Super Bowl.

Dr. John's Super Bowl 12 Lesson

"If you want to lose, turn it over 8 times!"

Denver Quarterback Craig Morton's passer rating was 0. Dallas committed 12 penalties and Denver 8, but Denver also turned the ball over 8 times versus Dallas' 2. The team with the least mistakes in this mess won.

Dr. John's Super Bowl 13 Lesson

"When two great teams collide, the one that takes the pressure better is left standing"

These were two of the finest teams ever assembled, but Terry Bradshaw, Lynn Swann and John Stallworth made more plays in key pressure moments of the game, and the Steelers became champions.

Dr. John's Super Bowl 14 Lesson

"Never let your last mistake spoil your next achievement!"

Quarterback Terry Bradshaw threw three interceptions and still won the MVP award for coming through when it counted. This is what I call short-term memory and resilience in action.

Dr. John's Super Bowl 15 Lesson

"Never give up hope"

Jim Plunkett's career was long considered dead. He had never lived up to his Heisman Trophy hype. He got one final chance when the starting quarterback was injured. He came in and most wrote him off … but not Tom Flores. A former star quarterback himself, he saw hope. A dynamic Hispanic coach/quarterback combo started winning. The backup blossomed under Flores. Jim Plunkett would go on to throw 4 touchdowns with no interceptions, winning two Super Bowl titles in four years. Tom Flores rediscovered Jim Plunkett by not giving up on him.

Dr. John's Super Bowl 16 Lesson

"Looks are deceiving! Calm execution in pressure looks natural to the unaware eye, but is earned with hard work and great effort"

What is missing in the final product of a great clutch performance are the hundreds of hours of work, imagery, review, and planning. Joe Montana and his team worked so that they could execute more easily when it counted."

Dr. John's Super Bowl 17 Lesson

"When you are better like the Redskins you are still vulnerable."

You need to scrap, claw and fight even harder like the Hogs, John Riggins and Joe Theismann because your opponent will be even more aggressive, creative and resourceful.

Dr. John's Super Bowl 18 Lesson

"Put the past behind you and make a total commitment"

The Redskins were the favorite, they had beaten the Raiders in the regular season and most thought they would do so again. Rather than be intimidated, the Silver and Black bought into Tom Flores' "total commitment" message and just went out and gave the Redskins a good old fashioned whipping.

Dr. John's Super Bowl 19 Lesson

"Diversify your weapons. A balanced attack with multiple ways to win defeats a one-dimensional foe."

The 49ers crushed one of the best offenses assembled with a more diverse attack that would produce 4 NFL titles in 11 seasons. Miami, lacking as balanced an attack, never returned to the Super Bowl.

Dr. John's Super Bowl 20 Lesson

"There is no such thing as the greatest football team of all time"
- Chicago Bears Head Coach Mike Ditka

Coach Ditka is entitled to his view, but there is such a thing as the "Best Team Ever" on Super Bowl Sunday and his Super Bowl 20 Chicago Bears were best.

Congratulations to the Super Bowl XX Champion Chicago Bears!
You have also Become the Champions of
MPI Bowl I

The MPI Bowl is the Super Bowl of Super Bowls

Dr. John's Super Bowl 21 Lesson

"Nothing limits how good you become when you eliminate negative thinking"

For one day Phil Simms only entertained positive thoughts, and he almost achieved perfection. It was plenty enough to lead his team to a Super Bowl title.

Dr. John's Super Bowl 22 Lesson

"Once you stop making excuses you start making history!"

Doug Williams had a daunting task ahead of him. He was to become the first African American quarterback to start in a Super Bowl. How would he handle that pressure? He had just had a root canal the day before and his knee that had been surgically repaired and hurt from hyperextension. Did he make excuses? What pressure? What pain? He went out and threw for 602 yards. Nobody has matched him since. Go beyond the excuse and find a reason to win!

Dr. John's Super Bowl 23 Lesson

"Joe Montana"

Need I say any more?

Dr. John's Super Bowl 24 Lesson

"Wear out the defense and freeze the offense by stealing time"

This 49ers team had everything, especially on offense, and their demonstration of steady ball control and punishing possession offense was exemplary. Add the fast strike ability of Joe Montana and this offense was almost unstoppable. Possession offense is very effective against a team with a top quarterback like John Elway. The offense only gets better as the game wears on and the defense wears out. It puts a chill in the opposing offense which can't do anything from the bench.

Dr. John's Super Bowl 25 Lesson

"Stop Blaming Scott Norwood!"

He almost won it for the Bills, but Scott Norwood did not by himself lose this game. Since when is a 47 yard field goal a sure bet? The Bills had been horrible in pressure situations before he missed, so Norwood would have only helped save his the team that had one of the worst pressure performances overall. The better team won this game, so it would have been more of a surprise if Norwood had made the kick. Scott Norwood should not be blamed even if he could have been praised as the hero.

Dr. John's Super Bowl 26 Lesson

"When you think you are on top of the world, watch out!"

The Bills might have appeared a little overconfident before this game whereas the Redskins kept a lower profile and went about making headlines on the field. Jim Kelly, a wonderful quarterback, perhaps showed some overconfidence in throwing into double coverage on two of his four interceptions in this game. It's better to appear humble and then surprise your opponent with your intense resolve on game day than to project an image of being on top of the world with only one way to go … and an opponent motivated to lead you there!

Dr. John's Super Bowl 27 Lesson

"Fumble 8 times and you don't win"

The Dallas Cowboys won this game decisively, but they were also aided greatly by the self-destructive Buffalo Bills in their third straight Super Bowl loss. The Bills turned the ball over 9 times with 8 fumbles and 4 interceptions. Some truths do not require extra discussion.

Dr. John's Super Bowl 28 Lesson

"Appreciate who takes care of you"

The Dallas Cowboys escaped a bullet. Mired in pre-game controversy, they were 7 down in the third quarter to a team with the 28th ranked defense. While their rushing game got the most credit, Cowboy fortunes owe more to special teams and a fumble returned for a touchdown. Dallas' special teams ranks 4th in history and one play would have made them 1st. Dallas ranked 28th in rushing and 37th in total yards. That doesn't come close with how well their special teams played in Super Bowl 28!

Dr. John's Super Bowl 29 Lesson

"Give credit where due. After you've tried everything, it's ok at the end to admit that a higher force reigned supreme."

Only a handful of players in history have had the talent and smarts of Jerry Rice or Steve Young. To have had to face them together when they were in sync with one another was a challenge almost too great to overcome, and better to appreciate.

Dr. John's Super Bowl 30 Lesson

"Are you starting to see a trend here?!"

Your author is dumbfounded. The Dallas Cowboys hold the top two takeaway minus giveaway (T-G) performances in Super Bowl history and here they do it again with a +3 that wins a game that they should have lost! In this Super Bowl 30 lesson I give up and ask you the reader to tell me why the Cowboys are so good at taking the ball away and not giving it up. I am sure every football team in the country would like to improve on this one and if you know and can tell me I will share it with others. Email your ideas to me for this rare trend to info@johnfmurray.com because I have no idea why they have mastered this so well!

Dr. John's Super Bowl 31 Lesson

"What you don't do may help most"

Desmond Howard was the recognized star in this Packers Super Bowl victory for what he did. What many do not realize is that what the Packers did not do helped them even more. They did not turn the ball over and they did not commit more than 3 penalties and these were huge.

Dr. John's Super Bowl 32 Lesson

"Be Courageous! Just one act of selfless courage in a critical moment of battle inspires your team 10 times more than talent"

John Elway flung himself fearlessly into the air for a first down. Terrell Davis played well after being hurt. The inspiration of courage spread wildly and paid off well as the Broncos become champions.

Dr. John's Super Bowl 33 Lesson

"To upset a superior opponent you first need to get your own house in order. Start by reducing distractions and mistakes."

The Atlanta Falcons did neither. They made themselves vulnerable to Elway & Davis with off-field controversy and on-field turnovers. The Broncos even failed to clinch the game several times, but the weakened Falcons never posed a threat.

Dr. John's Super Bowl 34 Lesson

"Out of the muck appears a blue lotus"

Mike Jones is the hero of this chaotic Super Bowl for making his game winning tackle and preserving victory for the Rams. In chaos individual heroes often arise. Examples include Jim O'Brien for his game winning kick in Super Bowl V, Joe Montana for his calm demeanor during the final touchdown drive in Super Bowl XXIII, or David Tyree's clutch helmet catch in Super Bowl XLII. The legend of the blue lotus in eastern cultures signifies wisdom of knowledge and the victory of the spirit over the senses. It is said that "out of muck will appear a lotus," a beautiful flower that is a symbol for goodness. Out of the muck of uncertainty and fear one special player, like the blue lotus, emerged as a symbol of strength. Mike Jones played the role of blue lotus for the St. Louis Rams in Super Bowl XXXIV.

Dr. John's Super Bowl 35 Lesson

"Who needs offense?"
-Coach Billick's parrot

Every so often one side develops a weapon so superior to its rivals that nothing else matters. The 2000 Baltimore Ravens defense was one of those weapons … like cannons against bows and arrows!

Dr. John's Super Bowl 36 Lesson

"Teamwork trumps individual glory every time"

Teamwork requires sharp timing, consistent effort, reduced mistakes, and big plays when it counts. The New England Patriots played smart football and stole the Rams' budding dynasty, replacing it with a New England Patriots dynasty that is still thriving a decade later.

Dr. John's Super Bowl 37 Lesson

"Win the psychological war beforehand and your chances in battle improve remarkably"

Oakland knew nothing about one of their own starting players. Tampa Bay knew everything about all of Oakland's players. While Oakland came in distracted and confused, Tampa Bay was mentally quick and two steps ahead with intelligence briefings all week by the perfect spy … an ex head coach!

Dr. John's Super Bowl 38 Lesson

"Act rather than react to be resilient"

Tom Brady is far from perfect, but he does bounce back! After he threw a critical interception in the 4th quarter to Reggie Howard, and after the impressive Panthers came back to score a touchdown and take the lead, Brady had a choice with less than 7 minutes left. He could get upset and "react" to this disappointment in any number of ways that would make his job more difficult. Or he could "act" instead by just directing his offense down the field. He chose this latter path and after an 11 play drive, short touchdown pass, and run for two, the Patriots led by 7. When Carolina tied the game up, Brady again just "acted" as a resilient quarterback does. He led his team into the winning field goal position. That is resilience and that is Tom Brady.

Dr. John's Super Bowl 39 Lesson

"Before you learn to win, learn not to lose"

Tom Brady, Deion Branch and the Patriots were a well oiled machine of efficiency and smarts who knew not to give it away. The Eagles might have had more talent and performed well in pressure moments, but all that talent and skill was negated by critical mistakes.

Dr. John's Super Bowl 40 Lesson

"Pay attention to details"

The Seattle Seahawks played well enough to beat the Pittsburgh Steelers in Super Bowl 41 but did not pay attention to details, especially on special teams. They lapsed in focus on three big plays that reversed their fortunes. That is the nature of mental mistakes. Just one bug ruins a meal no matter how good the food might be. The Steelers creatively cooked up success in a few key plays to beat a higher performing team.

275

Dr. John's Super Bowl 41 Lesson

"Keep a low profile and just Win"

The Colts were long known for their big passing game, and it led them back from an 18 point deficit to beat the Patriots to reach the Super Bowl, but it was a relatively unknown group of defensive players who really made the difference in winning this Super Bowl. Credit the coaching leadership of Tony Dungy and the personnel moves of Bill Polian, but credit mostly a defense that decided to make a name for themselves with a championship rather than individual awards.

Dr. John's Super Bowl 42 Lesson

"When others say you'll win, prepare as if you need a 110% effort to stay in the game."

When others say you'll lose, smile knowing you have nothing to lose and will play the game of your life. Victory occurs on the field, in the moment, and one helmet catch at a time.

Dr. John's Super Bowl 43 Lesson

"Sometimes being bad pays off"

Mistakes happen and 70% of perfection in any area is rare. Rare instincts at times win. When James Harrison intercepted Kurt Warner's pass and ran it back for a touchdown, some credited Harrison's instincts. He might have had a hunch about where the ball was coming. However, experts claim he blew his assignment and should have blitzed. His mistake of staying back paid off when the ball came to him wrapped in a gift box made of steel with a yellow and black ribbon. Had Harrison not been bad, his Steelers might have lost. It was a 14 point swing.

Dr. John's Super Bowl 44 Lesson

"Take smart risks to change your fate"

Saints coach Sean Peyton should have received the Super Bowl MVP award for ordering an onside kick to start the third quarter to beat another Peyton named Manning. It gave the Saints the ball, took it out of Manning's dangerous hands, led to points, and boosted the confidence of the number two ranked special teams unit in Super Bowl history.

Appendix II

How does Super Bowl XLV change the rankings?

This book went to press just a couple days after Super Bowl XLV was played in Dallas between the Green Bay Packers and Pittsburgh Steelers. I went to Dallas to promote this book and had a great time fighting the ice and snow, seeing The NFL Experience in the Dallas Convention Center, and meeting some of the truly great players from the past including Nick Lowery and Bill Romanowski. Both gave their wholehearted support for mental coaching and the idea of measuring mental performance. Romanowski went so far as to say that the mental game is what separates the good from the great and I did a video with both Romanowski and Lowery talking about how truly important the mental side of football and sports psychology is today and into the future. I then conducted an interview on several stations including ABC Network Radio with Todd Ant, and did several other interviews as well.

It only makes sense to include a brief update with the most basic MPI data from Super Bowl XLV. MPI Bowl II will be given much more coverage in future editions of this book, but for now let's just look at the most basic MPI data and see if the Packers were able to dethrone the Chicago Bears as the best team ever on Super Bowl Sunday.

Super Bowl 45 – February 6, 2011 – Cowboys Stadium, Arlington, TX

Green Bay Packers 31 (.516) Pittsburgh Steelers 25 (.505)

---

7 MPI Statistics

	MPI-T	MPI-O	MPI-D	MPI-ST	MPI-OP	MPI-DP	MPI-TP
SB45 Packers	.516	.543	.515	.447	.450	.519	.489
SB45 Steelers	.505	.525	.446	.603	.538	.450	.500

Brief Findings

Chicago Bears fans, players and coaches rest easy. The Packers' .516 MPI-T score was not even close to removing the Bears from their vaunted spot atop the rankings. In fact, no team was removed from the list of 32 best performing teams on Super Bowl Sunday. The 2010 Packers should be very proud, however, because they tied the New England Patriots of Super Bowl 38 to share the #32 spot. They are the 32nd best performing team out of 90 teams in Super Bowl history after a very close game with the Steelers.

Looking at the data, it is clear why Green Bay won this passing contest in a game that had the fewest rushes in Super Bowl history. The Packer's offensive dominance was decisive (.543 to .446) and Aaron Rodgers obviously earned his Super Bowl MVP award by going 24 of 39 for 304 yards (15th most yards in Super Bowl history) and no interceptions with a 111.5 quarterback rating! A relatively weak Pittsburgh defense is certainly a new idea in Super Bowl history. As usual, turnovers were decisive and Green Bay's +3 score on Takeaways minus Giveaways probably made the most difference in this game.

In addition to the 2010 Packers sharing the #32 spot now with the 2003 Patriots as overall best, here are two more updates to the MPI statistics after this game:

(1) Pittsburgh's .603 score on MPI-ST is ranked #15 overall, so the Steelers gain a position on the list of Top 25 best performing special teams units and no team is removed since there was a tie for #25 on this list.

(2) Pittsburgh's .156 on MPI-STD is ranked #10 overall, so the Steelers gain a position on the list of Top 25 most dominant special teams units, and the Super Bowl II Green Bay Packers are removed from this list as they were previously the #25 most dominant unit and now rank #26.

Table Defining the MPI Variables

VARIABLE	ABBREVIATION	MEASURES
MPI TOTAL	MPI-T	TOTAL TEAM PERFORMANCE
MPI TOTAL DIFFERENCE	MPI-TD	DOMINANCE OF TEAM OVER OPPONENT (MPI-T1- MPI T2)
MPI TOTAL PRESSURE	MPI-TP	TEAM PERFORMANCE IN PRESSURE
MPI TOTAL PRESSURE DIFFERENCE	MPI-TPD	DOMINENCE OF TEAM OVER OPPONENT IN PRESSURE (MPI-TP1 - MPI-TP2)
MPI OFFENSE	MPI-O	OFFENSIVE TEAM PERFORMANCE
MPI OFFENSE DIFFERENCE	MPI-OD	DOMINANCE OF TEAM'S OFFENSE OVER OPPONENT'S DEFENSE (MPI-O1 - MPI-D2)
MPI OFFENSE PRESSURE	MPI-OP	OFFENSIVE TEAM PERFORMANCE IN PRESSURE
MPI OFFENSE PRESSURE DIFFERENCE	MPI-OPD	DOMINENCE OF TEAM'S OFFENSE OVER OPPONENT'S DEFENSE IN PRESSURE (MPI-OP1- MPI-DP2)
MPI DEFENSE	MPI-D	DEFENSIVE TEAM PERFORMANCE
MPI DEFENSE DIFFERENCE	MPI-DD	DOMINANCE OF TEAM'S DEFENSE OVER OPPONENT'S OFFENSE (MPI-D1 - MPI-O2)
MPI DEFENSE PRESSURE	MPI-DP	DEFENSIVE TEAM PERFORMANCE IN PRESSURE
MPI DEFENSE PRESSURE DIFFERENCE	MPI-DPD	DOMINENCE OF TEAM'S DEFENSE OVER OPPONENT'S OFFENSE IN PRESSURE (MPI-DP1 – MPI-OP2)
MPI SPECIAL TEAMS	MPI-ST	SPECIAL TEAMS PERFORMANCE
MPI SPECIAL TEAMS DIFFERENCE	MPI-STD	DOMINANCE OF TEAM'S ST UNIT OVER OPPONENT'S ST UNIT (MPI-ST1 - I-ST2)

John F. Murray, Ph.D.

Dr. John F. Murray is a licensed clinical and sport psychologist in Palm Beach, Florida who has been in private practice since 1999 working with a wide variety of amateur, junior, Olympic and professional athletes, as well as business executives and corporate groups, to enhance performance and well-being. Dr. Murray earned a Bachelor's degree in Psychology from Loyola University New Orleans, and two Master's degrees and a Ph.D. from the University of Florida, specializing in both clinical psychology and sport psychology. For his doctoral dissertation, Murray examined injury coping responses of the members of the 1996 national champion Florida Gators football team. As a sport psychologist, Murray has worked with NFL teams and players, helped reverse the longest losing streak in pro tennis history, and filled in as a coach at many tournaments like the 2007 Australian Open. He served as a sport psychologist at the 2008 Summer Olympics in Beijing and at UFC 100 in Las Vegas. His first book "Smart Tennis: How to Play and Win the Mental Game" published by Jossey-Bass in 1999, bears an endorsement by the world's #1 ranked tennis player at the time, Lindsay Davenport. Murray has been described as "one of the major psychologists in sports" (Fox Sports), "the Freud of football" (Washington Post), and "the Roger Federer of sport psychologists" (Tennis Week Magazine). He has published hundreds of articles and has contributed to thousands of stories in the popular media. He has been profiled in ESPN The Magazine, Sports Illustrated ("Work in Sports" special), the Detroit Free Press and in a cover story in Canada's biggest tennis magazine, Ground Strokes, in December, 2009. Dr. Murray has appeared on many broadcasts such as ABC Good Morning America, MSNBC with Allison Stewart, the FOX Network with Neil Cavuto and John Gibson, NPR, the BBC, ESPN's Mike and Mike Show, CNN Radio ABC Network Radio, Bloomberg Radio and more. Dr. Murray can be reached at: info@johnfmurray.com and his web site can be found at: http://www.JohnFMurray.com.

Lightning Source UK Ltd.
Milton Keynes UK
14 March 2011

169219UK00001B/251/P